Arthur Gould

Rugby's First Superstar

Arthur Gould

Rugby's First Superstar

Gwyn Prescott

ST DAVID'S PRESS
Cardiff

Published in Wales by St. David's Press, an imprint of

Ashley Drake Publishing Ltd
PO Box 733
Cardiff
CF14 7ZY

www.st-davids-press.wales

First Impression – 2023

ISBN
Paperback: 978-1-904609-12-4
eBook: 978-1-904609-13-1

British Library Cataloguing-in-Publication Data.
A CIP catalogue for this book is available from the British Library.

Typeset by Prepress Plus, www.prepressplus.in
Cover design by Welsh Books Council, Aberystwyth, Wales

Contents

Dedicated to all Newport RFC players, past and present, for their long-standing contribution to the game and, in particular, to my greatly missed brother, Colin Prescott, who played for the club

Acknowledgements

No book is ever the work of one individual alone and that is certainly true in this case. In tackling the story of Arthur Gould, I was fortunate to benefit from the help and generosity of many. Without their contribution, this book could never have been written, though any errors it may contain are, of course, entirely my responsibility. I apologise unreservedly if I have inadvertently omitted anyone from these acknowledgements for their assistance during my research.

Firstly, my special thanks must go to the hugely supportive members of the Gould family. I shall be forever grateful to all of them for all their help and patience.

In particular, the enthusiastic and continual support of Gareth Harvey throughout this project proved to be invaluable. Arthur Gould's great-great-nephew invariably responded cheerfully and speedily to my frequent requests for clarification or additional information. The many images credited as "courtesy of the Gould family" came either from his own collection or were sourced by him from his contacts within the family. I am deeply indebted to Gareth.

Arthur's grandson, Robert Gould, generously gave me unrestricted access to one of rugby's great historic artefacts, Arthur's personal scrapbook, which contains many fascinating press cuttings and images relating to the great man's career. As the reader will quickly recognise, I made extensive use of this unique source. Robert also kindly provided me with photographs of many important family heirlooms which once belonged to his grandfather. I cannot thank Robert enough for allowing me to make use of these precious items.

I should also like to extend my thanks to Bruce and Christine Chubb who willingly shared their researches into the Gould family history. They also furnished me with an extensive collection of press articles and other published materials which they had collected on the rugby careers and lives of the Gould brothers. This was of great help in my research.

I very much appreciate the assistance which I received: from those indefatigable Newport RFC historians and researchers, Stephen Bennett, Mike Dams, Kevin Jarvis and Graham Sully; from the ever-supportive WRU Rugby Heritage Manager, Peter Owens; and from Philip Atkinson, John Hitchings, John Jenkins, Eric Lemon, Phil McGowan (World Rugby Museum), Richard Steele (World Rugby Museum), Professor Chris Williams (Cardiff University and University College Cork), Professor Gareth Williams (University of South Wales), and the staff at Cardiff and Newport public libraries, Cardiff University library and the National Library of Wales.

With regard to the images, I must express my gratitude not only to Gareth Harvey, Robert Gould and other members of the Gould family; but also to David Dow (Swansea RFC Memorabilia CIC); and to Kevin Jarvis (Newport RFC) who all generously provided many of those used in this book. In addition, my sincere thanks to Stephen Bennett, Bruce and Christine Chubb, Duncan Hockridge, Tony Lewis, Peter Owens, Graham Sully, Siân Prescott, John Taylor, Richard Tyrrell (Portsmouth RFC) and Dick Tyson who all obligingly agreed to let me include their images. Every reasonable effort has been made to obtain copyright clearance for the images used.

I greatly valued the writing of three journalists in particular whose articles appeared under pen names. For reference, these were: W J Townsend Collins, "Dromio" of the *South Wales Argus*; J R Stephens, "Old Stager" of the *South Wales Daily News*; and H W Wells, "Welsh Athlete" of the *Western Mail*. Though their estimates of crowd sizes were admittedly often very speculative, I have taken these at their face value throughout.

I am also grateful to Ashley Drake, my publisher, who has eagerly supported the project from initial proposal to publication and who, with his customary patience, has steered me with professional expertise at each stage. I know that, like me, he regards it a considerable honour and privilege to be involved in a book about one of the most iconic sportsmen that Wales has ever produced.

Finally, of course, *Arthur Gould: Rugby's First Superstar*, would never have been finished had it not been for the constant support and encouragement of my family. So my heartfelt thanks must go to my daughters Sarah, Anna and Siân for their practical and technical assistance, and to my wife Catherine for her invaluable help and advice and her unwavering support at all times.

Gwyn Prescott
September 2023

Introduction

"Arthur Gould Stands Alone"

In 1896, a journalist on the *Hull News*, writing under the pen name of "An Old Sportsman", published a handsome appreciation of Arthur Gould. What is intriguing about this article – which was picked up by other newspapers around Britain – is that it was the handiwork of a north-countryman rather than a partisan Welsh columnist. It is noteworthy too because it appeared towards the very end of Arthur's career, only a year before his retirement. And, in just a few lines, the writer manages to sum up Arthur's qualities as a player and as a personality, and also the marked impact which he had on the Victorian rugby world.

Arthur J Gould [is] without question the greatest three-quarter back Wales have ever boasted ... So widespread is his fame that thousands who never dream of visiting a Rugby Union game in the ordinary way are tempted by the presence of A J Gould. And seldom does he disappoint the onlookers, for the tackling has to be exceedingly clever and the "smothering" more than usually effective to prevent him getting away.

In some of the ordinary club games so masterly is his knowledge of every point of the game, and so cool and collected are his movements that really smart players are tricked so effectively as to appear little better than beginners. It must not be supposed, however, that this deliberation and deadly sureness slows his game at all; on

Arthur Gould. Siedle Brothers of Newport cabinet card. (Courtesy of the Gould family)

the other hand, some of his cleverest moves, feints, passes, and kicks are taken when travelling at top speed, and so adroit is he at dropping goals that his opponents seldom know "what to make of him" until the ball has left his hands.

... As a scientific exponent of three-quarter play, there is no better man playing ... Too often the Rugby game palls upon the spectators by reason of the tugging and tearing tactics brought into play; but there is nothing of this harum-scarum business about the Welsh hero; always avoiding a tackle if possible, or drawing a couple or more opponents on himself in order to ensure a better opening for his comrades. Too often, however, his opponents realise that to stop him by no means stays the advance of the enemy, the ball having been dextrously transferred in the twinkling of an eye.

This lithe, sinewy Gould possess ... gracefulness ... in a marked degree, and having been well favoured in face and form by Dame Nature, his wonderful popularity is easily understood. What he has done for Welsh football generally, as well as for his club ... cannot well be over-estimated ... Possessed of a charming personality, he is a general favourite wherever he goes, and it will perhaps be not too much to say that he is worshipped at home.

... I consider him to be one of the greatest players in the position we have ever seen.[1]

It is something Welsh rugby has a habit of doing. Sometimes it bestows on its besotted followers moments of sublime elation. Saturday 7 January 1893 was one such occasion. It was a freezing, bitterly cold day, yet it turned out to be one of the most exhilarating in the long history of Welsh rugby. The country had been in the grip of a hard frost for weeks but, with the over-night installation of coal fired braziers around the ground, the Arms Park pitch was in a playable if slippery condition.

Cardiff had never hosted an English international before, while Wales had only beaten England once in their previous nine meetings. Despite the state of the ground, however, the match has been remembered as one of the most sensational internationals ever played; and the Welsh victory was to herald Wales' first ever Triple Crown success.

---

1   "An Old Sportsman", *Hull News*, 7 March 1896.

Captaining his country in this famous triumph was a player who was one of the greatest ever to grace a football field. The victory was achieved principally as result of his matchless individual skill, his tactical alertness and his confident leadership. This game confirmed (if confirmation were still needed) to all those present – whether Welsh or English – that, in Arthur Gould, Newport had produced a rugby genius.

England dominated early on and were soon leading by three tries and a conversion to nil. Many no doubt now expected yet another hefty drubbing. But not the Welsh skipper, who stepped up and took personal responsibility for the fight back. With one of his characteristic and "phenomenal" corkscrew runs from half way, he dodged player after player to place the ball under the posts. The conversion was successful. This inspired piece of individualism now put new life into the whole of the Welsh team while England began to flag. Just a few minutes later, Arthur made a crucial break at centre during a magnificent round of passing which resulted in the winger Norman Biggs going over in the corner. But then, against the run of play, England grabbed another unconverted try and extended their lead to 11 points to 7. Wales, however, were not disheartened and they continued to attack fiercely. Always confident of victory, Arthur again made things happen. Receiving the ball in a good position and using all his speed and guile, he slid through the cover defence to register his second try under the posts. Agonisingly, Billy Bancroft missed the conversion but the fullback more than made up for this with a well-placed penalty in the dying moments to put Wales into the lead for the first time by 12 points to 11.

The crowd went wild at the final whistle. The hero of the match, who had had led Wales to a momentous victory, was cheered enthusiastically as he was hoisted onto the shoulders of the crowd and carried along Westgate Street to the Angel Hotel. There was widespread agreement in both the Welsh and the English camps that, undeniably, Arthur had been the best man on the field and that he was also the inspiration behind the historic win. This was just one of the record 27 internationals in which he appeared for Wales over 13 seasons. So dominant and experienced was he in domestic and international rugby at the time that no account of the Welsh game in the 19th century can ignore his towering presence. When he eventually retired, no-one had played in more internationals or first

Arthur's World Rugby Hall of Fame cap, awarded in 2016. (Courtesy of Robert Gould)

class matches; and no-one had scored more tries or dropped more goals. Arthur Gould made rugby history.

Although sporting fame is fleeting, Arthur's name still resonates in rugby circles even to this day, over 100 years after his untimely death. In 2007, he was finally inducted into the Welsh Sports Hall of Fame, though it did take an inexplicable 17 years for the organisation to do this. He was similarly honoured by World Rugby's Hall of Fame in 2016. As a result of an initiative by his great-great-nephew, Gareth Harvey, a blue plaque has proudly adorned "Thornbury", Arthur's old home in Newport since 2018. Fittingly, just like the testimonial which acquired the house for Arthur 121 years earlier, this too was funded by a public appeal. It is not difficult to account for his lasting renown. Possessed of undoubted footballing, tactical and leadership skills, he stood head and shoulders above his fellows during the Victorian era and, if the journalist W J Townsend Collins' judgement is accepted, for at least the next 50 years as well.

Arthur wasn't the only talented member of the Gould family. His father, Joseph, was a well-known Newport cricketer, who skippered the town club for eight consecutive seasons. At least six of Joseph's sons played rugby for Newport. The oldest, Harry, was the youngest player ever to represent the club. Besides Arthur, both Bob and Wyatt also captained Newport. Arthur was a Welsh international, of course, but so too were Bob and Bert, while Gus and Wyatt, were Welsh reserves. In athletics, Arthur (twice), Gus and Wyatt were all bronze medallists in the Amateur Athletic Association (AAA) hurdles championships; and Wyatt was also an Olympic hurdler. This then was a quite exceptional sporting family.

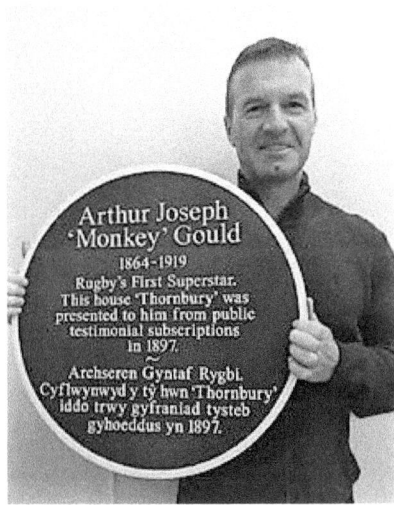

Gareth Harvey with the blue plaque. (Courtesy of Gareth Harvey)

However, despite the Goulds' unrivalled contribution to the popular sporting culture and life of Victorian and Edwardian Newport, the brothers also had a hankering for a more exotic life. It is well known that Arthur spent some time working abroad, but four of his rugby-playing brothers did so too: three of them died overseas.

Whilst the number of Arthur's international caps was a record for the time, what is perhaps even more impressive is that he was a member of the Welsh team over 13 seasons. During that period, Wales played only 34 times and Arthur was virtually a regular in

The Gould brother's Welsh caps reunited: Bob's on the left, Arthur's in the centre and Bert's on the right. (Courtesy of Robert Gould)

the team throughout, appearing in 80% of their matches. He was never dropped and only missed seven internationals because of unavailability, including three when he was out of the country. Anyone taking part in 80% of Wales' matches over the 13 seasons from 2009-10 to 2021-2 would have 130 caps to their name.

Comparing those who played at different periods throughout the history of the game, of course, is ultimately an impossible task. Given differences in player physique, in training and fitness regimes, and in the way that rugby has been organised and played under a constantly changing body of laws, it is a futile quest to try to determine, once and for all, who were the greatest players or what was the greatest ever Welsh XV. Not that this ever stops the media regularly having a go, usually only selecting players from within very recent memory.

Apart from relying on dry statistics, all that can be realistically achieved when attempting to assess the relative merits of any players from the past – in particular the distant past – is to seek out the views of those who actually witnessed them play. Highly subjective, of course, but so too are most assessments made of any more recent players. In the case of Arthur Gould, there is so much contemporary evidence available, it is undeniable that he was venerated, even hero-worshipped, by the Victorian rugby public; while in the eyes of those who recorded their impressions, his standing could not have been higher. Because Arthur played a great deal of club and county rugby in England, he came to the attention of a very much wider audience than most of his Welsh contemporaries. At times it seems that he was just as popular in English circles as in those at home. In addition to his footballing skills, he was also admired for his sportsmanship, his good humour and his geniality, not forgetting his good looks.

Celebrated in poems, in music hall and pantomime routines, and in specially composed songs, Arthur Gould was, both to his public and to the print media, a "celebrity" and a "superstar", although the expressions would not have been recognised in his day. Such was his widespread fame and popularity and such was his exceptional skill and talent that by any modern definition he was a "superstar". He was the first Welsh player – and arguably the first player – to achieve superstardom.

Despite his fame, however, apart from a few glimpses in the sporting pages, we know surprisingly little about the private Arthur. After his early death, his widow remarried and moved to Cardiff, so unfortunately few stories of Arthur's life and memories of him as a family man and as a father have passed down to his living descendants. Even where he was educated remains something of a mystery.

No contemporary rival matched his achievements: holder of the then world record for international caps; holder of the Welsh captaincy record not surpassed until 1994; captain of Wales in their first ever victory over England and also later in their first Triple Crown season; an astonishing 17 years of top flight rugby; a playing career which lasted from the late 1870s until the 20th century; the inspiration and mainstay of Newport during one of their finest ever periods when they became the most successful club in the land; undefeated seasons with Newport, Richmond, Middlesex and Wales; and scorer of more tries and dropped goals than any contemporary. On top of all this, he was one of Britain's leading hurdlers and sprinters, as well as a Minor County cricketer. Such was the extent of his extraordinary popularity that, uniquely, his admirers clubbed together to give him a testimonial in the form of a house. And such was his importance to rugby in Wales that this event almost resulted in a rupture which could have torn the game apart, had not wiser counsel prevailed.

He is probably best known in the 21st century by too many rugby followers for that controversy, over which, after all, he had no direct responsibility. This is a great pity, since there is so much more to his rugby career which deserves to be celebrated. It does Arthur's memory no great service to be mainly remembered as the Welshman who was gifted a house which, as a consequence, almost caused a serious breach in the sport. In any case, he was never directly involved in the testimonial campaign, which was, after all, a public-inspired response to everything he had done for the game over many years. As for accepting the testimonial, as one English official said at the time, he would have been a fool not to have done so.

This account of Arthur Gould's rugby career draws heavily on the writings of many of Arthur's contemporaries. A few brief examples of their comments on him speak powerfully as to just how much he was venerated by those who saw him play:

> *the prince of centres; the prince of players; the prodigy of football; the football King; the greatest three-quarter who ever donned a shirt; unquestionably the finest exponent of the Rugby game Wales has ever*

"The Football King": Arthur is presented with "Thornbury" while the jesters representing England, Scotland and Ireland disapprove. (London Star, 30 January 1897: Arthur Gould's scrapbook)

produced; his name will be handed down as one of the most skilful exponents of the three-quarter game ever seen; as pre-eminent in football as W G Grace is in cricket; the central figure in the football world – the greatest centre three-quarter that has ever played; the greatest player of all time.

Perhaps, however, final judgement of Welsh rugby's first superstar is best left to his most loyal admirer, W J Townsend Collins ("Dromio") who, towards the end of his life in 1948, wrote with sure conviction:

In the early 'Nineties I thought Arthur Gould the greatest Rugby player I had ever seen. Today after sixty years of football criticism I think of him still as the greatest player of all time ... Those who never saw him in his heyday can have little conception of his physical powers and the keen brain which directed and controlled them.

As a footballer he had all the gifts, and they had been developed by thought and constant practice ... dash and unselfishness, cleverness and coolness, judgement and resource, combined with peculiar grace ... no threequarter I have known has maintained the high level of attainment in attack and defence so long and so consistently as Arthur Gould – no man has shown such uniform brilliance and resourcefulness over so long a period of years. Arthur Gould is to me the greatest Rugby footballer who ever played ... When every deduction is made, Arthur Gould stands alone. [2]

---

2   W J Townsend Collins, *Rugby Recollections*, (Newport, 1948), pp. 7-9.

1

A Sequence of Chance Events

The story begins during 1854 with an ambitious and enterprising 21-year-old setting out on the long journey from the East End of London to south Wales. He had only recently completed his apprenticeship as a gas fitter, and was travelling with his young wife and daughter to start a new life in the rapidly developing town of Newport. This was a move which was destined to have a profound effect on the sporting life of Newport and Wales and indeed on the game of rugby football itself. It was just one in a sequence of chance events which would ultimately produce a sporting genius.

Joseph Gould had been born in 1833 in Curbridge, an Oxfordshire village just south of the modern A40 and the town of Witney. The Goulds had deep roots in this area. Nonconformity was strong around Witney in the 19th century and the family were active in the local Methodist community. Joseph's parents were William and Sarah (*née* Batts). William was the local blacksmith and indeed there were still Gould blacksmiths in Curbridge in the 20th century, well after Arthur had retired from rugby. Joseph, however, was not destined to follow in his father's footsteps, perhaps because his older brother was already working in the family business. As will be seen, it is quite possible that it was a neighbour who had advised Joseph that gas was "the coming thing". Familiar with working in metal from tending his father's forge, Joseph decided to take up an apprenticeship as a gas fitter in London. In 1853 at Lambeth, he married Matilda Wyatt, a childhood sweetheart from Minster Lovell, near Curbridge. Both were 19. By the end of the year, Matilda had given birth to a daughter, Alice Josephine. Matilda had not been born into wealth, however. Her father was a road labourer and she had previously been employed as an outworker in the notoriously hard and poorly paid Witney glove making trade. No doubt, then, she and Joseph were full of hope about the challenges and new opportunities which were on the horizon for them in Wales.

"Father of a stock of athletes", Joseph Gould (1833-1892). (Courtesy of the Gould family)

Joseph had found work as a foreman with the Newport Gas Company. This had been established in 1824 in Mill Street and – responding to the growing economic prosperity of Newport – by the mid-1850s the company's business was booming. But what attracted Joseph to Newport in particular rather than any other economically thriving urban area? The 1851 census provides an answer. The manager of the gas works during the 1850s was Joseph Bryan and he and his family had all been born in Bampton, the Oxfordshire village immediately to the south of Curbridge. Perhaps it was Bryan – in all likelihood an acquaintance of the blacksmith William Gould – who had advised Joseph to become a gas engineer. Maybe he even promised Joseph a job after he qualified. If he did, all Welsh rugby followers should be grateful that by 1854 Bryan had moved from his previous place of employment in Cheltenham to Newport. The two families may even have been related: Joseph Bryan's wife's shared her maiden name, Batts, with that of Joseph Gould's mother. There is further evidence of a possible relationship between the Bryans and the Goulds in the 1851 census. This reveals that the Bryans' house servant in Newport was a 13-year-old Elizabeth Gould. Her place of birth is recorded, like that of all the Bryans, as Bampton but this may well have been Joseph Gould's sister who had also been born in 1838. Joseph's decision to move to Newport is therefore typical of the process of migration: a newcomer is drawn to a location where a relative or friend has previously settled. It was a connection, therefore, which was to serve Newport and Wales well.

In 1855, the Newport Gas Company secured additional powers under Act of Parliament which allowed them to extend their activities outside the Borough to the immediate surrounding areas. It also gave them the authority to require their customers to consume their gas by meter. Prior to this, a complicated system in which consumers were only allowed to use gas at certain times had been the norm. Joseph no doubt saw a great opportunity here, realising that domestic and commercial users would need to engage fitters to install their new meters. So, after less than three years with the company, Joseph decided to set up his own business. Forty years later, the names "Gould" and "Nicholls" would resound throughout the rugby world, but in December 1856 it just happened that "Gould and Nicholls" was the trading name of a new gas fitting and brass furnishing business, reported in the *Monmouthshire Merlin* as operating from 119 Commercial Street in Newport. Nothing is known about Joseph's partner, Charles Nicholls, but it is unlikely that he was related to the Gloucestershire family into which another "Prince of Centres", Gwyn Nicholls, was born in Westbury-on-Severn in 1874.

However, just as Joseph was beginning to climb the business and social ladder in his adopted town, he suffered a grievous loss. In December 1857, Matilda died at their home in Commercial Street. She was just 24 and the couple had been married only five years. It was a devastating blow for Joseph. His ninth son by his second marriage, Edward, born 22 years after Matilda's death, was given the second name of "Wyatt" by which he became universally known.

To add to Joseph's problems, the partnership with Charles Nicholls was in trouble and in May 1858, there was an announcement in the press that it had been formally dissolved, with the comment "debts by Gould". From now on, Joseph ran his business on his own but financial difficulties continued to haunt him.

Those years as a widower must have been hard, with a young daughter to care for and a new business to manage. The early death of a spouse, of course, was an all too sad experience for Victorians, and remarriage was a common event. Joseph was no different from many of his contemporaries. In 1859, he married again.

It was Elizabeth Richards, who had been born in Newport in 1839, who gave the Gould brothers their Welsh ancestry and, presumably, at least some of their sporting prowess too. Her father Thomas Richards was a stonemason who had migrated from the Llanddarog area in rural Carmarthenshire. Like the Goulds, the Richards family were nonconformist artisanal working class, aspirational and upwardly mobile. Thomas was a building contractor in Newport and, therefore, probably knew Joseph professionally. His brother James was an eminent Welsh Baptist minister, while one

Elizabeth Gould (1839-1909), from whom the brothers inherited their Welsh roots. (Courtesy of the Gould family)

of Elizabeth's cousins became a doctor in London. Elizabeth was only half Welsh though, as her mother Ann came from Appledore in Devon. Years later, after Arthur had played against Devon for Newport, one west country journalist had done his homework and suggested that he might consider playing for the county of his forebears. Always tactful in handling the press, Arthur gave a noncommittal response.

Like many Victorian couples, Joseph and Elizabeth had a very large family. Arthur was born in 1864, the fourth of their 13 children. The American Civil War was still raging; while also that year, in Wales, David Davies of Llandinam took out a mineral lease on land at Upper Rhondda, an event of enormous significance for the future Welsh economy. And despite it being a Monday, on 10 October 1864 – the actual day of Arthur's birth – rather appropriately, a "football" match took place at Rugby, where the "Sixth" drew no score with the "School".

Arthur's birth certificate, however, confirms that his name was registered as *Joseph* Arthur Gould. Like many a son named after his father, he was known by his second name within the family and this stuck with him throughout the rest of his life. Given its association with ancient Welsh legend and the Victorian public's fascination with romantic tales of the mythical king, perhaps "Arthur" turned out to be a far more appropriate name for an idolised Victorian footballer than the more prosaic "Jo" Gould. Confusingly, Arthur's younger brother Gus (Augustus) was also given the first name of Joseph but, even more confusingly, he too was sometimes referred to, like his brother, as "A J" Gould in match reports.

Arthur's 12 siblings with year of birth were: Henry William ("Harry") (1859); Charles William (1861); Robert ("Bob") (1863);

George Herbert (1866); Clara Gwenllian ("Gwen") (1868); Lily (1869); George Herbert ("Bert") (1870); Ethel Annie ("Effie") (1872); Ivor Llywelyn (1873); Joseph Augustus ("Gus") (1875); Edward Wyatt ("Wyatt") (1879); and Trevor (1881). Three of the boys – George (born 1866), Ivor and Trevor – did not survive childhood, whilst Charles died when he was 21.

While Arthur's father enjoys a prominent place in some accounts of the remarkable Gould family's exploits, his mother's influence is largely unrecorded and overlooked. The novelist Hilary Mantel once said of her great grandmother, "I suppose that when a woman has ten children, she ceases to have a biography."[1] And Elizabeth Gould, of course, had 13 of her own, as well as her step-daughter Alice, to look after. Between 1859 and 1881 Elizabeth was almost always either carrying a child or recovering from childbirth. Yet, while Joseph was indulging himself at cricket; helping to run the Newport club; or enthusing his athletic boys with a love of sport, it was Elizabeth who was left to manage the large household, full of her energetic and boisterous offspring. Nevertheless, she still took pride in her sons' sporting achievements and managed to regularly attend their matches at Rodney Parade.

As his business prospered, Joseph had more time to devote to sport, particularly cricket. It was a shrewd move. By taking up the game, Joseph greatly widened his social circle as he came into contact with many of the town's leading civic, business and professional community. Developing such networks did his business no harm.

His first known involvement in the game in south Wales occurred in 1859 when – only five years after his arrival – he and some fellow local tradesmen founded the Newport Commercial Cricket Club. By 1864, he had moved on to the more prestigious Newport Cricket Club and one of his very first games was against Cardiff at the "Cardiff Arms field". At this time he batted and bowled but, as he grew older, he generally concentrated on being a middle order batter. After serving as club secretary from the mid-1860s, he was eventually elected captain and made a success of this, as he led Newport for eight successive seasons up to 1880. In 1874, he represented the Gentlemen of South Wales in their innings victory over the Players of South Wales in Cardiff. He was moving in more elevated social circles now. It must have given him great pleasure towards the end

---

1   Hilary Mantel, *Lecture 1, The BBC Reith Lectures*, 13 June 2017.

of his career to play for the Newport XI alongside his son Bob and even, occasionally, a very youthful Arthur. Bob took part in Joseph's last major match held in September 1881, in which he made a couple of runs for a Newport District XXII against W G Grace's All-England XI. The Newport scorer for this contest was a 16-year-old Arthur and evidently, during the event, a now lost photograph was taken in which the two most famous sportsmen of the late Victorian era appeared together. After retiring, Joseph continued to remain closely involved with the game, serving on the match committee of the South Wales Cricket Club and on the management committee of the Newport Cricket, Athletic and Football Club, later renamed the Newport Athletic Club (hereafter NAC).

Joseph even had a brief flirtation with a rather different ball game. In 1867-8, a "Newport Football Club" had been set up by a group of local "gentlemen" who played several games on the Marshes. One of the participants was Joseph Gould. The version of football played was a hybrid of rugby and association: running with the ball was allowed but goals were scored by kicking it between the posts. One match report noted that there were few spectators. "In this game, as in cricket, the inhabitants of Newport display very little interest, and are generally conspicuous by their absence"! The enterprise was evidently a little premature and no more was heard of the club after only one season.

Father and son with Newport Cricket Club, 1886. With his distinctive beard, Joseph is easily identified on the left; while Bob is seated front row centre. (W J Townsend Collins, Newport Athletic Club: The Record of Half a Century 1875-1925, p.112)

It would take another seven years before the Newport rugby club was established. By then, Joseph was too old to give the game a go, but he nevertheless occasionally umpired rugby matches, including an early Newport-Swansea contest held in March 1876. He remained closely involved with the rugby club throughout the rest of his life through his management role in the NAC. When Newport won the first South Wales Challenge Cup in 1878, for instance, Joseph was one of the speakers at the celebratory banquet held at the King's Head Hotel. It was in recognition of his contribution to the NAC that he was later made a life member. And as the reputation of the Gould brothers grew, so too did Joseph's standing in the town. His prominence in Newport's sporting community does suggest that Joseph had a good way with people, a skill which his famous son certainly possessed.

Like many Victorian tradesmen, Joseph seems to have sailed close to the wind on a number of occasions. He appeared in court several times for obstructing the highway with goods displayed on the pavement and, more bizarrely, on one occasion for storing an excessive stock of fireworks on his premises. In 1871, he was summoned for non-payment of wages, when he admitted the debt but claimed he had no money to pay it. Then in 1876, his business was liquidated by arrangement, but this does not seem to have resolved his difficulties as, in 1881, his gas business was finally liquidated and all his stock in Commercial Street was disposed of, by forced sale. It was probably no co-incidence that in May 1881, he resigned the captaincy of Newport Cricket Club, after eight seasons at the helm. He managed to continue with contract work, however, laying water pipes around south Wales for a while but was eventually forced to give this up to become a commercial traveller for a Birmingham brass founding company.

Newport RFC pioneer, Harry Gould (1859-1928): Kingston Gleaner 14 October 1925. (Courtesy of Bruce and Christine Chubb)

It was during Joseph's working career that rugby became a cornerstone of life in the quickly growing and economically dynamic towns and valleys of late 19th-century south Wales. In so doing, the game helped to shape a binding sense of civic and national pride and identity. Nowhere was this more true than in Newport, where Joseph's sons – and in particular Arthur – were enthusiastic participants in the town's evolving sporting culture. Joseph was a keen and active sports devotee himself and it was as a result of his encouragement that all the brothers became involved in sports from an early age.

1875-6 to 1879-80

The first Gould to play rugby was the eldest son, Harry. His father must have been deeply proud when Harry started turning out for Newport but little did Joseph know then that, in all, five more of his sons would eventually play for the club. Of the six, Harry's record, it has to be admitted, was the least distinguished. However, as the very first Gould to represent Newport, his role was not an insignificant one. His participation in club matches, initially played at the Marshes, would surely have inspired his younger brothers to take up the game; whilst later he would also strongly influence their working lives too.

There can be little doubt that Joseph persuaded Harry to take up sport as soon as he was old enough. And get involved Harry did, becoming one of the pioneers of Newport rugby, representing the club over five seasons from 1875-6 to 1879-80. His Newport playing career began, therefore, before the Cardiff club was formed and before Rodney Parade existed; and he retired before the Welsh Football Union[2] (hereafter WFU) was founded.

Privately educated at Devon County School, West Buckland, Harry probably had his first taste of rugby there. It would seem, though, that because of Joseph's financial circumstances, he was the only son sent away to school. There were even rumours of non-payment of Harry's school fees. All the other brothers were educated locally, though precisely where – including in Arthur's case – remains unknown. In an interview with the rugby administrator and writer Rev Frank Marshall, in *Chums* in 1893, Arthur confirmed that he had been

---

2   The Welsh Football Union did not change its name to the Welsh Rugby Union until 1935.

educated in Newport. He was always at pains to make it clear that he never went to public school, so he was presumably educated at a Newport municipal or church school or perhaps at a small private fee-paying establishment of which there were many in the town. He told Marshall, "I learned my football here and never had the benefit of a public school. My football was not learned so much at school as with the Newport Club. They have a third team, known in the district as the Newport Juniors. I played with this team when I was 13."

Some of Newport's early team lists are incomplete, so there is no record of exactly how many games Harry had for the 1st XV, though he is credited with playing at least 13 times. He did not take part in Newport's first ever and only fixture in the 1874-5 season against Glamorgan Football Club. However, despite his youth – he was only 16 years and four months old – he first played for Newport against "Cardiff" on 20 January 1876. As the Cardiff club was not formed until later that year with the merger of Glamorgan FC and Cardiff Wanderers, this fixture must have been with one of these teams. Harry's involvement marked the first sporting achievement of the Gould brothers because it is believed that, since then, no younger player has ever represented Newport's 1st XV. Harry played in half of Newport's matches in 1875-6 and this was the first of *29* consecutive seasons – and *31* in total – in which at least one member of this extraordinarily talented family played for the 1st XV.[3] The last to represent the club was Wyatt, whose final game for a Newport XV – the Reserves – took place on 12 March 1910, 34 years after Harry's debut.[4]

During the following four seasons, Harry appeared occasionally for the 1st XV and sometimes for the Seconds, alternating between fullback, three-quarter or forward. Such positional changes were not at all uncommon at this time as the game was still very much in its infancy and individuals and clubs were constantly experimenting to find out what worked best.

In 1877 Newport moved from the Marshes to Rodney Parade, which was officially opened with a club sports day on 24 May. Years later, the indefatigable rugby correspondent of the *South Wales Argus*,

---

3   This assumes that Harry represented the 1st XV in 1878-9. See below.

4   Even the Gould family's remarkable achievement was later surpassed by the eight Williams brothers of Cardiff who played for the club over a 40-year period between 1934-5 and 1973-4.

"Master A J Gould". (Arthur Gould's scrapbook)

W J Townsend Collins, discovered a reference to a performance at this event which is of particular interest. "Mr J Horner jun. and Master A J Gould were attired in motley, and amused the crowd with droll capers." Arthur would have been 12 and by this time was already being referred to as "Monkey". In his 1893 interview with Marshall, he revealed how he acquired his famous nickname. "That has nothing to do with football. It was given me at school, and has its origin in my fondness for climbing trees. An old school-chum of mine, Edgar Evans, dubbed me 'Monkey'." Marshall commented, "this origin of the soubriquet by which Arthur Gould is universally known will be news to many, as the general idea is that it was bestowed upon him for the activity he displays in the game. Tree-climbing gave him the title, his extraordinary agility had caused it to be continued and perpetuated. Arthur Gould will be "Monkey" or "Monk" Gould to the end of his days."

While "Monkey" was being initiated into the game with Newport Juniors in 1877-8, Harry was playing for Newport in the inaugural South Wales Challenge Cup. He took part in the second round cup victory over Llanelli in the December 1877 but did not play in the final, which Newport won.

Harry probably played for the 1st XV in 1878-9, though because of incomplete records, it isn't possible to confirm that he did so. However, he certainly turned out for the 2nd XV on occasion that year, as did his brother Bob, so the Gould presence at the club was maintained.

The Gould brothers accumulated a profusion of sporting achievements, of course, but Harry was the first to win representative honours in 1878-9, which suggests that he was indeed a 1st XV player that season. In the November, he was selected at forward

First winners of the South Wales Challenge Cup. Newport 1877-8. Back: G Harding, J Goss, Will Phillips (captain), G Phillips, Arthur Goss; Middle: D Loane, W Ponsford, T Spittle, G Rosser, E Jenkins, J Bothomley, W Mitchell, Richard Mullock (standing); Front: Alfred Goss, C Newman, W C Phillips. (Courtesy of Kevin Jarvis at Newport RFC)

for the Rest of South Wales XV against Glamorgan County. Held at Swansea, this match was organised by the South Wales Football Union, the forerunner of the Welsh Rugby Union. Nineteen year-old Harry would have been in the thick of things, since it was a forward dominated game, which Glamorgan eventually won by a goal to a try. Newport's end of season victory over Chepstow on 28 February 1880 marked Harry's last recorded 1st XV appearance. It wasn't long, though, before another Gould was making his presence felt at the club. As will be seen, only seven months later, in October 1880, Bob was playing for the Firsts.

Like all the Goulds, Harry didn't confine his sporting interests to rugby. He was a cricketer and an athlete, often racing over hurdles. In some athletics meetings, while competing against Bob and Charlie, yet another brother, Arthur, was beginning to make a name for himself as an athlete by regularly picking up cash prizes in boys' races.

Harry initially worked as a gasfitter for his father but, when he was 18, he began a pupillage with a Newport civil engineer and he was soon engaged on contracts around the country. These largely involved the design and construction of water supply, drainage and sewerage projects. It was this work which would periodically take three of his brothers, including Arthur, away from Wales and eventually overseas. By 1885, Harry was engaged on several contracts in the Southampton area, where he was joined by Arthur. Later in the 1880s, Harry went out to the Caribbean and spent most of the rest of his working life there. He initially lived in Barbados where he was appointed resident engineer of the water supply works there. Then he was engaged on construction projects in Antigua and in St. Kitts, where the Gould Brothers won the contact for the new Treasury Building in 1893. Eventually, Harry was appointed the City Engineer for Kingston, Jamaica and worked on the building of the island's Heritage Dam. He was also responsible for the reconstruction of Kingston after the 1904 earthquake. Harry retired in 1925 and returned home to live in Edgware, where he died three years later aged 68. He may have been the least well known of the rugby playing Gould brothers, but it was Harry who spearheaded their long association with Newport RFC.

As we have seen, Arthur referred to Newport Juniors as the 3rd XV of the Newport RFC, though whether at that time they were officially organised as such is not known. One very early reference to Arthur playing rugby is found in a *Western Mail* report of January 1879, where he is named at half-back in the Newport Juniors team which lost to Cardiff Juniors. He was then 14, and 15-year-old Bob was also in the side, but what makes this brief report even more intriguing is that a "C Gould" played in the forwards that day. This was almost certainly Charles, who would have been 17 at the time. If this was indeed him and if the Juniors *were* a team organised by Newport RFC, then it could be argued that *seven* Gould brothers, rather than six, represented the club. Charlie, though, may not have been as robust as his brothers, and he suffered from ill-health. In the 1881 census, he is described as an unemployed engine fitter. Perhaps he was too unwell to work by then, because, sadly, he died of consumption just over a year later, aged only 21.

With Harry's departure from Newport, the stage was now set for the dramatic entrance of his much more famous rugby playing brothers.

2

Bob Leads the Way

Harry may have been the Newport ground-breaker but it was Bob's meteoric rise in the game which demonstrated to the young Arthur that anything was possible. Given the latter's subsequent pre-eminence, it is not surprising that Bob's standing in the sport is sometimes overlooked. Yet Arthur's older brother was a distinguished pioneer of Welsh rugby. He deserves his place in the pantheon of the game, not just because he was a Gould, but for his role in establishing rugby as the most popular sport in both Newport and Wales during the crucial 1880s. A talented, skilled and consistent forward, Bob was ever-present in the national team for six seasons, at a time when other Welsh players were selected and discarded with regularity. His Newport and Wales team-mate, Tom Baker Jones described Bob as immensely strong, as hard as nails and – real praise this – "as good a forward as his brother was a back."[1] He was also an inspiration, of course, to his younger brother.

Bob (never Robert) was born in Newport on 26 February 1863 and by 1881 was working as a brass finisher, probably in his father's business. Like other Goulds, he was a precocious youngster and a natural sportsman. A keen gymnast and a more than competent cricketer, he played for Newport Cricket Club from a young age and later for the embryonic

Bob Gould (1863-1931) captained both Newport and Wales, and held the then Welsh record of 11 caps. (Courtesy of Swansea RFC Memorabilia CIC)

---

1   Quoted in: Duncan Pierce, John M Jenkins, Timothy Auty, *Welsh International Rugby Players 1881-2018*, (Charlcombe Books, Bath, 2018), p. 101.

Monmouthshire XI as well as for the prestigious South Wales Cricket Club.

Arthur too, of course, was an early cricketer and, by the time he was 14, he was playing occasionally alongside Bob for Newport. In June 1879, for instance, they were in the same XI which drew with Cardiff. Arthur's performance that day resulted in his being singled out for the very first time in the columns of the *Western Mail*. Apparently, the match was:

> a very tame affair, the only redeeming feature in it being the remarkably smart all-round play of A Gould (a lad, who shows every promise of developing into a first-rate cricketer) ... Newport ... were rather summarily dismissed for 29 runs, their gallant little batsman A Gould holding his own famously at the wickets and scoring 5 not out.

When Cardiff turned up short a month later, they were grateful to Arthur for making up their numbers. Guesting for Cardiff at cricket was one thing, but the blue and black rugby jersey would never sully his skin. However, it was as a cricketer, two years later, that Arthur first trod the Arms Park turf for Newport; while, by the time he was 19, like Bob, he was also representing the Monmouthshire XI.

Having cut his teeth at rugby with Newport Juniors, Bob had his first experience of the senior game at 16, when he played for "The Rest" against the Newport 1st XV in March 1879. This was a specially arranged run-out for the Newport team before the South Wales Challenge Cup final, in which they triumphed over Cardiff. The following November, the *Western Mail* reported that Bob – still only 16 – had "played very well" for Newport Seconds in their victory over Chepstow.

1880-1

Within less than a year, he was in the First team. Bob came into the side for Newport's third fixture, against Merthyr in October 1880 and retained his place for the rest of the season. Just as his more famous brother later made an extraordinary early impression for the club, in only his second match, Bob converted all six of Newport's goals in very windy conditions in their easy win over Rockleaze at Clifton. The press reported that "the Newport team never played so well together". Despite being a mere 17-year-old, Bob had arrived.

He was a quick learner. Newport had been the strongest club in Wales in these early years but the greatest disappointment of 1880-1 came with their first-ever defeat at the hands of Cardiff. To make matters worse, it occurred in an early round of the South Wales Challenge Cup, a tournament dominated by Newport, who won it five times in the first eight seasons. Even though it was no place for the fainthearted – some of the Cardiff players were attacked by the Rodney Parade crowd after the match – Bob took it in his stride. Many of the participants were later included in the first Welsh international team a few weeks later. He was still a bit too young yet for consideration but, during the following season, with consistently impressive performances, Bob forced himself into contention.

1881-2

Although rugby had arrived in Wales only around ten years earlier, by 1881 the organisation of the sport *was* improving. The game's administrators were learning. The 13 try to nil debacle in Wales' international debut against England the previous February had been a deeply shocking and embarrassing affair. Consequently, the newly-formed Welsh Football Union resolved to arrange a series of special fixtures in an attempt to improve both playing standards and selection practices. Despite his youth, Bob was a beneficiary of these initiatives and 1881-2 turned out to be his breakthrough season. Still only 18, he gained his first representative experience with the South Wales XV which won a close game by a try to nil against the "Irish Rovers", an unofficial touring team containing several internationals.

Over the next few weeks Bob played four times for Monmouthshire in home and away fixtures with Glamorgan and Gloucestershire. There was little surprise, therefore, when he was included in the Wales team to meet the North of England on 14 January 1882 at Newport. As the match against England a year earlier had taken place before the formation of the WFU, this was the first ever *officially* selected Wales XV. Caps were not awarded but the team still played in scarlet jerseys emblazoned with the three feathers. Because of the pasting handed out a year before, the RFU declined to send a full international team this time. However, the North of England XV included over half the team which had recently inflicted defeat on the South for the first time in five years and it was a powerful enough combination of experienced county players and internationals. Wales put up a stout fight and went down narrowly by only a converted try to a try. It was a very encouraging performance and a huge improvement on 1881. Importantly, it surprised and impressed the officials of the RFU.

1882: Ireland v Wales – Bob's First Cap

Bob retained his place in another non-cap fixture a week later. This time Wales thoroughly overwhelmed a Midlands XV by three goals and three tries to nil. A couple of days later, there was great delight in the Gould household, when his family read in the local press that he had been included in the team to meet Ireland in Dublin. After Edward Treharne in 1881, Bob was the second 18-year-old to be picked by Wales. Of the 1,177 men who had played for Wales by March 2022, only 12 – and some by a matter of days – were younger than Bob when they won their first cap.[2] In comparison, Arthur had turned 20 when he later became an international.

Only Newport's George Harding, Charlie Newman and Frank Purdon and Cardiff's Bill Phillips remained from the XV which had lost so badly to England the previous season. At half-back was Ronald Bridie, who came with a complicated rugby background. Working for a short period in Wales, he was currently playing for Newport. Ron was Scottish by parentage but had been born at sea. So, crossing their fingers, the Welsh selectors gambled that he was sufficiently qualified by temporary residence. In the meantime, he was selected for the West Scotland v East Scotland trial. However, this match was fixed for the same day as the Ireland game, so Bridie decided to opt for Wales instead. Obviously, a cap in a Welsh hand was worth two in a Scottish bush.

The Ireland fixture became a regular headache for Wales in these early years. With the Welsh arriving late at the international table, the Irish rugby fraternity did not seem over-keen to welcome Wales into an otherwise cosy arrangement with England and Scotland. When the WFU was founded in March 1881, the newly-elected secretary, Newport's Richard Mullock, was charged with arranging a fixture with Ireland in Dublin before the end of the 1880-1 season. This he claimed to have done, fixing a date (9 April 1881) and selecting a team, only then to be told by the Irish that the game had to be cancelled

---

2   Duncan Pierce et al, p. 229. Thanks to John Jenkins for updating to March 2022.

A very youthful-looking Bob wins his first cap against Ireland. Wales 1882.
Back: C Newman, H Vincent, G Harding, Richard Mullock, S Clark, W F Evans,
T B Jones; Middle: F Purdon, W D Phillips, T Williams, C P Lewis (captain), Bob
Gould, W Norton; Front: T Clapp, G Morris, R Bridie. (Courtesy of Swansea RFC
Memorabilia CIC)

with the feeble excuse that "no ground could be obtained". It would
happen again. Even the Irish RFU historian refers to their attitude
towards the Welsh at this time as being "something approaching
condescension", which was probably an understatement.

So the match was eventually rearranged for the following
season on 28 January 1882, to be played – at the insistence of the
Irish – in Dublin. This time Lansdowne Road *was* available. Though
Wales won at a canter by two goals and two tries to nil, there was
still controversy. For a start, most of the selected Irish team were
distinctly underwhelmed about playing against Wales and only four
of the originally named XV took the field. The *Belfast Newsletter*
declared that "the so-called Irish team made a miserable exhibition
of themselves". The result had been "totally unexpected" because
Wales had been "much underrated". In fact, the *Newsletter* noted,
somewhat patronisingly, "the visitors were not at all a bad side".

The Welsh forwards "worked hard" and they "passed right
well". Their defence was sound even "if not always in accordance

with the rules" (always a good excuse for defeat). But apart from the "penchant for offside play" by the Welsh forwards, what really infuriated the Irish press was the "questionable" umpiring of the wily WFU secretary, Richard Mullock. By half time, Wales were already in the lead, the Newport forward Tom Baker Jones having burrowed his way over the line to become the first-ever player to score a try for Wales. Then, from a throw-in from touch near the half-way line, the ball was passed to Ron Bridie who, it was claimed, was in an offside position. Bridie, however, ran in unopposed to score. Mullock ruled that the try was good; the Irish umpire said he was unsighted; so the try was allowed to stand and the conversion was taken. The Irish could have appealed to the referee but they left it too late to do so. According to the *Newsletter*, Mullock's decision "was not endorsed by a single other person on the ground". From then on the result was never in doubt. The Irish seem to have given up the fight and four of them left the field at various points, either in disgust or through injury. Tom Clapp and Bill Evans added two more tries to Wales' total. It was an excellent win but the match had done little to enhance the reputation of Welsh rugby in Ireland.

Irish pride was partially salvaged, however, the following Monday, when Newport became the first Welsh club to play in Ireland. Their opponents were Dublin Wanderers who beat them by a goal and a try to nil. Barely recovered from the post-match celebrations, Bob was one of eight Newport internationals who dragged themselves onto the Lansdowne Road pitch for the second time in three days. The "Mustard and Blackings" lost only two other games in 1881-2 but perhaps they can be excused for this defeat. The *Irish Times* conceded that "allowance must be made for men who are combining a little rational amusement with the duties of the football field".

The season's success for Bob continued with Newport's defeat of Llanelli in the replayed final of the 1882 South Wales Challenge Cup at Swansea. The first match had ended in a no-score draw and it was while reporting this that the local press (though conveniently ignoring what was happening in north Wales) began referring to rugby as the national game. In front of upwards of 5,000 supporters, the replay was another close contest, the "most exciting ever seen in Wales", with Newport winning by 7 points to 5 under cup rules. But the growing enthusiasm for the game in Wales also heralded its darker side. During the first half, trouble erupted in the crowd and "a free fight [broke out], in which a large number of persons participated ...

Violent blows were exchanged, sticks used with effective force, and hats unceremoniously "blocked" ... the police interposed." Happily, at least the match itself passed off without incident.

Judging by the reaction in Newport to the cup win, there was no doubt about the growing enthusiasm for rugby amongst the Welsh general public. The team was greeted at Newport station by a vast crowd. Joseph and Arthur would have witnessed the scenes, along with

Arthur in his teens. (Arthur Gould's scrapbook)

other members of the Gould family who now lived less than one of Arthur's drop kicks away at their new home in Bridge Street. Amid great cheering, the local drum and fife band escorted the players from the station to the King's Head Hotel in High Street. Six-times captain Will Phillips was shouldered all the way and, at the entrance to the hotel, he thanked the supporters for their reception. Then the trophy was displayed to the crowd who reacted heartily.[3] We can only imagine what an impression these scenes must have made on the 17-year-old Arthur, who followed all Bob's success on the field with great pride. It would not be long, though, before he would emulate – and then surpass – him.

With the season over, in April 1882, both brothers attracted much attention at a gymnastic event held at the Victoria Hall. Bob demonstrated his expertise on the rings and on the double trapeze, while he and Arthur gave a display of "tumbling somersaulting". "Monkey" also performed "some very neat clever tricks" on the flying trapeze. But perhaps what is most telling about the evening is that "A J Gould went through some tricks as a clown". An unimpressed *Star of Gwent* reporter did not find them "mirth provoking" in the

---

3   Missing for many years, the South Wales Challenge Cup was returned to the custody of the Welsh Rugby Union in September 2021. A magnificent trophy, it cost 50 guineas (£52.50) when the tournament was introduced in 1877.

slightest but grudgingly admitted that as gymnastic feats, they were very clever.

In his column in the *Western Mail* in 1894, "Welsh Athlete" (H W Wells) claimed that, in the early 1880s, Arthur had been apprenticed as a plumber, (though the 1881 census shows his occupation as a clerk and gas fitter in his father's business). However, "Welsh Athlete" revealed that in order to earn a few extra shillings at this time, Arthur played "the cymbals and other high-sounding instruments" in the band at the Newport Theatre. Local newspapers reveal that he also strutted his stuff on the stage as a teenager, performing the role of the "Printer's Boy" in a Newport Histrionic Club comedy which was attended by a large audience. Arthur's self-confidence and his strong urge to entertain, then, evidently emerged at an early age.

1882-3

"Kick, You Young Devil"

From the late 1870s, Arthur had been honing his skills with Newport Juniors but it was during the 1882-3 season that he first took his place alongside Bob in the Newport XV. The story of Arthur's arrival is well known but worth repeating. Most accounts (including some by Arthur!) claim that he was only 16 at the time but he was actually a month over 18. Had there been any portents in the Newport sky the night before 18 November 1882, none was recorded. It appeared to be just another ordinary rugby day, with Weston-Super-Mare the visitors at Rodney Parade. However, a brilliant new star was about to be discovered in the sporting firmament. According to Townsend Collins, full back Fred Dowdell had failed to confirm his availability by the morning of the match. So the Newport groundsman, John Butcher, was urgently despatched to his house to find out if there was any problem. Dowdell, it transpired, had gone to a funeral, so Butcher decided to hang around for his return. Arthur must have got wind of this because, according to Collins, Butcher then noticed him anxiously pacing up and down in the street. The teenager then plucked up courage and approached Butcher, who asked Arthur if he would cover for Dowdall should he not be available. There could only have been one response. When Butcher later reported to the captain Charlie Newman and the secretary Richard Mullock, he persuaded them to give Arthur a chance. And it was a decision that none of them, or Townsend Collins for that matter, would ever regret. Remarkably, Dowdell was selected as the reserve back for Wales later that season, but still lost his regular place as the Newport fullback to the youngster.

Even though Arthur more usually played at three-quarter, his debut at fullback was a triumph. Ignoring his captain's admonishment, "kick, you young devil", he sliced through the Weston defence to score two of Newport's three tries. This was not what was expected of fullbacks, whose role was essentially a defensive one of tackling and kicking. However, "Monk" ignored accepted practice and, in so doing, helped Newport to a trouble-free win. He kept his place from then on and was never dropped.

Bob's form was better than ever and he was included the East team to meet the West, prior to the England international at Swansea. The trial was fixed for 2 December 1882 but, the week before, tragedy struck the Gould family, when 21-year-old Charles succumbed to tuberculosis, the scourge of Victorian Britain. The funeral took place on the day of the trial, so there was no question that Bob would play. Even so, he was already held in such regard by the selectors that he was still picked for the international. Charles' prolonged illness

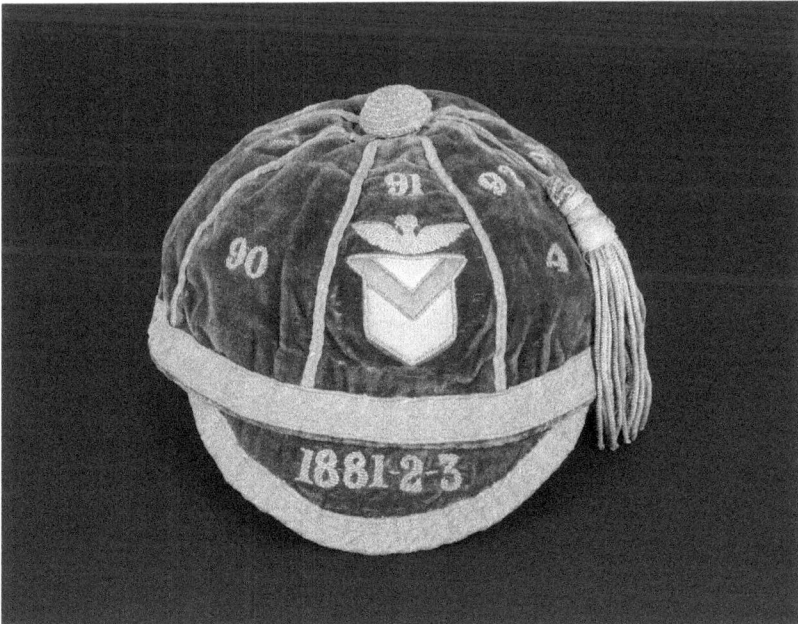

Arthur's Newport cap, which records all the seasons he played for the club. (Courtesy of Robert Gould)

must been a very difficult period for the Gould family and no doubt celebrations over Arthur's elevation to the Newport team and Bob's re-selection for Wales were muted.

1882: Wales v England

Hard to believe when compared to the almost hysterical level of pre- and post-match media attention today, but when the *Western Mail* reported the very first international held on Welsh soil, their account of the game was actually delayed until the following Tuesday. This was because priority was given to its extensive Monday coverage of the death of the Bishop of Llandaff. England were again much too strong for Wales who went down by two goals and four tries to nil. Despite this, the Welsh performance was acknowledged to be an improvement, especially up front. According to the *York Herald*, "The two fifteens were well matched at forward, but in passing and pace England were far superior." The defence struggled to cope with Greg Wade, a big winger who was to cause Wales further heartache in later internationals. He was on fire in this match, scoring a hat-trick of tries, and one in each of the following three meetings of the sides. Given that no-one expected Wales to win in 1882-3, there may have been some irritation that England had selected an Australian, though no objection was made about Wade's inclusion. Nor, perhaps with even greater justification, was there any complaint about the three-quarter who kicked the two English conversions. Not only had Arthur Evanson been born at Llansoy in Monmouthshire but he had also turned down invitations to play for Wales on two previous occasions.

Over the Christmas, it was Arthur's turn to have his first taste of representative rugby when he was selected for South Wales against Old Monmothians. Though only a few weeks into his senior career, he was already demonstrating his characteristic quick-wittedness, speed and self-confidence. South Wales had scored a try but missed the conversion. However, Arthur followed up the kick "with great quickness" and fell on the ball before any of his opponents did. Under the laws as they then stood, it was a legitimate try. The original RFU laws of 1871 stated:

> *53. The ball is dead whenever a goal has been obtained, but if a try at goal be not successful the kick shall be considered as only an ordinary kick in the course of the game.*

Arthur also dropped a "neat goal" and so gave victory to South Wales by a goal and two tries to two tries. He was getting noticed.

1883: Scotland v Wales

The first ever meeting with Scotland took place shortly afterwards. This was to involve Bob in the most hectic and draining few days of his rugby career. The international was held at Raeburn Place, Edinburgh on 8 January 1883 which was, unusually, a Monday. However, on the previous Saturday, Newport had a home fixture with Gloucester who had beaten them twice the previous season. Presumably Mullock persuaded the Newport men selected for the international that they were needed against Gloucester before they headed north. Incredibly, this meant that half the Welsh XV, eight players in all – Bob Gould, Charlie Newman, Bill Evans, George Harding, Tom Clapp, Tom Baker Jones, Horace Lyne and Frank Purdon (guesting now that he had transferred to Swansea) played in a tough club encounter only *two* days before meeting Scotland. It didn't do Newport much good, either, as they still lost to Gloucester. The players surely grumbled about the wisdom of this as they headed north on the long and tiring journey to Edinburgh.

This certainly took its toll on the Welsh performance. Scotland won by three converted goals to one converted goal. Tom Judson finished off a spectacular try, after the Welsh forwards ran the length of the field in possession. Gould, Clapp and Judson were reckoned to be the pick of the Welsh pack. It is sometimes claimed that the Scots objected to the drafting in of Ron Bridie at half-back. Resident again in Scotland, only a week earlier he had played for the South of Scotland against the North. Bridie is mentioned in a number of match reports but other sources suggest that it was Cardiff's William Norton who played, possibly as a result of the Scottish protests. With no Welsh qualifications, John Griffin, who was studying medicine at Edinburgh University, also came into the team as a late replacement.

But the ordeal wasn't over for Bob yet. Mullock had arranged a fixture with Halifax who had overcome a full strength Newport earlier that season. Mullock agreed – foolishly as it turned out – to play the return match on the Wednesday as the players travelled home from Edinburgh. At the best of times, this was no easy task, as Halifax were a very strong side. Bob now found himself taking

A reorganised Welsh team lost in their first meeting with Scotland. Only twelve in this line-up played. Wales 1883. Back: G Rowland Hill (RFU, referee), H Lyne, W F Evans, F Purdon, T Clapp, G Harding, T B Jones; Middle: Richard Mullock, Bob Gould, G Morris, C P Lewis (captain), C H Newman; Front: T Judson, R Bridie (later withdrawn after protest), W Norton. Missing: A Cattell, J Griffin, J A Jones. (Courtesy of Swansea RFC Memorabilia CIC)

part in his third tough encounter in five days. With only 13 players available (and no Arthur), Newport had to borrow a couple of local men. But even with seven members of the Welsh team, Newport were simply too tired to put up much opposition. Townsend Collins commented that Halifax "made mincemeat of 'The Tired Thirteen', some of whom had hardly been to bed from the time they set out from Newport." They lost heavily by three goals and six tries to nil. Apart from their catastrophic loss to Blackheath in 1879, this was the heaviest defeat suffered by the club for a very long time. A shattered Bob was must have been glad to get home.

He should have added another Welsh cap to his total before the season was over. Ireland were due in Cardiff on 27 January 1883. The team was selected, club fixtures cancelled, special trains organised and the post-match banquet booked. Then, just two days before the game, the Irish contacted Mullock to say that, yet again, they couldn't raise a team. Such were the sentiments in Ireland about playing Wales that a motion was even carried at an IRFU meeting from one half into the other, and the game was full of interest to the onlookers. The following are the names of the teams:—*Harlequins:* A. J. Gould, back; A. E. Stoddart, F. T. Watts (captain), and W. H. M'Mahon three-quarter backs : F. Watts and T. Harding, half-backs; H. L. Stoddart, H. K. Gow, J. Trotman, G. L. Jeffrey, H. Inman, L. Weber, C. S. Kohler, J. G. Scott, and E. A. Jackson, forwards. *Cardiff :* T. M. Barlow, back ; C. H. Newman, T. Williams and W. B. Norton, three-quarter backs ; W. Douglas and Herbert Jones, half backs ; W. D. Phillips (captain), J. S. Smith, H. J. Simpson, E. Laybourne, J. Hinton, W. P. Phillips, J. A. Jones, M'Connochie, and Treatt, forwards.

The only appearance Arthur made for the Harlequins. (Weekly Mail, 24 February 1883)

that selection against Wales would not merit the award of a cap. These difficulties continued to fester for some time.

A couple of weeks later, Cardiff were hosting the Harlequins who turned up two men short. Newport happened to be without a fixture, so Arthur and Theo Harding were invited to fill the gaps in the Quins' ranks. The match was an "exhibition of really good play" in which Arthur "rendered valuable service" to the London club, who managed to hold Cardiff to a scoreless draw. Cardiff had been involved in a couple of fractious cup matches in the weeks leading up to the visit of the Harlequins and this appears to have finally convinced the club that they could find far more attractive fixtures elsewhere. As a result, from the following season, Cardiff took no further part in the cup, something they had been considering for a while, as indeed had Newport, though they rejected a motion to pull out. The competition then began to lose some of its momentum. Perhaps Arthur's performance that day contributed to this.

The brothers' season ended on a very high note. Newport again reached the final of the South Wales Challenge Cup. This time the opponents were Swansea, who had the advantage of playing at home. The *South Wales Daily News* match report provides further evidence of rugby's growing influence on the shared experience of life in south Wales.

Such popularity has the game attained that it would have been difficult to meet anyone during Saturday morning who did not make enquiry respecting the probable result ... long before [kick-off] the roads leading to the St. Helen's ground presented a very animated sight; crowds of people, young and old, ladies in almost summer costumes, busied along, eager to obtain a good place on the field.

For fully an hour a continuous stream of people passed along St. Helen's Road ... The ground ... looked like a billiard table. On one side the beautiful bay studded with craft, on the other the gorse covered mountain, and between some thousands of people discussing eagerly the approaching game. There were hundreds who "cheated the gate" by getting a good view from the railway bridge or any eminence that commanded the sight of the ground.

Such scenes at major matches might seem hardly worthy of much attention today but what must be remembered is that at this time they were still something of a novelty. A mere ten years earlier, they would have been unimaginable. No wonder the reporter felt the need to comment on them. He continued:

The moralist might moralize, the cynic might sneer, or the pessimist might grumble, yet the sight on the ground ... was proof positive that the game of football is appreciated by thousands of all classes, and that also a match can be played without the slightest ill feeling.

Rugby was clearly capturing the hearts and minds of the Welsh public and it was in this sporting arena that Arthur Gould was beginning to make his presence felt. Very soon his performances would enrapture his fellow countrymen.

The cup final must have been one of the brothers' most enjoyable experiences. Newport had evidently learned the lesson of England and Scotland's passing and backing up. They took control of the second half and:

passed the ball back and fore with great skill – long and short passes – followed up by runs ... the striped figures of the Newport forwards spread out in one thin line, and the passing and running commenced in earnest, which completely baffled the Swansea men, they not knowing where to look for the ball. If one of the visitors was ... tackled, another was ready to receive the ball, and so on until some half a dozen handled it ... It was evident that the Newport men were adepts in this part of the game, indeed no passing like that witnessed on Saturday has been shown on the Swansea field since the Englishmen played there.

Under the cup scoring rules, Newport won 28-12. It was their fourth win in the competition in six seasons.

A year earlier, Arthur had merely been an excited onlooker at Newport station when the victorious team returned home. This time, he was at the centre of the celebrations. Again the team were met by over a thousand well-wishers, who cheered the players all the way to the King's Head. Charlie Newman thanked them for the reception and then Bob Gould, generous and big-hearted as ever, took it on himself to call for three cheers for Swansea.

1883-4

The next season was another one of success for Newport, who lost only twice in their 19 fixtures. The two Goulds played in all of them, with Arthur featuring at both fullback and three-quarter. After only two years of senior rugby, it was realised that, in Arthur, Wales possessed a rare talent. In December 1883, he was selected at fullback for Monmouthshire against Glamorgan and then for the East v West trial, though he would have to wait another year before making his international debut.

1884: England v Wales

That season's England match was held on 5 January at Leeds where Wales gave their best international performance so far. Although Yorkshire was a hotbed of the English game, this was the first international staged in the county but locals were understandably irked by the fact that there were no Yorkshire representatives in the English XV. The Welsh forwards played especially well and more than held their own

Charles Taylor was an officer in the Royal Navy, serving from the 1880s until his death in action in at the Battle of Dogger Bank in 1915. (Courtesy of John Taylor)

in the tight. According to *The Referee,* "though much lighter than the Englishmen, [the Welsh] played splendidly in the packs ... Gould, Lyne, Margrave and Clapp showed dribbling and tackling powers of great merit". Controlled dribbling was a common feature of the game at the time and it was a skill at which Bob was expert. The *Leeds Mercury* reported that, in spite of the English weight advantage, the Welsh pack "played throughout with more determination and spirit, following up and tackling firmly". Wales lost, scoring one goal to England's goal and two tries. They might have even felt they were a little unlucky. At one point, the new cap and soccer convert from north Wales, Charlie Taylor – a three-quarter renowned for his kicking – attempted a long range drop goal. It was adjudged to have been just wide, but the English fullback, Henry Tristram, later sportingly conceded that he was standing under the goal and clearly saw Taylor's kick going over the bar and *through* the posts. Had that drop-kick been awarded, Wales would have achieved their first victory over England under the then laws by two goals to one. And no doubt Charlie Taylor, who became a naval casualty of the First World War, would be a household name to this day.

1884: Wales v Scotland

Arthur and other members of the Gould family were amongst the spectators a week later to watch Bob win his fifth cap against Scotland on his home ground. Following the much improved display at Leeds, there was an air of confidence about Welsh prospects this time. The *Western Mail* reported that the "common belief was that Scotland would be beaten". All week, rail companies had been advertising cheap fares and special trains to Newport from towns throughout south Wales. Entrance to the match cost sixpence (2½p) for the ground; one shilling (5p) for the enclosure; and two shillings (10p) for the stand. The enclosure was free for ladies, Newport club members and season ticket holders, though they had to pay a shilling if they wanted a seat in the stand. While 4,600 paid for admission and 800 entered by ticket, it was reckoned that another 600 rushed the gates. This would become a common occurrence at Welsh matches, which sometimes resulted in serious injuries to spectators. The total attendance, described in one report as "immense", was much bigger than that at Leeds.

However, despite the pre-match optimism, there was disappointment again for Wales, who went down by a dropped goal and a try to nil. But it could have been so different. Wales did play well and their passing and backing up was good. Bob was prominent amongst the forwards, as they frequently broke through their opponents. Charlie Taylor's kicking was "uncommonly sure and powerful". Both Scottish scores were regarded as dubious and were disputed by Wales, (appeals were an accepted part of the game then). To make matters worse, Wales missed what looked like a certain try after half-back Bill Gwynn sold a dummy and then took off on an inspired run. However, with the line at his mercy, he hesitated while looking round for support and was bundled into touch. "A groan of despair arose from the mass of spectators".

But Wales were definitely improving. The *Glasgow Herald* was sure that they had stepped up from their performance against England; while the *South Wales Daily News* proudly boasted that the match "proved one fact conclusively, that the Welshmen are making rapid strides in the game".

Wales v Scotland 1884. Back: H Simpson, F Musgrave, W D Phillips; Middle: G Morris, T B Jones, H Lyne, T Clapp, F Andrews, Bob Gould; Front: C. Newman (captain), C Allen, W Gwynn, C P Lewis, C Taylor, W Norton. (Courtesy of Swansea RFC Memorabilia CIC)

1884: Wales v Ireland

The 1883-4 season was the first in which Wales played three times and all three Home Unions played each other. At last, the Irish managed to bring a team to Wales – well, a team of sorts. We should sympathise with Herbert Cook, the hard-pressed Irish RFU secretary, who was doing his best not to let Wales down yet again, even to the extent of agreeing to play himself in his only international appearance. However, although a team was selected, only nine men were prepared to travel. The match was arranged for 12 April, but just a few days before, Cook was forced to appeal desperately in the Irish press for interested players, "especially forwards". The response was disappointing and thus it was that the Irish team arrived in Cardiff with only 13 players, including Cook. So Ireland were obliged to borrow two, what were then referred to as, "substitutes". Cook afterwards wrote that the Irish Union wanted to abandon the game but "as the Welsh Union had almost besought them to send over a team, it was decided to play the match at all hazards".

The two Welsh replacements played in the Irish pack and both were old team-mates of Bob's. Charles Jordan was a good journeyman forward who played six seasons for Newport. Welsh press reports confirm that it was Charles who played and not, as often claimed, Newport's tiny international wing H Martyn Jordan. The other replacement was the experienced and versatile Irish-born Welsh international, Frank Purdon, formerly of Newport but now with Swansea. Discarded by Wales that season, Purdon must have relished the opportunity of playing against them. Despite the evidence of several Welsh match reports which confirm that Purdon played, the Irish RFU and many others still do not acknowledge him. They prefer instead to rely on the much later dubious claim that it was another of Bob's Newport team-mates, Harry McDaniel who represented Ireland, even though his name is not mentioned in *any* press reports. It is a shame that Purdon has so far been denied official recognition as he was rugby's first dual international.

The match, however, was memorable for rather more important reasons. This was the very first time that the Arms Park hosted an international; and, just as significantly for the future of the game, it was also the first occasion on which a genuinely working-class player represented Wales. Forced to make their own late changes – four altogether – Wales brought in Cardiff's "Buller" Stadden at half-back. Stadden, a general labourer, later became the first Welsh international to move north to better himself financially.

As the teams gathered at the Angel Hotel to change, it is possible that Arthur Gould was anxiously pacing up and down, just as he had done before beginning his Newport career only 17 months earlier. Despite being only 19, he had been selected reserve fullback for Wales, though on this occasion there was to be no fairy-tale call-up for him. His time would come soon enough, however. It is just as well, perhaps, that he didn't have any Irish ancestry!

Every effort was made to give the visitors a warm welcome on their very first visit to Cardiff. Mullock had even gone to the trouble of printing green coloured handbills advertising the match, with the heading "a hundred thousand welcomes" in Gaelic. The *South Wales Daily News* noted that "the devotees of the national winter game" had been long and ardently looking forward to the match. The crowd of around 5,000, boosted by members the town's large Irish community, were generous in their appreciation of the performance of the depleted Irish XV.

Wales were much stronger on the day and won relatively easily. Surprisingly, though, given their selection difficulties, up front the Irish matched their opponents well. But behind the scrum Wales were far superior. Their backs "worked together like a machine" and the passing was "of a very high order", whereas that of their opponents was "wild and uncertain". Bob Gould was again praised for his good play. His automatic selection, as others came and went, demonstrates that he was now one of the most consistent of forwards in Wales. The final score-line was a drop goal and two tries to nil. It was a creditable performance and after the two good displays against England and Scotland, there was a sense of satisfaction amongst the devotees of what the *South Wales Daily News* was already referring to "as the national winter game." Three years would pass before Wales met Ireland again.

The 1883-4 season was a good one for the Gould brothers at club level too. Newport again reached the final of the South Wales Challenge Cup, having suffered only one defeat up to then at the hands of Cardiff by a try to nil. The venue for the final was Neath. The "Mustard and Blackings" had already beaten their opponents Llanelli twice, so there must have been some confidence in their ranks that they would make it three cup wins in a row. There was bitter disappointment, however, when they went down by 11 points to 2. The only try of the match was disputed by the Newport umpire, but the referee, George Rowland Hill, ruled in the Scarlets' favour. Arthur would be confronted with rather more controversial decisions of the RFU secretary later in his career. Llanelli deserved their first cup success and the town also outdid Newport's previous efforts at celebrating victory. The Llanelli XV received a huge ovation when they arrived home. A tramcar, "heavily leaden" with supporters, led the procession. They were followed by a brass band. Then came the team who were carried in a brake pulled by supporters rather than horses. Finally, bringing up the rear, was a crowd estimated at 2,000 amongst whom were "innumerable" torch bearers. The windows of all the houses along the route were lit up with lamps and candles, while fireworks illuminated the sky around the town. The return of the Newport team was not recorded.

3

"Monk" Breaks Through

1884-5

The 1884-5 season was to witness Arthur's breakthrough as an international. Still only 19 when the season opened, he was nevertheless ready to come out from under his brother's shadow. Match reports now frequently praised his overall play and in particular his drop kicking. Unquestionably, Bob was still performing extremely well and he was clearly regarded as one of the finest forwards in Wales. But forwards rarely received the same coverage as backs in match reports and, when the back was Arthur Gould, it was inevitable that he would eventually become the more prominent in the eyes of the press.

Newport 1884-5. Back: H Lyne, F C Jones, J Webb, T Newcombe, G Harding, T Clapp (captain), H Briggs, E Bellerby, L Williams, T B Jones; Middle: H Martyn Jordan, W Bailey, T Harding, F Dowdall, Arthur Gould; Front: Charles Jordan, T Barfoot, H McDaniel, Bob Gould. (Courtesy of Kevin Jarvis at Newport RFC)

Another significant change for Arthur was that, after two games for Newport at fullback, he switched to three-quarter and thereafter that became his permanent position, for his club at least. Never short of self-confidence, it is quite likely that he had requested this change to his preferred position, where he could take on a more influential and creative role. Both brothers again played in most of the club's 26 fixtures but it was a somewhat less successful season for the "Black and Ambers" in which they suffered more defeats than ever before, six in all. They were beaten by Wakefield Trinity, Llanelli, Weston, Cardiff and twice by Neath. However, Newport *did* manage to reclaim the Challenge Cup, gaining revenge in the final for their previous reverses against Neath, though the competition was now definitely beginning to lose its shine.

The 1885 final was held at Cardiff Arms Park. The modern-day Welsh Rugby Union may like to think that they were innovators when they pioneered the "double header" at the Stadium but, as so often is the case in many other areas of life, it was the Victorians who got there first. Newport defeated Neath by a try and three touch downs (7 points) to nil in a match dominated by scrums and described "as dull as ditch water" by "Old Stager" (J R Stephens) of the *South Wales Daily News*. However, that contest was then immediately followed by a much more entertaining exhibition between Cardiff and Gloucester. This was "far and away a superior game", with scarcely "a dull interval". Cardiff had been experimenting with four three-quarters for a while now and other clubs were beginning to take note, including Gloucester who played four against them. So too did Neath in the final, though interestingly Newport still defiantly stuck to three. The comparison between the boring final and the thrilling "friendly" probably convinced even more followers that the Challenge Cup had had its day.

The only try of the final was made by Arthur who, on receiving the ball from Bob, made a decisive break and eventually passed to his wing Martyn Jordan who crossed to score. For Newport, this was the fifth time they had won the cup in eight seasons: for Bob, it was his third win. The cup was finally withdrawn two years later, so Bob was one of a select group of only five – all Newport men – who played in three successful Challenge Cup teams.[1]

---

[1]   The others were Will Phillips, Horace Lyne, Harry McDaniel and Tom Clapp.

From the start of the season, the brothers had been putting in some impressive displays for their club, and so both were selected to represent South Wales in a pre-international fixture with Oxford University in early November. Shortly afterwards, Arthur came in for some criticism in the *Western Mail* for his passing in a match with Gloucester. Newport won easily enough, and Arthur and Martyn Jordan played "splendidly" in the three-quarters but "sometimes the ball was thrown a little too high ... in good passing, the ball should not be thrown higher than the head". Rather than tucking the ball under his arm, Arthur had a preference for running with the ball in both hands which he felt gave him more options when attacking. Townsend Collins later recalled, "as he side-stepped an opponent, he would raise the ball at arm's length above his head; sometimes from that height he gave a downward untakable pass." This tendency was something for which Arthur was occasionally criticised in his more mature years. He and Jordan, however, "showed fine form, and their runs and kicks proved of immense service" against Gloucester.

Then came a controversial meeting with Cardiff, in which "the younger Gould" dropped a magnificent goal "eliciting a tremendous outburst of enthusiasm". Cardiff scored three tries but none was converted, so Arthur's solitary score of a goal gave Newport victory even though, as the Cardiff press were keen to point out, had Challenge Cup rules applied, the "Blue and Blacks" would have won by 14 points to 9. Arthur was to be involved in a remarkably similar outcome for Wales against Ireland only a couple of years later.

1885: Wales v England – Arthur's First Cap

It was only a little over two years since Arthur had made that unforgettable 1st XV debut for Newport but now, at just turned 20, he was to represent Wales for the very first time. There was some criticism about the selection of the team to meet England, especially over the number of Newport men chosen. However, this doesn't seem to have been directed at Arthur's inclusion at fullback, nor indeed at that of his brother who would be winning his seventh cap. One correspondent to the *South Wales Daily News* even suggested that there wasn't a "better back in Wales, or England ... than "Monk" Gould, the man who beat the Cardiff team." Another thought that, rather than picking him at fullback, it would have been better to have placed him at three-quarter where his "invaluable services

Arthur's Welsh cap. (Courtesy of Robert Gould)

are required more". As for Bob, "Newport have certainly a splendid forward in Gould". It is instructive here, too, to note that Arthur was now being publicly referred to by his nickname, a sure sign that he was already becoming a household name in wider rugby circles.

Arthur launched his 27-cap international career at Swansea on 3 January 1885. There was certainly a feeling in the air that things were on the move. Pre-match, the *South Wales Echo* referred to the rapid increase in rugby's popularity in Wales over the previous few years, commenting that "it is now recognised as a national pastime". The *Western Mail* claimed that the Welsh were "improving almost daily in their style of play". And the magazine *Land and Water* gave Welsh rugby a patronising pat on the head when it declared: "it says a good deal for the vitality of the game in that district that the Taffies can manage to make the good fight they always do against their more numerous and more powerful rivals".

Wales did indeed perform well enough but any over-confidence soon evaporated. Both up front and behind, England were far better organised and they hammered Wales by five tries to two, with Greg Wade in particular completely dominating his opposition. Both sides managed only one conversion. Newport's diminutive Martyn Jordan was responsible for the two Welsh tries while Arthur recorded his first international score with a conversion. The *Western Mail* was somewhat critical. There was a "lack of combination" and "little passing worth speaking of". But "Old Stager" in the *South Wales Echo* took a more sanguine view. He recalled the disaster only four years earlier in 1881 and, comparing it to this display, concluded that there was "very much to make us hopeful, if not confident, of the future". He went on to describe the scenes in Swansea before and during the match and these gave him further cheer. "It was a grand and impressive and ... encouraging spectacle, speaking volumes for the future of Welsh football". He was right to be optimistic, not least because that future would involve Arthur Gould.

"Old Stager" thought that Bob Gould had played consistently well. As for Arthur, "no better choice could have been made. He played splendidly, collared well and dropped well". "Old Stager" repeated these views a week later before the Scotland match, saying that his display at Swansea fully justified his keeping his place. "He runs and tackles

Arthur's first international. Wales v England 1885. Back: T B Jones, S Goldsworthy, E S Richards; Middle: L C Thomas, H Lyne, T Clapp, J S Smith, Bob Gould, E M Rowland; Front: H Martyn Jordan, C Taylor, W Gwynn, C Newman (captain), Arthur Gould, F Hancock. (Courtesy of Swansea RFC Memorabilia CIC)

well, while in dropping goals from the field he has lately exhibited some startling performances". Though naturally both left-handed and left-footed, Arthur had tirelessly practised kicking off either foot, which gave him a great advantage in deceiving opposition defences.

1885: Scotland v Wales

A week later, there were four changes, all in the pack, for the game in Glasgow at the Hamilton Crescent cricket ground. The weather was poor which partly accounted for the small crowd of only 3,000. The pitch was in a wretched state and the greasy ball may have helped Wales. The Scots had a powerful side – they hadn't lost in three seasons – but Wales held their own to achieve their best international result so far. The forwards matched the Scots and, if anything, had the edge in the scrums and mauls. Again Bob led from the front. The backs defended staunchly and Charlie Taylor's magnificent drop kick, which could have won the match, passed just under the bar. But it was Arthur who most impressed the *Scottish Athletic Journal*: "Gould is one of the best full-backs I have seen for many a day and Wales is in possession of a treasure in the person of that individual." Not bad coming from a neutral, especially as it was only Arthur's second international, and fullback was not his preferred position.

The forward-dominated game ended in a scoreless draw. Not a victory it is true, but still a result for Wales to celebrate. "Old Stager's" earlier optimism proved to be well-founded and he gleefully revealed that, when the result reached Cardiff, the rejoicings were "great and manifest". Naturally, the players celebrated too. It was reported in the *Scottish Athletic Journal* that the post-match dinner was a quiet affair, though "afterwards there was some rather lively work". The *Journal* went on to criticise some of the Scottish team for not attending the dinner and contrasted their behaviour with the "unbounded" hospitality which they had received in Newport the previous season. We don't get much information from the press about after-match activities but these comments give us just a few hints.

Unfortunately, the difficulties with Ireland continued and there was no game with them in 1884-5. Arthur, therefore, had to be content with just two caps in his first season. Nevertheless, it had been an unforgettable one for him and he was now already acknowledged in Wales, and indeed beyond, as an exceptionally promising player. At the end of only his third season with Newport, "Old Stager" reckoned that "If the Newport Club do not in some form or other show their appreciation of the wonderful service Arthur Gould has done them this year, they will be – well, most ungrateful". Little did this journalist suspect that, a little over a decade later, he would be at the forefront of just such a show of gratitude – one which would push Welsh rugby into a mire of dispute and threaten the whole future of the game.

1885-6

Up to now, Arthur had missed only a few of Newport's matches since his arrival at the club. But, with his work commitments taking him around the country and eventually abroad, he was seen less frequently in black and amber colours over the next five seasons. He played at Rodney Parade in the opening two fixtures in 1885-6. These were a victory over Cardiff Harlequins and a defeat by the Yorkshire Cup holders, Batley. However, after this match, "Old Stager" warned readers that Arthur might be moving away and indeed he then missed five games on the trot. He was now working with his brother Harry in the south east and south coast areas, mainly on water supply and sewerage projects. Nevertheless, he still managed to play plenty of rugby and, at the end of the season, he claimed to have travelled over 4,000 miles by train to do so. It was this period spent working in England which, in the words of David Smith and Gareth Williams in *Fields of Praise*, "turned him from a local phenomenon into a national sensation."

His arrival in London was timely. There had been several earlier attempts to found a London Welsh club. However, in the summer of 1885, a number of prominent players finally got round to organising a permanent club. By the time they had arranged their first fixture, Arthur was available and so, on 24 October 1885 at Walthamstow, he was the London Welsh fullback in their inaugural match against

Arthur when a young man. (Arthur Gould's scrapbook)

London Scottish. They fielded a very talented side, in which Arthur would have recognised many familiar faces, including international team-mates Charlie Taylor and Martyn Jordan. Poor Welsh combination, however, allowed the very strong Scottish XV to run out winners by a goal and try to nil. Arthur played occasionally for London Welsh over the next couple of years but never on a regular basis. When in London he preferred to play his rugby elsewhere, perhaps considering that the Welsh were not quite strong enough.

However, for much of this season, Arthur was working on water supply projects around Hampshire. One day he went to watch a midweek game between Winchester Training College and the Trojans club of Southampton. A college team member recognised "Monk" and invited him to play for them. He accepted, though Winchester still lost. However, the Trojans were quick to realise their good fortune in having someone of Arthur's talent staying locally. For the rest of the season he turned out for Trojans whenever he was available, playing against teams of the calibre of Portsmouth Victoria, Salisbury and HMS Marlborough. This also meant that he became eligible for county rugby and so he managed to fit in several games for Hampshire too.

Though he was away for much of the year, Arthur was still involved in three games for South Wales held prior to the internationals. This time, however, Arthur was selected at three-quarter. He was now considered to be of more value to Wales in what was, after all, his regular club position. In front of 3,000 spectators at Oxford, the University were well beaten by four goals and a try to one goal and a try. Arthur contributed a "capital drop" and also ran the length of the field for a try, scoring "amid loud applause". "The play of the two Goulds was especially fine".

But then back in Cardiff, South Wales were defeated by Blackheath. In very wet and muddy conditions, the nine Blackheath forwards overwhelmed the lighter Welsh eight-man pack. Even so, the play of the four South Wales three-quarters – where Arthur had been added to the Cardiff trio of Frank Hancock, Charlie Arthur and Billy Douglas – simply astonished the London pressmen. Their "precise and rapid" passing was an eye-opener for the *Pastime* reporter who also commented that "foremost and best was Gould". The South Wales three-quarters were demonstrating the new "Cardiff game" which was proving to be such an emphatic success for the "Blue and

Blacks" that season. This was Arthur's first experience of the new four three-quarters system.

Despite Arthur's preference for the three man line-up in his early career, it is interesting to note that the four played so well against Blackheath. However, there were still doubters. "Honestas,"writing in the *South Wales Echo*, was concerned that, no matter how good their four three-quarters might be, if Wales were to field an eight-man pack, they had to be robust enough to take on their opponents' nine. Otherwise, he argued, they might end up having to pull a player out of the backs to shore up the forwards, and that would be worse than selecting nine forwards in the first place. It was both a perceptive and prophetic observation. It would be over a decade before the arrival of the rather loosely described "Rhondda forward" enabled Wales to prove beyond doubt the superiority of their new "scientific" system at international level.

That Christmas, London Welsh enjoyed a successful tour of Wales. Arthur took part in all four of their matches, though only twice *for* the London club. He kicked a crucial conversion for them to defeat Swansea; then switched sides and was irrepressible in Newport's victory over his "other" club. However, his presence in the South Wales XV didn't prevent London Welsh from gaining an impressive second tour victory. Finally, presumably nothing would stop him helping out London Welsh in his fourth match in six days against a still unbeaten Cardiff, though even with Arthur, the now physically and socially exhausted tourists went down by two tries to nil.

1886: England v Wales

The steadily growing interest in rugby is revealed by a poll which the *South Wales Daily News* then decided to conduct to select the readers' favourite team. Arthur came fourth in overall popularity, behind Charlie Newman, Frank Hancock and "Buller" Stadden. Bob was seventh. For the actual team to play England, Arthur was partnered at three-quarter by Cardiff's Billy Douglas and Blackheath's Charlie Taylor. Hancock was only selected reserve and there was some criticism over the preference given to Arthur at centre. It was argued that he was more selfish and more reliant on kicking than Hancock and so should have been more usefully selected at fullback.

The England game at Blackheath on 2 January 1886 was Arthur's fifth in ten days. It was another defeat for Wales, though

THE " OLD STAGER'S " POLL.

Our contributor the " Old Stager " writes :— In fulfilment of the promise made in the " Athletic Notes " in yesterday's issue, I have now to announce the result of the poll taken by me, on the question of selecting the above team. In all 649 lists of teams were sent in. After going through these carefully, I find that in the opinion of the majority, the following are best qualified to receive caps. Back, D. H. Bowen, Llanelly (353 votes). Three-quarter backs, F. E. Hancock, Cardiff (599) ; A. J. Gould, Newport (560) ; and C. Arthur, Cardiff (532). Half backs, C. H. Newman, Newport (601) ; and W. Stadden, Cardiff (576). Forwards, A. F. Hill, Cardiff (536) ; R. Gould, Newport (518) ; T. J. S. Clapp, Newport (511) ; D. H. Lewis, Cardiff (505) ; D. Morgan, Swansea (484) ; E. P. Alexander, Llan-dovery (470) ; E. S. Richards, Swansea (449) ; A. J. Hybart, Cardiff (437) ; E. Roberts, Llanelly (436).

The votes recorded in "Old Stager's" poll demonstrate that, as early as 1885-6, the Welsh rugby public already regarded Arthur as an exceptional player. (South Wales Daily News, 22 December 1885)

not a crushing one. Had England's Andrew Stoddart not kicked a long-range goal from a mark, the result might have been different. "Buller" Stadden's spectacular try was converted by Taylor, but neither of England's conversions was successful. So under the then scoring system, without Stoddart's exceptional goal, Wales would have won by a goal to nil. However, England deserved their victory. There was a marked disparity in the size of the two packs and, despite working hard, the Welsh forwards were too light for their opponents. Even so, according to the *Yorkshire Post*, Bob Gould stood out as one of the best men on the field.

The backs performed well and *Athletic News* thought that had the forwards matched them, then Wales might have won. Their defence was sure: they kicked and tackled superbly. "Taylor and Gould more than realised expectations", the *Yorkshire Post* reported, but added, "in the matter of passing they were not the equal of [England] and at this particular point, they have a good deal to learn." The *Hull Daily Mail* agreed. The tackling of the Welsh backs was "the leading feature of their play, but they were sadly deficient in the passing department". *Sporting Life* argued that "the play of the Welshmen behind the scrummage lacked the science of the opposite side". Given that Cardiff were thrashing all-comers this season with their innovative "scientific four three-quarter passing game", these comments may have cut the Welsh selectors to the quick.

"Old Stager" was evidently impressed by the conduct of the 6,000 spectators at Blackheath. He confessed that he had never witnessed such a well-behaved audience. "Their applause was bestowed irrespective of side and there was an utter.... absence of that hooting and groaning much too frequently indulged in by football onlookers nearer home." Welsh rugby was noticeably developing its own distinctive personality.

There were four Richmond men in the victorious team that day, including forwards Charles Gurdon and William Clibbon and the herculean Greg Wade on the wing. The fourth was the half-back and World Rugby Hall of Famer, Alan Rotherham, regarded as the man responsible for changing the way half-backs played. Before him, they usually made individual runs or kicked. Under Harry Vassall's captaincy at Oxford, Rotherham initiated the idea that the *primary* role of the half-back was to act as the connecting link between the forwards and three-quarters. He was perhaps the original outside-half. More than anyone else present at Blackheath, Arthur would have realised the potential of Rotherham's ability to create openings for fast, elusive and intelligent three-quarters such as himself. Arthur later spoke of him as the greatest half he ever saw. No doubt he had some interesting conversations with the Richmond contingent after the international because before the end of the year, Arthur was playing outside Alan Rotherham for the London club.

1886: Wales v Scotland

Wales met Scotland a week later on 9 January 1886 at Cardiff. Welsh history was made that day when the first ever train ran through the Severn tunnel, dramatically reducing travel time from south Wales to the west of England and to London. That day is also remembered in the history of rugby as the first occasion on which an international team fielded four three-quarters. The Severn tunnel had an immediate impact on rugby, greatly improving the ease with which Welsh teams could arrange fixtures in southern England. It would take a little longer, however, before the adoption of four three-quarters became an accepted practice in the international game, even by Wales. What *Sporting Life* declared a "dangerous experiment" was judged to be a failure.

Hoping to replicate Cardiff's stunning success with the new system, their captain Frank Hancock was drafted in to partner Arthur in the centre. Charlie Taylor and Billy Douglas on the wings completed this history-making quartet. The forwards, of course, had to be reduced to eight. Practice was one of the cornerstones of the "Cardiff system", as it was already being called, but unfortunately the Welsh team had no time to train together. Arthur had only extremely limited experience of the new system and, as far as is known, Taylor had never played in a four-man line-up and was better known for his kicking than his "combination".

In addition, their prospects had already been greatly weakened by the withdrawal of two key players and both were badly missed. Bob Gould was injured and so was absent for the first time since making his international debut four years earlier. To add to Wales' difficulties, Charlie Newman was unable to travel down from Durham, where he now lived. He was replaced at half-back by another clergyman, Alfred Mathews (Lampeter College), who won his only cap that day. Thirty-three years later, he would read the lesson at Arthur's funeral.

Nevertheless, there was still optimism at the Arms Park. Regular observers of the ground-breaking Cardiff team hoped to witness the superiority of the four three-quarters system being demonstrated in the international arena. Since Wales had managed a draw in Scotland the year before and had also made a good fight of the match with England a week earlier, expectations were understandably high. An "immense" crowd, over 5,000 fans was reported. To increase standing capacity, rows of carts had been lined up behind the ropes so spectators could get a better view of the play. The *Western Mail* also observed, perhaps with some condescension, that "the poor unfortunates unable to pay the price of admission ... seized upon every point of vantage where a sight could be got, the house-tops and the walls surrounding being literally packed".

All expectations, however, were soon dashed. Scotland won by three tries and two conversions to nil. Wales were extremely disappointing, in particular at forward. The backs though played much better. The *Yorkshire Post* thought Arthur never put a foot wrong throughout; while both he and Charlie Taylor were praised in many match reports, suggesting that the result would have been worse without their kicking and tackling. Wales were never really in it, though they were unlucky on two occasions not to score, particularly when, from half-way, Taylor ran through the entire Scottish defence only to have the ball knocked out of his grasp in a last ditch tackle as he dived over the line.

The Welsh decision to select four three-quarters is usually blamed for the nature of the defeat that day and certainly Wales did not adopt it again for another three years. "Old Stager", however, saw things differently, though we must remember that the Cardiff journalist was not unbiased when it came to the new system. With Wales struggling, in the second half they reverted to the conventional line-up of nine forwards and six backs. Fullback Harry Bowen was moved to shore up the pack; while Arthur was switched to fullback. However, "Old Stager" thought this was a mistake which only made matters worse.

> During the first half, the four three-quarters did excellent work in stopping the rushes of the opposing forwards, but in the concluding half, when Bowen had been sent forward and A J Gould back, the character of the game changed. The forwards did not seem to be in the least bit strengthened by the advent of Bowen in their midst while, with one man missing behind, the tackling of the team was distinctly weakened. Scotland scored twice in the second half, only once in the first, thus proving that playing four three-quarters is not so mistaken a policy as some imagine.

However, the new system was introduced to enhance its *attacking* rather than just its *defensive* potential. Of the three-quarters, only Hancock and Douglas were regular exponents. Lacking time for adequate practice and, with the eight forwards unable to provide sufficient ball, the experiment was bound to fail against a decent side. Did Arthur have any part in the half-time decision? He is said to have opposed the selection of four three-quarters in subsequent internationals for some time. However, seven years later in an interview with Rev Frank Marshall, Arthur claimed that he thought the decision to move Bowen up to the forwards was a mistake. "I think it would have been better to have stuck to the original arrangement, and have made the best of a bad bargain. I am not in favour of selecting

Wales v Scotland 1886. Back: Bob Gould, E Alexander, T Clapp, A F Hill, G Young, C P Lewis, D H Bowen, W A Bowen, Dai Morgans, C Newman; Middle: A Duncan, W H Thomas, C Taylor, F Hancock (captain), Arthur Gould, W Douglas, A A Mathews, W Wilkins; Front: D H Lewis, W Stadden. (Courtesy of Swansea RFC Memorabilia CIC)

a team to meet contingencies. I prefer to settle with what game you mean to play, and play it throughout." But was this hindsight?

Unfortunately, there was no Irish fixture this season in which to experiment with the new system again. However, at club level, an opportunity to assess the efficacy of four three-quarters arose exactly a week after the Scotland defeat. Hancock's unbeaten Cardiff XV had so far *averaged* five tries a match and they had conceded *only* two tries all season. They had earlier hammered Newport by eight tries and six conversions to nil at the Arms Park. And this time at Rodney Parade they recorded another clear-cut victory by five tries and four conversions to nil. To face Cardiff's regular three-quarter line-up of Angus Stuart, Frank Hancock, Charlie Arthur and Billy Douglas, Newport selected three. Partnering Arthur was Martyn Jordan, who had only played twice for Newport early in the season, and Charlie Newman who hadn't been a regular "Black and Amber" for three years. This was Newman's only game for the club in 1885-6. So Newport lacked Cardiff's well-honed combination behind the scrum and it showed.

"Old Stager" thought the Newport forwards played well enough and reckoned that Bob Gould, "although not fully recovered from his recent accident, was particularly prominent all through", adding "Wales can ill afford to lose her most brilliant forward." The backs, however, were far from impressive. "If they could only ... emulate the smart passing and perfect combination of the Cardiffians, the latter would soon find their work cut out."

Selecting Charlie Newman was a mistake. He spent much of his time looking round before passing and this was in marked contrast to the Cardiff backs, who seemed able to "shoot the ball without even glancing around." Indeed, Cardiff owed their victory "in great measure to the brilliancy and accuracy of their passing". Jordan tackled well but otherwise "was a complete failure. He never ran a yard." And following Arthur's heroic performance a week earlier in difficult circumstances against Scotland, he failed to produce anything like his usual form. "His kicking was tame and feeble and he never seemed able to get clean away". Even Arthur had his off days and this was one.

"Touchstone" in the *Western Mail* was largely in agreement with this assessment of the match. "Behind the scrimmage they hadn't really a look in." Newport "trotted out their very best stuff, but still looked like raw recruits. What the team wants is a really good drilling." Whenever Newport attempted to pass, their three-quarters were standing too far apart and before they could do anything with the ball the Cardiff defence was on to them. "With plenty of weight forward, the home men might with advantage have followed the example of Cardiff and played four three-quarters." Even allowing for the bias of two Cardiff journalists, if the new system had failed against Scotland, it evidently worked well a week later in the east Wales derby.

"Monk" played for Newport for most of the remainder of the season, though he still had the occasional game for Trojans and Hampshire. There was also an unusual outing for a combined London Scottish and London Welsh XV against a London XV in the Charity Festival held at the Oval in March 1886. Over 8,000 spectators, including the Prince of Wales, attended, no doubt also attracted by the Gentlemen v Players soccer game. The London XV proved to be far too strong for the Exiles, who were overwhelmed by three goals and six tries to a goal and a try.

Arthur ended his season for Newport in the final of the South Wales Challenge Cup. Held at Swansea, this was the ninth year of the competition and Newport's seventh final. However, this time the holders were completely outplayed by Llanelli, who won by 44 points to 15. The conditions were awful. A strong cold wind combined with snow, sleet and hail resulted in a game dominated entirely by scrums and mauls. With little ball, the backs were "relegated to the ranks of the great unemployed." Captained by Harry Bowen, Llanelli fielded four three-quarters, though their eight man pack held their own in the forward battle. "Old Stager" thought "Monk" was the best of the backs but "he did scarcely anything but tackle showing little of the kicking power rightly attributed to him."

1886-7

Bob was rewarded with the captaincy of Newport for the forthcoming season and he skippered the side well. They remained unbeaten at home and only lost three times, to Swansea twice and to Llanelli. Unfortunately, though, his brother was only able to assist him on six occasions. After four successful years for the club, Arthur's work now took him away from Wales more regularly and this meant that he had to play most of his rugby elsewhere. Over the next four seasons, Arthur's club was essentially Richmond, though this is not always credited in international match reports and records. He was the regular centre for Richmond during this period, participating in about two-thirds of their fixtures. He usually featured in their keenest matches, especially those with their oldest adversaries Blackheath, as well as with Harlequins, London Scottish, Oxford University, Cambridge University and Bradford.

"Swansea v Arthur Gould"

He was present, however, in Newport's opening game of 1886-7 – a victory over Swansea – and, judging by his performance, he was going to be seriously missed. "Old Stager" believed that he had never played better. He scored the only try "after a clinking run" and time after time he prevented Swansea from scoring. His brother "worked like a giant" but, even so, Arthur was peerless that day: "in short, the match very might be styled 'Swansea v Arthur Gould and 14 others' ... How the team are to fare without him I fail to see ... Newport's loss is destined to be Richmond's gain. Gould has just joined the latter's "crack" organisation." As it happened, Bob proved to be an effective captain and the club managed to enjoy a successful year, even without Arthur.

So in mid-October, Arthur joined Richmond, one of the oldest and most fashionable clubs in Britain. They were indeed a "crack organisation" at this time. Full of internationals,

1886–87.

Captain : E. T. GURDON.

From the beginning of this season a match was decided by a majority of points. A goal counted as three points, and a try as one point. All goals were of equal value.

Date.	Ground.	Opponents.	Result.	For. Goals	For. Tries	Against. Goals	Against. Tries
1886.							
Oct. 2	Richmond	Croydon	W	–	4	–	–
" 9	Cooper's Hill	R.I.E. College	W	4	–	–	–
" 16	Chiswick	Harlequins	W	2	–	–	–
" 23	Richmond	Old Cheltonians	W	6	–	2	–
" 30	Wandsworth	Clapham Rovers	W	3	2	–	–
Nov. 6	Sandhurst	Royal Military College	W	2	1	–	–
" 13	Surbiton	Marlborough Nomads	W	2	2	–	–
" 20	Cambridge	Cambridge	W	1	–	–	1
" 27	Oxford	Oxford	W	4	1	–	–
" 30	Richmond	Edinburgh University	W	–	1	–	–
Dec. 4	do.	Blackheath	W	–	1	–	–
" 11	Lee	London Scottish	D	–	1	–	1
1887.							
Jan. 22	Richmond	Old Cheltonians	W	6	1	–	–
" 29	Blackheath	Blackheath	W	–	1	–	–
Feb. 5	Richmond	Clapham Rovers	W	2	3	–	–
" 12	do.	R.I.E. College	W	2	–	–	–
" 19	Spring Grove	International College	W	2	3	–	–
" 26	Richmond	London Scottish	W	–	1	–	–

Richmond's invincible season, 1886-7, though perhaps their fixture list was not as demanding as that of Newport when they were unbeaten in 1891-2. (E J Ereaut, The Richmond Football Club, p.215)

county players and Blues, they had lost only once during the previous season and, with Arthur now on board, they would remain undefeated throughout 1886-7. Richmond played a high standard of rugby but, even so, their fixture list perhaps lacked the intensity of Newport's. Norman Biggs, the Cardiff and Wales wing who played for Richmond a couple of years later, spoke to the Welsh press about his experiences. "What is the great difference between the London match and a Cardiff game? At Richmond there was no need to exert myself, and nobody cared much who won, that's the difference."

"This Dazzling Player was Arthur Gould"

Arthur's celebrity status was already spreading well beyond Wales, and his move to Richmond brought him to the attention of a much wider audience of players, administrators, journalists, spectators and the general public. His fame now breached the very heart of the game's establishment. One of his new admirers in London was W J Townsend Collins, later to become "Dromio" of the *South Wales Argus*. Writing in 1948, he recalled one Richmond v Blackheath match in particular which he had witnessed 60 years earlier:

The play was the best I had ever seen till then. The length and accuracy of the kicking especially impressed me: the passing and tackling were supremely good; and till late in the game neither side could pierce the defence. Then there was a hush, a shout, a triumphant roar – a threequarter in amber, red and black jersey – graceful, swift, elusive – swerving left, dodging right, went through the defence without a hand being laid upon him, and by the try he scored Richmond won. This dazzling player was Arthur Gould ... So I saw for the first time the man whom I regard as the greatest Rugby player who ever took the field.

Arthur made his Richmond debut on 16 October 1886 in a two-goal victory over the Harlequins. After the match, he may have reminded his opponents that, three years earlier, he had "substituted" for them against Cardiff. The Quins must have kicked themselves for what they had missed. Then followed one of those periods which reveal just how much Arthur loved playing, when he took part in five games over two weeks.

Pastime – The Football Journal recorded that, on Saturday 30 October, he was "a model of fine kicking and accurate passing" and that he dropped two superb goals for Richmond when they defeated Clapham Rovers. Four days later on the Wednesday, "Monk" scored a try and conversion for London Welsh in their win over East Sheen. The following Saturday, he dropped a goal in Richmond's victory at RMC Sandhurst; then on the Monday, he was on the losing side for South Wales against Oxford University. The Welsh selectors were still toying with four three-quarters, because Arthur was included in an all-international four man line-up, alongside Charlie Taylor, Martyn Jordan and Billy Douglas, though only the latter was a regular practitioner of the system. South Wales fielded a very weak pack so Arthur and his fellow backs were given few opportunities. Finally on Saturday 13 November, Arthur needed little persuasion from Bob to travel home for Newport's much anticipated derby with Cardiff.

"Newport Partisan", writing in the *Western Mail*, was relieved before the match to spot "that almost unique young athlete Arthur Gould" amongst team at the Angel Hotel. His presence certainly boosted the numbers in what was the season's largest crowd at the Arms Park. Such was the congestion that, just before kick-off, a wooden standing area collapsed under the weight of over 100 spectators, but fortunately no-one was seriously hurt. The stoicism of the Victorians has to be admired: this incident produced little comment in the press.

A tense and hard-fought struggle, the game ended at nil-all. After suffering two embarrassing hammerings the previous season though, this was a moral victory for Newport. Bob's forwards outplayed the Cardiff pack and, with vigorous tackling, the backs had discovered a way of neutralising their opponents' speedy three-quarters. The *Star of Gwent* reported that Arthur "played the same cool, confident game ... as he always does." He kicked well, whilst his tackling "proved a rare stumbling block to the Cardiff three-quarters, who couldn't anyhow contrive to get past him".

Arthur was confident that he was now pivotal to the Welsh team. He was able to miss the trial, yet still keep his place for the Scotland match in Edinburgh arranged for New Year's Day. Before then though there was still the usual clutch of Christmas holiday fixtures. Over 11 days, there were games for Newport against Swansea and London Welsh; and for London Welsh at Swansea, Llanelli and Cardiff. "Monk" was certainly battle-hardened for the forthcoming internationals.

FOOTBALL PLEBISCITE.

The football plebiscite, for which a prize of one guinea was offered in the *Weekly Mail* of Dec. 25, has resulted as follows :—

	Votes.
Best football team—Newport	47
Worst football team—Neath	23
Best individual player—A. J. Gould (Newport)	75
Best captain—D. H. Bowen (Llanelly)	48
Best back—H Hughes (Cardiff)	52
Best three-quarter back—A. J. Gould (Newport)	63
Best half-back—O. J. Evans (Cardiff)	68
Best forward—R. Gould (Newport)	73
Best place kick—H. Hughes (Cardiff)	105
Best sprinter—G. Thomas (Newport)	75
Best umpire—A. Duncan (Cardiff)	77
Best referee—A. F. Hill (Cardiff)	33

According to the readers of the local press, Arthur was the best individual player in Wales and Bob the best forward during 1886-7. (Western Mail, 3 January 1887)

Over the Christmas, a "Football Plebiscite" published in the *Western Mail* and *Weekly Mail* revealed just how popular the Gould brothers had become. Bob was the readers' clear choice as the "best forward" and came second in the "best captain" category. However, Arthur was overwhelmingly voted the "best three-quarter" and, significantly, the "best individual player" in Wales.

But not everybody was happy with the choice of the three three-quarters for Scotland. "Old Stager" thought that the selection would offer little chance of "combination" and "the passing game". Whereas Cardiff's Billy Douglas, he believed, was "one of the best exponents of the new game", he criticised both Arthur and Charlie Taylor for their over-reliance on kicking at the expense of "running and passing". "Douglas will simply be out of it". However, as it happened, because of a heavy frost in Edinburgh, the game had to be postponed. Just as well perhaps, as it allowed Arthur an extra week's rest after his Christmastide exertions.

1887: Wales v England

That rest was needed because England were due at Llanelli a week later on 8 January 1887. This was Wales' 12th international and Stradey Park became the tenth venue at which they had so far played. The game should probably never have gone ahead. On the morning of the match parts of the pitch were frozen. England wanted to call the game off but the artful Richard Mullock came up with a solution. The adjoining cricket ground had not been so badly affected and he somehow managed to persuade the English to agree to shift the game there. It was hard luck, though, for those spectators who had bought grandstand tickets. They now found they would just have to take their chances watching the events from behind the ropes. Clearly concerned about the loss of revenue to the cash-strapped WFU if the match didn't proceed, Mullock refused to offer any refunds. Unsurprisingly, this did not go down very well. He must have had a very thick skin. It was worth it though. There was a "tremendous assemblage" of 8,000 spectators around the ropes and the match takings were high.

It was this game which gave rise to one of the most celebrated anecdotes about Arthur, when he was called on to justify his already popular nick-name. One of the cross-bars had blown down in the high winds and so "Monkey" volunteered to climb one of the uprights to re-fix it. Playing up to the crowd, to their great amusement he shinned up to the top of the post and called out, "How's this for high?" However, one Yorkshireman was unimpressed with his showmanship, and bawled at Arthur: "Come dahn, tha fathead and go on wi't game, or tha'll nivver be nearer 'eaven than tha' is nah".

The English author Rev Frank Marshall had this to say about the game:

> *The ground was not in a fit state for football, a morning's thaw supervening on a severe frost ... Not a player on the field could keep his legs on the skating rink, and both sides funked the hard frost-bound ground with a slippery top. Scientific football was out of the question and the game, which consisted of slipping and sliding, demands no serious comment.*

Really? No serious comment? Evidently, Marshall hadn't read the animated columns in the Welsh press. The result was admittedly a scoreless draw but it was a game in which Wales easily gave their best performance so far against England. Unlike Marshall, "Old Stager" had plenty of serious comment, which even included a parody of a popular religious poem of the day: "Sound the timbrel o'er the muddy wastes of the Bristol Channel, the Welshmen have triumphed, or virtually triumphed".

The home side decidedly had the better of the encounter. On more than one occasion, they, and Arthur in particular, "came within an ace of scoring". Though Wales gained five minor points to England's two, the official result was a draw. "Minor points" referred to touch downs in defence (hence the origin of the term "to *minor* the ball"). They didn't count but they gave rise to the concept of "a draw in favour of". So it was a draw in favour of Wales: they couldn't have come closer to winning.

For the first time – and to the surprise of the press – the Welsh pack outplayed their English counterparts both in the scrum and the loose, even though the visitors had the first man to captain the Lions, Robert Seddon, at forward. A fine drizzle in the first half, followed by heavy rain and sleet in the second, together with a greasy ball, meant that the game was largely confined to the forwards. Cambridge Blues Willie Thomas and Edward Alexander, Cardiff's Alex Bland, Swansea's David Morgans, and – inevitably – Bob Gould were all praised for their sterling performances.

Behind the scrum where, after all, England fielded the stars Alan Rotherham at half-back and Dicky Lockwood at three-quarter, matters were a little more even. Arthur was "a tower of strength" and "his play was worthy even of his high reputation." He and Charles Taylor kicked and tackled extremely well throughout the game (no "funking" on their part then), though "Old Stager" thought they over-did the kicking at the expense of passing. In his opinion, given their forward dominance, Wales were far too defensively minded and could have won easily had the backs been more adventurous. On a drier day, Arthur might have had more luck with the boot. Two drop goal attempts just scraped the upright, while on a third occasion he slipped backwards as he was dropping at goal. "How narrow a squeak the English had of being severely beaten" was the summary of the *Western Mail.*

Arthur came home only twice more this season for tough encounters with Cardiff and Swansea. Cardiff were outplayed but Swansea were victorious in the semi-final of the South Wales Cup. This was the last time Newport would participate in the competition. But it was one major event after another for Arthur. A week later, he was on tour with Middlesex. He had played county rugby for Hampshire the previous season, of course, but this time the standard was much more challenging. Middlesex's first opponents were Yorkshire. This was one of the biggest games in English domestic rugby in 1886-7. According to the local press, it was the season's most important fixture for Yorkshire and this was confirmed when Arthur ran out in front of a

To the delight of the crowd, "Monkey" shows off his superb gymnastic skills by re-fixing the cross-bar during the game at Stradey. (Weekly Mail, 15 January 1887)

massive 12,000 crowd at Bradford Park Avenue. It turned out to be an exciting game, throughout which Arthur ran, kicked and tackled magnificently. With the two packs evenly matched, he and his Richmond half-back partner, Alan Rotherham, completely outplayed the opposing backs. The sides were level at two tries apiece with five minutes to go, when Arthur sensationally sprinted down the touchline to score the winning try in the corner. He made something of a habit of recording memorable tries in this fixture.

There was further success at Sunderland on the Monday when Middlesex overcame Durham by a goal and two tries to a goal. Again Arthur was prominent in the victory. He "made the run of the day" when he collected the ball near the centre of the field and ran through the Durham defence to score amid hearty cheers.

1887: Scotland v Wales

Only five days after this strenuous tour, Arthur again headed north for the postponed Scottish match at Raeburn Place, Edinburgh. There were five changes from the side which had done so well against England. Charlie Taylor was injured and was replaced at three-quarter by Swansea's David Gwynn, who was moved from fullback. Arthur hadn't partnered him before. Hugh Hughes of Cardiff won his first cap at fullback. Charlie Newman was unavailable and so George Bowen, also of Swansea, came in at half-back for his first cap too. Bob Gould now took over the captaincy from Newman. There were also two changes in the pack.

Sadly, this was to be yet another example of what plagued Welsh international rugby until the turn of the century: inconsistency. The draw with England had been one of Wales' best performances. But this was followed on 26 February by a really crushing defeat from Scotland who inflicted the heaviest loss suffered by Wales since the slaughter at Blackheath in 1881. George Lindsay of London Scottish ran amok with five of Scotland's 12 tries, four of which were converted. Wales failed to score.

In a one-sided game, Wales were no match for their opponents. The ire of the Swansea-based *Cambrian* was particularly focussed on the three-quarter line-up of Gwynn, Gould and Douglas. They "completely broke down and seemed almost afraid to tackle the stalwart Scots ... Gould did little or no tackling worth noticing; in fact the Welsh backs exhibited poor combination and indifferent passing and were evidently not strong enough to withstand the rapid advances of the powerful Scotchmen."

"Old Stager" in the *South Wales Echo*, however, pointed out that most reports had ignored the fact that Cardiff half-back Jem Evans was badly injured and had to go off at half-time, reducing Wales to 14 men for the rest of the game. Consequently, Tom Clapp had to come out of the forwards to replace Evans. Furthermore, in the first couple of minutes, Billy Douglas had suffered a painful injury to his arm and shoulder which troubled him throughout. It is no wonder that the backs were disrupted and disorganised. Arthur had been playing really well all season, but this was one game in which even he was unable to exert any influence on the outcome. *The Cambrian* concluded with a depressing and rather despairing summary: "It is evident that the Scotchmen are far ahead of the Welsh in football. They are a hardier race [and] much stronger". However, within a year, Wales and Arthur would force the writer to revisit this very pessimistic judgement.

1887: Wales v Ireland

After five years in the Welsh XV, Bob had played his last international, as injury cost him his place for the next match. Because of Ireland's previous reluctance to play Wales, the teams had not met for three years. Surprisingly, however, this season the Irish RFU agreed unanimously to play Wales, though even by late January 1887, no date had yet been finalised. This change of heart, however, might not have been entirely due to magnanimity. Trouble had been brewing between the RFU and the three Celtic Unions over the establishment of, what later became, the International Board; and in 1887-8 and 1888-9, the three broke off fixtures with England over the issue. So Ireland's agreement to meet Wales again might have had more to do with keeping the Welsh on side for this boycott rather than anything else. The match couldn't be held in Ireland because they had already played two home fixtures in 1886-7 against Scotland and England. Mullock, therefore, proposed Newport as the venue. Yet frustratingly, this didn't suit the Irish who responded that they preferred Manchester as it was more convenient! Despite this being a "home" fixture for Wales, the WFU were anxious to resume fixtures so they accepted this rather arrogant "take it or leave it" demand. When it transpired that the

Manchester club's ground was not actually available on 12 March, the agreed date, there were press rumours that the game would not take place at all (again). However, it was eventually discovered that Birkenhead Park's ground could be used (and it is hard not to see Richard Mullock's hand in this). The IRFU's excuse for this arrangement was it would save them the expense of travelling to south Wales; but, as a "home" venue, Birkenhead Park was scarcely more convenient for many Welsh players and supporters than it was for any Dublin-based Irish.

"The Memory of Gould Will Take a Long Time to Eradicate"

It turned out to be a strange but highly entertaining match played in front of 5,000 supporters, a decent enough crowd considering the circumstances, especially as it had snowed heavily the night before. Wales made eight changes, one of which was positional, as George Bowen of Swansea was moved from half-back to three-quarter. Fully recovered from his injury, Charlie Taylor re-joined Arthur in the threes. The highly talented "Buller" Stadden, not always available now that he was playing for Dewsbury, returned at half-back. The experienced Tom Clapp took over the captaincy.

Wales dominated the first half. After 15 minutes of play, Stadden passed out to Arthur following a scrum and "Monk" dropped a magnificent goal. Wales kept up the pressure after half-time and this soon produced a try. Again the move involved Stadden, who had "a remarkably fine game". He passed to the Swansea forward, Dai Morgans, who with great self-assurance, dummied to Arthur and crossed over himself. Arthur's thoughts about this were not recorded. Even though the conversion was missed, the outcome was beginning to look like a forgone conclusion. But the game now swung heavily in favour of Ireland, as the wing Robert Montgomery grabbed three tries. Crucially, though, Ireland failed to convert any of them. Just one conversion would have been enough to give Ireland victory, but under the scoring system still prevailing in 1887, Wales were the winners because they had scored a try *and* the only goal, and a goal now counted as three tries. Arthur's drop goal had, therefore, won the match.

The *Yorkshire Post* thought Arthur was absolutely the best Welshman on the field, while he and Stadden also impressed the *Liverpool Mercury*:

Wales won a beautiful game ... It is really difficult to say which was
the better team ... O'Connor [at half-back] was completely outwitted
by Stadden, whose passes to Gould were in number legion, and in
execution perfect. The last named kicked with great effect, most of
his punts being into touch, and gaining much ground ... he dropped
a goal with perfect nonchalance ... Gould was vastly superior to [the
Irish three-quarters] ... The memory of Gould ... will take a long time
to eradicate.

Scotland won the Triple Crown in 1887, though this victory by Wales
at Birkenhead Park was sufficient for them to achieve second place in
the International Championship, their highest in the competition so
far.

There was no let up for Arthur throughout the summer of
1887, as athletics took over. He made regular appearances at sports
meetings around the country but there were two particularly
outstanding performances deserving of mention. In July, he competed
at Stourbridge in the national AAA championship finals, finishing
third in the 120 yards hurdles and fourth in the 100 yards sprint.

*Newport 1886-7. Back: R Powell, T Clapp, T Lockwood, H Pepperall, F Stone,
J Young; Middle: H McDaniel, J Webb, Bob Gould (captain), H Martyn Jordan,
George Thomas, J Hannam, T Edwards; Front: Arthur Gould, T Harding, T Downe,
C J Thomas. (Courtesy of Kevin Jarvis at Newport RFC)*

In addition, at the popular Private Banks Athletic Club meeting at Catford Bridge, Arthur won the 120 yards hurdles, defeating Sherard Joyce who was the runner-up in the AAA race and who became AAA champion the following year. Arthur also won the 100 yards sprint that day from a large field of nearly 80 runners. More typical of the meetings he attended that summer was the one held at Rodney Parade over the August Bank Holiday. Arthur picked up several cash prizes including those for the steeplechase and the high jump. He gave the 120 yards smokers' race a miss, though. Provoking a good deal of laughter, the competitors were required to wear tall hats and carry umbrellas. At half way they had to fill their pipes with tobacco and light and smoke them to the finish. Arthur missed out on the winner's prize of a guinea (£1 1s) this time.

4

History at Crown Flatt

1887-8

There was no more experienced international in Wales than Bob Gould when he had led his men out at Edinburgh against Scotland in February 1887. In the 13 matches Wales had played, they selected 67 men. This was Bob's 11th cap – more than any other player had so far won, apart from his fellow Newport team-mate Tom Clapp, who equalled him at this stage.

However, the 1886-7 season had also effectively marked the end of Bob's Newport career. For seven seasons, he had been a constant and consistent presence in the 1st XV, only ever missing a handful of games. However, in the autumn of 1887, the *Western Mail* announced that Bob had become the latest of Newport's "departing heroes". He had left to work with his brothers in the south-east of England for a few months prior to going abroad. So for the first half of 1887-8, he joined Arthur in the highly successful Richmond XV, who were in the middle of a two-year undefeated run. Although only at the club for three months, he still made an impact, not only as a hard-working and mobile forward, but also as a reliable goal-kicker.

He was with Richmond when they made their first visit to Yorkshire to meet Bradford at Park Avenue in November 1887. With both clubs bristling with internationals, this was a serious North v South confrontation. The Yorkshire press acknowledged that Richmond were one of the strongest teams in the country at the time and they attracted so much local interest that the attendance was even larger than for the previous season's Yorkshire v Middlesex clash. At 15,000, it would have easily been the biggest crowd Bob had ever played in front of. Even so, Richmond dominated the game, particularly in the scrums, and ran out winners by two tries to nil.

A week later, the brothers travelled home to play in another tough and competitive encounter, this time against Cardiff. It was Bob's only game for Newport this season and also the very last occasion on which he appeared in black and amber colours alongside Arthur. The match was drawn. In early January 1888, just before he went overseas, Bob was selected for Middlesex in another major North v South battle, the return fixture with Yorkshire. It would have been the last time that the brothers played together, but unfortunately the match had to be postponed because of the death of the president of the Yorkshire RFU. A few days later – and before the fixture had been rearranged – Bob left Britain for Barbados to help set up the family's construction business there.

A great servant to his club and Wales, Bob was a popular favourite in Newport. Before sailing for the Caribbean, he was given a rousing send-off by his many friends and "lovers of football" at a local hotel. They presented him with a ring inscribed "To Bob, from Newport", as well as (and presumably the RFU never got to hear about this or there might have been an earlier "Gould Affair") a purse containing 20 sovereigns. He gave a short speech, reminiscing about his earliest days at the club "and promised on his return to England [yes, that is what he said] the first match he would play in should be for his old club".

Apart from that draw with Cardiff, Arthur's only outings for Newport during 1887-8 were in the Christmas victories over London Welsh and Kensington. Clearly, though, Arthur's game hadn't suffered at Richmond. The *South Wales Daily News* reported that against Cardiff:

> *Arthur Gould played a wonderful game. He kicked with unnerving effect, collared safely and ran better than ever. The brunt of the tackling fell on him and it was marvellous how he got at his men. Pass after pass was intercepted by him, and more than once he alone was responsible for spoiling a certain try ... From what one has read of his recent exploits with the Richmond team, one might have looked to seeing him in good form, but I, for one, did not anticipate seeing such startling form as that actually displayed by him. He, more than any other man in the team, saved the match for his side.*

Following this performance, *Athletic News* declared that he was now without doubt the finest three-quarter in the game.

It was another highly successful season for Richmond who lost only once, to Blackheath by a single goal, in a match unluckily cut short because of a dangerously hard pitch. This was Richmond's first defeat for exactly two years. Remarkably, it was also the *only* time during 1887-8 when Arthur was on the losing side. A week later, playing against Clapham Rovers, *Pastime* described his form as wonderful. "His accurate and well-timed punts [were] equalled by the power and speed of his runs". This was typical now of how the press was regularly praising him.

Having experienced an invincible season with Richmond the previous year, Arthur now enjoyed similar success with Middlesex. Again he had a prominent role in this. At Old Deer Park in November 1887, Arthur's try and conversion were enough to secure victory over Durham by a goal and a try to a try. Then in February, on the Monday after his exceptional display against Scotland, Arthur scored both a try and a "splendid drop goal" to defeat Yorkshire at Queen's Club by two goals and a try to a single try. "A J Gould deserves special notice for his really grand play all through". His try was again the best of the match. According to the *Yorkshire Post*, following a forward dribble, there was some "really brilliant passing ... by Rotherham, Gould and Lindsay, the ball changing hands with lightning-like rapidity, until Gould planted it firmly between the posts." For Rev Frank Marshall it was a "glorious try" which he remembered in more detail. "Roberts gave Gould a pass, by no means a good one, but it was taken with that peculiar celerity so characteristic of the Welsh crack and he was bowling along before his opponents realised the ball was away from the scrum. Then came a series of passes: Gould to Lindsay, Lindsay to Rotherham and finally back to Gould who cantered over ... The bewildered Yorkshiremen never had a chance of stopping the quick passes."

Arthur spoke of Alan Rotherham of Richmond, Middlesex and England as the greatest half-back he ever saw. (F Marshall (1892), Football: The Rugby Union Game p.123)

Late in the season, Middlesex took part in the London Charity Festival at the Oval where, in front of 8,000 spectators, they defeated Somerset by a goal and two tries to one goal and a try. Arthur's "play was especially

brilliant" and, "rounding his opponents", he scored what turned out to be the winning try. A week later, Arthur was in Manchester where he helped Middlesex beat Lancashire by a goal and a try to a try and in so doing record an invincible season. With four wins out of four, including victories over the northern powerhouses, Middlesex were the effective county champions of 1887-8.

Arthur won only one cap in 1887-8. The dispute with England over the formation of the International Board had escalated. At a meeting held at Newport on 4 February 1887, the RFU were invited to join the Board but they declined. As a consequence, there were no fixtures between any of the Celtic unions and England both this season and the next. When considering Arthur's total number of Welsh caps, it should always be remembered how relatively few international matches were arranged during his career.

1888: Wales v Scotland

Following the hammering in Edinburgh a year earlier, there was some trepidation about the visit of Scotland to Newport on 4 February 1888.The *Western Mail* confirmed the downbeat expectations, revealing that, on the morning of the match, most of the Welsh supporters were decidedly pessimistic about Wales' prospects and that "not a few of the 'knowing ones' predicted another massacre."

Despite the prevailing gloomy mood, there was still a big crowd, though "Old Stager" thought it would have been even larger had Mullock not increased the admission prices. He also commented on the growing passion for the game in Wales. "Passing through the crowd, one could not help observing the vast hold football has attained on the affection of the Welsh public [even though] the vast majority ... thought Scotland would win."

Rodney Parade was packed. The stands were over-flowing; the boundary ropes were lined six or seven deep; and the raised banks behind them were fully occupied. So was the temporary standing area, which had been erected behind the town end goal. And even though he was a Cardiff journalist, "Old Stager" reckoned that the Newport ground was then "out and away the best in Wales". With a swipe at the Arms Park, he noted from personal experience that the cycle track around the pitch enabled the crowd to watch a match without "standing ankle deep in mud".

The pitch itself, though, wasn't in great shape. Five tons of straw had been laid to protect it from frost. In addition, salt had been strewn over the ground so, following a rapid thaw, it became heavy and sticky. "Imagine a farmyard pond drained dry, and you have a pretty accurate conception" of the conditions, wrote "Old Stager". Despite this, however, the play was fast, furious and exciting.

There were no pre-match rituals. "A particularly cordial welcome was given to the visitors as they stepped onto the arena. No time was lost in commencing". Even allowing for the fact that Wales unexpectedly won, the match reports do agree that it was an exceptionally fine game. According to the *South Wales Echo*:

> There was a sustained dash and brilliancy about the play from beginning to end. The tackling of the Welshmen was effective in the highest degree ... the most notable characteristic of the game was the excellent combined play of the forwards, who contrary to anticipation, managed to hold their own against their doughty and powerful opponents.

Early in the game, and with the Welsh backs combining well, Stadden threw a long cross-field pass, which was collected by the debutant wing, Tom Price Jenkins of London Welsh. Facing him was the Scottish three-quarter and later World Rugby Hall of Fame inductee, Bill Maclagan, normally "a pillar of strength when repelling attackers". Not this time, however, as Price Jenkins danced past him and then "slipped in and out of the Scottish backs and fell across the line with a Scotchman on his back" to record a wonderful try. It was the only score of the match. Three years would pass before Newport hosted another international when England were the visitors. By then, Price Jenkins had retired to become a comic actor and on that very day was appearing in *Sinbad* at the Theatre Royal Cardiff, where he delighted rapturous audiences with a song about the England game. But the reception he received for his on-stage performance didn't match that for his try at Rodney Parade against Scotland in 1888.

The Welsh supporters erupted. They "yelled, cheered, flung their hats in the air, flourished sticks and umbrellas and went off their heads generally for ... a minute or two. Even the occupants of the press table [on the touch line], cold and unexcitable enough as a rule, caught the popular infection and cheered as frantically as the most enthusiastic of those behind the ropes."

Despite the closeness of the score, Wales deserved their one try to nil victory. The Welsh pack outplayed their much heavier opponents and "in tricks and devices, the home side were long chalks ahead." Wales were also superior outside the scrum. At half-back, Stadden had lost none of his cunning and his performance "could not have been surpassed". The tackling of the three-quarters – Arthur, George Bowen and Tom Price Jenkins – was "was a treat to witness". But it was "Monkey" who came in for the highest praise. "He was ubiquitous. Running, kicking, tackling, he

> CARDIFF.
>
> **THEATRE ROYAL.**
>
> LESSEE AND MANAGER..Mr EDWARD FLETCHER
> ACTING MANAGER............Mr JOHN SHERIDAN
> TO-DAY (SATURDAY), at 2 ; EVENING, at 7.
> UNDOUBTED AND UNPRECEDENTED SUC-
> CESS of Mr EDWARD FLETCHER'S 10th MAG-
> NIFICENT COMICAL CHRISTMAS PANTOMIME,
> entitled—The Wonderful Adventures of
>
> **SINBAD THE SAILOR,**
> OR
> HARLEQUIN, THE WICKED LITTLE OLD
> MAN OF THE SEA.
> BY VICTOR STEVENS,
> Author of "Little Red Riding Hood."
> SUPPORTED BY THE MOST TALENTED COM-
> PANY EVER ENGAGED IN CARDIFF
>
> | | |
> |---|---|
> | Miss HETTY CHAPMAN. | The TWO MACNAUGH- |
> | Miss SALLIE WATERS. | TONS. |
> | Miss VICTORIA LYTTON | FULLER ALLEN. |
> | Miss NELLIE FLETCHER | TOM W. CONWAY. |
> | Miss RUBY DANA, | LLEWELLYN LLOYD |
> | Miss EDITH HUNTER. | (DIGRI GWYN). |
> | Miss JENNIE THOMAS. | PRICE JENKINS. |
> | SISTERS BLANCHE and | ERNEST E. PARKER. |
> | ROSE. | Major TITBITS. |
> | NEWHAM and LATIMER. | |
>
> The CONTINENTAL BALLET TROUPE—The PRIZE
> DANCERS of England and America.
> THE MAGNIFICENT AND GORGEOUS SCENERY,
> SPECIALLY PAINTED by Mr WILLIAM PHILLIPS
> from the Gaiety Theatre, London.

Exactly three years after scoring his spectacular winning try against Scotland, Tom "Price Jenkins" was again entertaining Welsh crowds, but this time as a cast member in "Sinbad the Sailor" in Cardiff. (South Wales Daily News, 3 January 1891)

was in the thick of the fray, and no man did more for the success of the side." Had there been a man of the match or *seren y gêm* award, it would have been conferred on Arthur without a murmur of dissent. He was "now recognised as one of the finest three-quarters in the Kingdom."

As soon as "no-side" was called, the Welsh players were mobbed and given a tremendous ovation. Arthur was lifted onto the shoulders of supporters who carried him away in triumph out of Rodney Parade, over Newport Bridge and back to the King's Head. All the streets to the hotel were thronged with happy supporters and, even after leaving the players to get changed, the cheering and yelling continued. It was an historic day for Welsh rugby, long remembered by all those who were lucky enough to be there.

The following Monday, proceedings were delayed at the Newport Police Court because one of the magistrates was late. It was reported that, while waiting, "the court gave itself up to decorous chat, principally about the football match of Saturday, the splendid display made by Arthur Gould, and the tribute borne to his powers at the dinner afterward by Charles Reid". The Scottish captain had evidently

WRU CENTENARY 1881-1981

Arthur (Monkey) Gould

"Monkey" Gould caricature by "Gren" of the South Wales Echo. One of a set of 50 cards of 'Great Welsh Rugby Players' produced by the WRU to celebrate its centenary in 1981. Arthur was number one in the series. (Author's collection)

admitted that he had never seen a man do so much for a team as Arthur did that afternoon. It is not known if the magistrate was delayed because he was still recovering from post-match celebrations.

1888: Ireland v Wales

The same team was selected to meet Ireland at Lansdowne Road in early March. Unfortunately, however, two of the stars at Newport had to drop out. Dewsbury had a Yorkshire Cup tie that day, so "Buller" Stadden opted to play in front of 10,000 spectators at Crown Flatt instead. But there was worse news for Wales. Arthur had informed the Welsh Union that he was unable to travel to Dublin, presumably because of injury or work commitments. After winning eight consecutive caps, this was the first time since January 1885 that he would not be in the Welsh line-up. It was also the first Welsh XV in six years which didn't include a Gould. He was replaced by Charlie Arthur of Cardiff.

Yet again, a good Welsh performance was immediately followed by a disappointing one. Wales experienced their first ever defeat to Ireland by a goal, a drop goal and a try to nil. In mitigation, the whole team had suffered from severe sea sickness in a rough crossing. In addition, fullback Ned Roberts of Llanelli, who had had a fine game against Scotland, was injured and had to leave the field for a period. However, undoubtedly Wales were not the same side without Arthur and Stadden.

66

1888-9

Bob Briefly Returns

Bob kept his word. Back in "England" by the opening of the 1888-9 season, he resumed his place at forward for Newport's first two matches, which involved Neath and Weston-Super-Mare. Both were comfortable victories. However, against Weston, while playing with all his old dash and enjoying "out and away the best game of his pack", he received a nasty kick which fractured his leg. As he left the field in pain, it was the last time he was seen in Newport's colours. After 136 1st XV games, Bob's rugby career was finally over. He was only 25.

In the history of the game, Bob Gould does not deserve to be relegated to the role of a mere spear-carrier in Arthur's story, for he was a great performer in his own right. Arthur was frequently proclaimed as the "Prince of Three-Quarters" but, even before being invested with that title, his brother was described by the *Western Mail* as "honest Bob Gould, that prince of scrimmagers". Admired by his contemporaries throughout Wales, he was by nature a modest and unassuming man. A player's player, he always pulled his weight in scrums and mauls, as well as in open play where he demonstrated his fine handling skills. He was a sound tackler; an expert at that long lost art of dribbling; and a very useful goal-kicker. His consistency and reliability can be judged by his six-year presence in the Welsh jersey, while many others lasted only a game or two. Townsend Collins remembered Bob as "a great forward, a fine, big-hearted fellow, good tempered, as big men often are, and capable of doing everything well. He was a wonderful man near the line, either from a line-out or from a scrum." In summary, as might be expected of a member of the Gould family, Bob was a complete "footballer". After returning to the West Indies, he later went out to South Africa to work in the gold fields with his brothers Bert and Gus, and eventually retired to Devon. He outlived Arthur, but with his health failing, Bob settled in the south of France where he died aged 68 in 1931 at the small hillside town of Vence near Nice. He was buried in the local cemetery.

Arthur may have had much to celebrate during the previous season, but 1888-9 proved to be a much less enjoyable one. Missing a number of key players, Richmond were not the side they had been and they lost eight of their 20 fixtures. At the same time, Newport suffered nine defeats this year, more than ever before, though Arthur only played five times for his old club. Two of these were in London, when the "Black and Ambers" beat Blackheath and when they lost heavily to Cambridge University at Queen's Club. Wales played three internationals in 1888-9, but Arthur figured in only one, and that resulted in failure. There were even occasional indications that he was not playing quite so well as before.

Even a fixture between his current clubs, which Arthur had helped to arrange, turned out to be a sour affair. Although Richmond had been in existence for over 25 years, they had not met any Welsh opposition until they entertained Newport at Old Deer Park in November 1888. Perhaps it was a condition of the fixture that Arthur would play *against* his home club. As it turned out, the event may have been somewhat embarrassing for him, as it did little to create any long-term good feeling between the clubs. Newport won the game by a goal from a mark to nil, but it wasn't so much their winning the match that upset the London club but more the manner in which victory was achieved – or so was claimed.

Newport fielded four three-quarters to Richmond's three but, in a forward dominated game, the backs were given little to do. Arthur seems to have had a quiet time, perhaps missing the service of the inspirational Alan Rotherham at half-back. *Sporting Life* thought that Arthur was not at his best, though it is scarcely credible that he was holding himself back. He came close to saving the game for Richmond on two occasions. Firstly, he dropped a goal which was disallowed because of an earlier knock-on; and then he crossed for a try, only to be brought back after the Newport umpire noticed a touch-line infringement. It was a hard and well-fought game but it was the second-half "roughness" which the English press condemned. Whatever happened at Old Deer Park that day, predictably it was the visitors who bore the blame. *Sporting Life* claimed, "play was generally of a very rough description ... Newport being the chief offender", while *Athletic News* declared, "Londoners think Newport play a very rough and unscientific game". No return fixture was arranged and Richmond thereafter side-stepped Welsh clubs, apart from London Welsh, for over 30 years until they lost to Swansea in November 1919.

The First Tourists

The organisation of rugby in Victorian times can sometimes appear rather perplexing to the modern follower. After Middlesex had been acknowledged as England's leading county team, it might be assumed that they would have arranged a series of attractive fixtures the following season. But that is not what happened. Only *one* was played in 1888-9 and that took place under the most extraordinary of circumstances.

Even though the international programme was still riven by dispute, the 1888-9 season saw a new major attraction in the rugby calendar: the visit of the first international touring team to Britain and Ireland. This was the ground-breaking – and almost body-breaking – tour by the New Zealand Native Football Team or the "Maoris" as they were more generally known. Most, but not all, of the 26-strong party were either Māori or of mixed descent. Like the visit to the Antipodes of the 1888 Great Britain team, the Maoris' tour was more of a commercial venture than an official one. It took in New Zealand and Australia as well and, in all, they played 107 matches, of which 74 were in Europe. And even the Goulds never managed to include five brothers in one team as did the Maoris' Warbrick family. The players wore black kit with a silver fern badge and they were also the first to perform a haka to a curious British rugby audience. This was introduced partly as an attraction to increase match gates, though Rev Frank Marshall was a bit sniffy about it and recorded in his 1892 book that the Maoris gave up the haka after a few matches. "Later, when the real merit of their play was recognised, *they discarded these advertising spectacles*, and depended upon their genuine exhibition of football to attract spectators." He must be spinning in his grave today.

They arrived in September 1888 and won their first three games against county teams, then lost to Moseley and Burton-on-Trent, before defeating Midland Counties. Their seventh fixture was arranged with Middlesex. The venue, though, was in rural East Sussex at Sheffield Park, the country seat of the Earl of Sheffield, a mad-keen patron of sport. His particular passion was cricket and he had previously hosted matches involving W G Grace's XI, as well as the Australian tourists.

The Maoris were under the impression that they would be taking part in a jaunt against a relatively modest scratch team, equivalent to the Earl of Sheffield's cricket XI. However, they discovered that they were facing a full strength Middlesex XV containing seven internationals. Arthur was partnered in the three-quarters by the Scottish internationals Billy Maclagan and George Lindsay; while Darsie Anderson, also of Scotland, was at half-back. The pack

The Maoris perform their haka or "war cry" before their first tour match, in which they defeated Surrey 4-1. (Illustrated London News, 13 October 1888)

contained two England caps in George Jeffrey and Rupert Inglis, as well as Tom Lockwood, a former Newport and Wales team-mate of Arthur's, now playing for Middlesex Wanderers. Throughout his lengthy career, Arthur never experienced anything quite like this day. Lavishly entertained by the Earl, the teams were met at the local country railway station where vehicles had been organised to convey them to the ground. Upon their arrival, the players were serenaded by the band of the Brighton Artillery Volunteers and invited to stroll around the Park to admire the extensive gardens, hot-houses and vineries. The Earl then hosted a sumptuous lunch in honour of both teams in the presence of his many aristocratic and titled friends. Rugby and alcohol have a long-standing relationship but usually they become re-acquainted *after* rather than *before* the game. Unfortunately, the Maoris tucked in to the food, wine and champagne with a gusto they had previously shown on the football field. With mixed feelings, one of them later exclaimed, "What a lunch it was to play football on!" When the time came for the pre-match photographs, two of the team were missing and were alleged to have been sleeping it off amongst the bracken.

Hard to believe it today, but the public were *deliberately* kept away from this match! Attendance was strictly limited to those personally invited by the Earl of Sheffield. So the only time Arthur played against an international touring team was in front of the smallest crowd of his entire adult career. It was not even a "modest" crowd. Some reports suggested that it was around 200 but others claimed that as few as half that were watching. A number of "rugby fanatics" did turn up hoping to see the Maoris but they were refused entry by police at the Park gates. Attempting to assure the Earl that they were respectable and well-behaved "gentlemen", they "sent their cards" to him and asked to be admitted, only for this to be denied and they were then forced to wait at the local station for three hours for a return train. Subsequently, there were some disgruntled complaints about this to the press, including one letter to *Sporting Life* from a John Dawes of Tunbridge Wells, possibly the first ever "Disgusted" of that locality.

If the county players had also been over-doing it at lunch, it was not apparent from their performance. Soon after the start, they scored two quick tries, the second originating from a "smart pass from Gould". Behind the scrum, the Maoris were entirely eclipsed by Arthur and his fellow backs. They spent much of the time defending and Middlesex eventually ran out as victors by two goals and three tries (9 points) to nil. That they also had the benefit of "five minors" is a further indication of their superiority. The New Zealand newspapers

Arthur in Middlesex colours, seated third from left (for the match against Yorkshire in 1892-3). (Illustrated Sporting and Dramatic News, 10 March 1893: Arthur Gould's scrapbook)

were impressed with the home team. "The Maoris frankly admit they have never previously witnessed ... such passing." But they also accused Middlesex of rough play, which injured several of the tourists. One Māori thought that the match had come close to a free fight.

1888: Wales v Maoris

The New Zealanders arranged five games in Wales over 11 days at Christmas. After losing 3-0 to Llanelli, they met Wales three days later on 22 December at Swansea. Arthur was not in the team. It is not clear whether he was unavailable because of work or injury or simply wasn't picked. What is known is that he hadn't played in the trial and that the selectors were keen to re-introduce a four man three-quarter line-up. Did Arthur inform them he wasn't interested because of this? Or was it because, as some accounts suggest, he had requested to be appointed captain? Whatever the circumstances, the experienced Cardiff forward, Frank Hill, was selected as skipper. The four three-quarters were George Thomas (Newport), Dickie Garrett (Penarth), Charlie Arthur and Norman Biggs (both Cardiff), and Wales would never again take the field with only three. The Maoris were beaten by a goal and two tries (5 points) to nil, a good result for Wales, especially as the tourists had previously beaten Ireland. Two days later the Maoris defeated Swansea 5-0. It was then announced that Arthur would play in a four three-quarter formation for Newport against the tourists on Boxing Day but he did not turn out. In front of the largest crowd to watch the Maoris so far – no doubt boosted by hopes of seeing Arthur in Newport's colours again – the home side lost 3-0. Without Arthur, the backs played very poorly. Evidently, the Maoris were not the only side to indulge in pre-match drinks, as one excuse for Newport's disappointing performance was the "free handed Christmas hospitality of supporters". Arthur did play for Newport the very next day, however, in a four-man three-quarter line-up in their victory over Moseley; and again two days later in the win over London Welsh. On the same day, the Maoris made their farewell appearance in Wales going down 4-1 to Cardiff. They were very complimentary about the warmth of the hospitality they had received during their brief and demanding visit to Wales. Evidently, they were not always made so welcome elsewhere.

1889: Scotland v Wales

Whatever the reasons for Arthur's absence against the Maoris, when the next Welsh team was announced, he was not only included but was also made captain. Again, Wales selected four three-quarters. However, a week after the team to play Scotland was published, it was revealed that Arthur had written to the WFU to inform them that he was unable to travel to Edinburgh. He did, though, play his final game for Newport that season on the same day as the international – again in a four three-quarter line-up – in a defeat at Moseley. In controversial circumstances, Wales were forced to make six changes as other players withdrew, and a depleted team lost by two tries to nil in a snow storm which reduced the game to 30 minutes each way.

1889: Wales v Ireland

Arthur's withdrawal at Edinburgh did not prevent the selectors from including him in the team to meet Ireland at Swansea on 2 March 1889. And he was again given the captaincy, although at that time he had not had a great deal of experience in the role. Not only was this the first time he had skippered Wales, Arthur had never regularly captained Newport, Richmond or Middlesex.

An extremely large crowd for the time, perhaps 10,000, attended St. Helen's. Many anticipated a straight-forward Welsh victory. But it was not to be as, in the second half, the Irish forwards "were allowed to do practically as they liked". The visitors won by two tries to nil. In view of Ireland's forward dominance, "Old Stager" thought it had been a mistake to play eight forwards against nine. Now this particular journalist was a true believer of the new system, but it appears that it was Arthur who was the cause of his apparent change of heart. Essentially, he was criticising the selection of "Monk" who, he argued, was "unaccustomed to ... the four three-quarter game."

He added, "Gould is a splendid fellow, but he is not, in my humble opinion, the best centre man at the disposal of the match committee. At any rate, he didn't show it on Saturday. He played a hard game and did a lot of useful work, but he didn't play the four three-quarter game." However, to be fair to Arthur, this time he was partnered at centre by Norman Biggs, while the wings were new caps Abel Davies (London Welsh) and Tom Morgan (Llanelli), neither of whom played for Wales again. "Old Stager" admitted that Arthur was "handicapped

... behind a beaten pack [and] by the very pronounced offside play of [his] opponents. Of the three-quarters, Arthur Gould alone did everything, but even he was a long way below his form."

Arthur was still essentially an individualist and this was one of the reasons why, at this stage, he favoured three three-quarters over four, since it gave him more freedom to operate. Of course, he did come round. However, whilst the system was already proven at club level – even Newport now seem to have been won over – its effectiveness depended on practice and combination and this was still lacking in the international team. To an extent, therefore, we can sympathise with Arthur's initial reluctance to embrace four three-quarters. In their three international matches in 1888-9, Wales fielded ten men at three-quarter and they were drawn from seven clubs, offering scarce opportunity for "combination". Rev Frank Marshall drew attention to this in his 1892 book, when he quoted an unnamed critic on the use of four three-quarters by Wales:

> Until Wales systematically practices the four selected three-quarters for some time previous to the match, she can never hope to show other countries what the system is capable of effecting. When her clubs play English teams they invariably either outplay the Englishmen or compel them to bring out a man as an extra three-quarter. The cause is obvious; the club mates are combined and in their right places.

1889-90

The following season was to be Arthur's last before he left to work overseas. It was also one in which he was partnered in the Newport XV by another of his brothers. But what Arthur prized most of all as he went into temporary rugby exile at the end of the season was that he had recently taken part in one of his most significant of victories.

His club commitments in 1889-90 were more or less equally divided between Richmond with 12 games, and Newport with 15. Arthur also continued to represent Middlesex in their victories over Kent and Surrey and in draws with Somerset and Yorkshire.

It was another disappointing season for Richmond, though Newport under T C (Tom) Graham were much improved and Arthur experienced defeat only once for the club. It was, in fact, under Graham's leadership this season that Newport laid the foundations for what would become their greatest period of success in their long history. It also was the year in which George Herbert Gould, six years younger than Arthur, arrived. On 4 January 1890 in a drawn game at Swansea, Bert partnered his older brother in the centre for the first time. They next played together in the final three games of the season – all victories – against Broughton, Manningham and Leicester.

The week after the Swansea game, Arthur scored the only try as Newport defeated Devon at Exeter. The *Star* enthused about his performance: "his graceful and refined action, superb judgement, running and passing, making him the

Bert Gould (1870-1913) played three times for Wales and was a member of the Triple Crown team in 1893. (Courtesy of the Gould family)

most conspicuous of all the players." Unsurprisingly, the Exeter press took pride in Arthur's Devon roots. "Gould fully came up to my expectations, for never have I seen a runner with such a slashing style. He goes with such propelling force that it seems as if only a miracle could check him, and he passes splendidly ... I hear his mother [sic] is a Devonshire woman, which accounts for the Devonshire grit he possesses."

1890: Wales v Scotland

The Welsh team to meet Scotland at the Arms Park on 1 February 1890 was announced two weeks beforehand. Again, it was an untried three-quarter line, with Garrett of Penarth partnering Arthur for the first time, and Newport's Charlie Thomas and Llanelli's Percy Lloyd on the wings. There was also some criticism that the James brothers had been split up, with only Evan being chosen as partner to Stadden. The Cardiff forward Frank Hill took over the captaincy from Arthur. Newport's Tom England had been selected at fullback for his first cap and it was a very good choice: he was a fine player. However, he was injured in a defeat at Penarth the week before the international and was replaced by Swansea's uncapped Billy Bancroft. Tom England played for Newport for another five years but – apart from being chosen as reserve – he never received a call from the Welsh selectors again. Billy Bancroft, on the other hand, eventually took Arthur's international appearance record, by playing in 33 consecutive matches for Wales, and became one of the game's all-time greats. Sport can be a cruel business.

A 10,000 crowd – the largest so far to attend a match in Cardiff – were present at the Arms Park for the Scotland international, though many "gate-cheaters" witnessed the events from outside the ground. Hundreds were perched on surrounding walls, trees and roofs while others stood on vehicles parked in Westgate Street. Such was the pressure from the packed crowd, however, that at one point the wire fencing around the pitch gave way and officials had great difficulty in keeping spectators back from the touchline. Otherwise, however, the behaviour was exemplary.

Two days earlier, the pitch had been completely covered by standing water. Despite the desperately muddy conditions, however, it was a high-tempo game. "From start to finish, the fight waged fast and furious", enthused "Old Stager". Scotland set off with a bang, racing to score under the post after just two minutes, though the conversion was missed to the accompaniment of not so exemplary "terrific cheering". A second unconverted try followed ten minutes later and the visitors went even further ahead with a third before half-time. This one was converted. However, Wales were not down-hearted and, soon after the restart, Penarth's Dickie Garrett broke away and shipped to Arthur who, running at top speed across field, carved through the Scottish defence and scored in the corner. His try "raised a cheer which might have been heard a mile away" but Bancroft missed the conversion and it was the last score of the match. Scotland won 5-1.

However, "Old Stager" argued that, though well defeated, "in one sense, the Welshmen scored a gigantic victory". Immediately following Arthur's try, Scotland pulled a man out of the scrum to play as a fourth three-quarter confirming, in the eyes of Welsh pundits, the superiority of the Welsh system. There was some difference of opinion though about Arthur's performance. "Goalpost" of the *Western Mail*, thought Gould played well, but was not up to his old form and added that his co-centre Garrett rarely passed to him. "Old Stager" agreed, "Gould was good, though not the Arthur of old, both he and Garrett were much too close to each other in the centre"; and when Garrett did pass, he passed too late. On the other hand, according to *The Scottish Referee*, "Gould was in great form and severely troubled [the Scottish three-quarters] ... the Welsh defence all round was very poor, Gould being a brilliant exception." Yet again, the combination of the four three-quarters – who had never played together before – failed to match the standard now regularly demonstrated to acclaim at club level.

1890: England v Wales

Following an historically important meeting of the International Board at the Angel Hotel on the day of the Scottish match, the two-year dispute with England was finally resolved. This was particularly fortunate for Wales as it meant that, just two weeks later on 15 February, they were able to resume fixtures with their oldest adversary. And what an occasion that turned out to be. Arthur reclaimed the captaincy and – apart from when he was unavailable – he never relinquished it again until he retired seven years later. Dai Gwynn of Swansea took over on the wing from the versatile Charlie Thomas who replaced Evan James at half-back.

The venue was Crown Flatt, the ground of the Dewsbury club, so one Welshman – "Buller" Stadden – didn't have very far to travel, though he still managed to miss the team photograph! As it was England's first Championship game in two years, a huge attendance of perhaps 15,000 was anticipated. However, on match day, the weather turned foul. "A more miserable February afternoon ... could not well be conceived", lamented the *Yorkshire Post*. Early morning rain had turned to driving sleet and snow, and by kick-off only 5,000 spectators were brave enough to tolerate the conditions. As in the Scottish game, the pitch was a quagmire but this time it proved to be advantageous for Wales. Despite the weather, it was a "wonderfully open" game with "scarcely a dull moment from start to finish. Instead of the slow scrummaging fight anticipated on the wet ground, the game was ... fast and furious all through" according to the *South Wales Daily News*. And this wasn't just Welsh bias. The *Yorkshire Post* agreed, "the match was wonderfully exciting."

With a strong cold wind behind them, if anything England had the upper hand in the first half. However, the Welsh eight were coping with the greasy conditions much better than the heavier

Wales v England 1890. Back: A Duncan, S Thomas, A Bland, W E O Williams, Richard Mullock, W A Bowen, J Meredith, W Treat; Middle: D P Lloyd, J Hannan, Arthur Gould (captain), W H Thomas, D W Evans; Front: C J Thomas, D Gwynn, W Bancroft, R Garrett; Missing: W Stadden. (Courtesy of Swansea RFC Memorabilia CIC)

English nine-man pack, who had more difficulty keeping their feet in the sludge. As a result, Wales managed to hold England to 0-0 by half time. After the interval, however, the balance swung decidedly in Wales' favour. Within minutes, "some beautiful passing" between Arthur, Dickie Garrett and Dai Gwynn led to a Welsh line-out close to the English goal-line. At that time, the throw-in was customarily taken by a half-back and what Stadden did next has been described by John Billot as "the awakening of thought for deception" in Welsh rugby. As the line-out formed up, Stadden seemingly prepared for a long throw, but then he suddenly dapped the ball in front of him, recovered it and dodged past a couple of defenders to score. A great cheer went up from the Welsh supporters. There was no appeal. It was a perfectly legal play and the English press later criticised the home forwards for not being alert enough. However, what was ignored in all the match reports, apart from that of an observant journalist on the *Yorkshire Post*, was Arthur's involvement in the subterfuge. When the forwards and backs began lining up for the throw in, Arthur was seen to "cleverly draw his men well out in the field", fooling the defenders about what was to come. While Stadden, rightly, has always been praised for his quick thinking in making this hugely important try, it is hard not to imagine him and his sharp-brained captain cooking up the ploy beforehand. For Stadden – one of the finest half-backs to play for Wales before the First World War – this was his greatest moment in the Welsh jersey but sadly it was to be his last international.

Bancroft just missed the conversion but Wales unquestionably took the honours in the second half, notwithstanding a desperate defence in a series of scrummages on their line in the last five minutes. At the final whistle, the score-line remained at 1-0 and Wales had defeated England for the first time. Understandably, as *Athletic News* reported, "the victorious side could scarcely contain themselves"; while, much to everyone's amusement, an emotional Arthur Gould grabbed the WFU secretary and covered him in mud as he embraced him. Richard Mullock probably didn't give a damn. It would have been a delightfully satisfying moment, as he reflected on the dismissive and patronising manner with which he had been treated by *some* English officials when, only nine years earlier, he had first had the brazenness to approach the RFU about a fixture. Wales had come a long way in that time and not least in developing a new style of play which was greatly improving rugby football as an attractive spectacle.

The *Western Mail* reckoned that the match had been regarded throughout the kingdom as a test of the four three-quarter system. Like Scotland at Cardiff, England had to acknowledge that there was something in this "Welsh" game. Following the Welsh try, England were "practically forced to admit its advantage" by bringing the versatile and mobile Sammy Woods out of the forwards. Since the Australian had a great deal of experience at three-quarter, his selection perhaps reveals that there was already some wariness on the part of the RFU about the new system. By including Woods, it allowed for the possibility of switching him to the backs should the need arise. The *Yorkshire Post* conceded, "it must now become an open question whether ... the proper number of three-quarter backs should not be four."

In common with most of the English press, the *Post* graciously admitted that, because of their superior all-round play, Wales thoroughly deserved their victory. The floundering nine-man English pack was routed while their backs were "over-run and swamped."

Even with the "greasiest of balls", the extra three-quarter made all the difference. The *Leeds Mercury* agreed with this assessment and argued that ultimately the Welsh success was due to the brilliant and faultless display of their backs, "whose running, passing and tackling has never been equalled in any of the historic games that have been played at Crown Flatt." Despite the dreadful conditions, all the Welsh three-quarters performed beautifully and passed superbly, but there was special praise for Arthur, who was "in his best form and was very smart in all he did." This was a truly historic moment for Welsh rugby and Arthur had been at its very heart.

Even several years later, Rev Frank Marshall recalled:

Englishmen will not readily forget the way he [Gould] bounded along in the quagmire of Dewsbury in 1890, when Wales first defeated England. That field was probably the worst that any international match has been played upon. The heavy, tall, stalwart English forwards were helpless in the mud. Gould seemed to revel in it, and the accuracy of the Welsh passing, considering the day, was something marvellous. The day might have been fine and the turf in good condition so far as the Welsh backs were concerned. The state of the ground and the greasy ball seemed to make no difference to their play.

T C Graham, whose "considerable skills as a forward were only surpassed by his capabilities as a captain" (Fields of Praise p.71). (F Marshall (1892), Football: The Rugby Union Game p.530)

1890: Ireland v Wales

Ireland proved to be rather more troublesome for Wales two weeks later on St. David's Day though. Stadden couldn't travel and was certainly missed. However, winning his first international cap was the clever and mobile Newport captain, Tom Graham, at forward. Leaving for Holyhead on the Friday morning, and enjoying an unusually calm crossing of the Irish Sea, the team arrived at their Dublin hotel at 9.30 in the evening. They spent the morning of the game sight-seeing. There was no pre-match practice.

For the third time this season, Wales were involved in a thrilling game. One Irish journalist wrote that it was "remarkably fast and well contested and the speed with which the ball travelled up and down the ground was simply marvellous – a faster and more entertaining international has never been witnessed in the Irish metropolis." On balance, it seems that Ireland were slightly the better side on the day. In particular, their nine-man pack overran the Welsh forwards in the loose and as a consequence they disrupted the play of Welsh three-quarters. Even so, the Welsh backs were superior to those of their opponents, with Arthur and Dickie Garrett passing, kicking and tackling well. Ireland scored a converted try early on and had it not been for the defence of the Welsh backs, according to *Athletic News*, they might have punished the visitors three more times.

So Wales managed to remain in the game. With only five minutes to go, Arthur brought the play to the Irish 25 yard line with one of his well-judged long-range kicks. Following a subsequent scrum, the nifty Charlie Thomas at half-back found himself in possession not far out. Arthur was positioned immediately outside him and was ready to pounce. Recognising the danger, the Irish defence, understandably, but fatally, concentrated on Arthur, and in so doing left a gap through which Thomas raced in to score under the post. Bancroft converted and Wales had grabbed a 3-3 draw at the death. As at Dewsbury, even though he didn't *score* the crucial try, as a watched man, Arthur's passive role was all important.

The awkwardness which had plagued Wales-Ireland relations in the early years thankfully now seems to have dissipated. The game was played without any rancour and the teams enjoyed a lively time together after the formalities were over. Indeed, they celebrated too well, as it was widely claimed in the press that "a spree on the part of the Welshmen ... led to the arrest of the team. They were brought before the magistrates and two of them fined." Other reports suggested it was *only* three Welshmen who were charged with being drunk and disorderly and two of them fined. The *Western Mail*, however, was at pains to refute the story that the *whole* team had been arrested, reporting that (of course) no-one was more surprised than the players when told of it on arrival in Cardiff on the Monday evening. Their version was that, in all, nine players had been arrested, but that eight of these had been Irish and only one was Welsh. Apparently, "small fines were inflicted on several of the irrepressible footballers". There was no denial that one of the "irrepressibles" was a Welshman but that name has forever stayed on tour.

Arthur now made plans to join Harry and Bob in the West Indies at the end of the season. With his work commitments in England winding down, he played the remainder of the season for Newport. He was sensational in the Easter fixture with Broughton, dropping two goals and scoring three tries. According to the *Star of Gwent*, he "fairly eclipsed himself. He was probably never seen to better advantage, not even in the great Scotch match at Newport two years ago." It was hardly surprising that he was loudly cheered as he returned to the pavilion: the Newport supporters realised how much he was going to be missed the following season. Three days later he made his final appearance for the club in their last match of 1889-90 as Leicester were crushed by five tries to one. Arthur hadn't quite finished with Rodney Parade yet, though. Just before going abroad, he dominated a two-day athletics meeting held there, winning five events in all: two 120 yards sprints; the 120 yards hurdles; the 400 yards steeplechase and the 440 yards. In so doing, he took home prize money of £22 to add to his travel funds.

The people of Newport weren't going to let him slip away quietly, however. In May 1890, 400 of his admirers gathered at the Albert Hall, Stow Hill to bid him farewell. As was customary at such functions in Victorian times, the event included a long programme of solo recitals and songs, one of which was performed by Arthur himself. Letters from the WFU president, J T D Llewelyn, and from the Llanelli secretary were read out. There was even one from the regulars at the Cottage Hotel in Cardiff, who promised to drink a toast to him, surely the only occasion on which a *Newport* player has been so honoured in this long-standing haunt of Cardiff rugby fans. There were speeches, of course, including one from the Cardiff and WFU committeeman, Bill Phillips, who testified to the high regard in which Arthur was held in Cardiff, both as a rugby player and for his "gentlemanly conduct in every form of athletic sport." To cries of "Hear, Hear", Phillips, who had played in Wales' first humiliating encounter with England in 1881, remarked that he took special pleasure in reminding everybody that Arthur was the captain of the only Welsh team to beat England.

The Mayor of Newport praised the contribution which the whole Gould family had made to the life of Newport, and we might reflect here on how much more was still to come. After paying tribute to Arthur's "personal character and varied gifts", he presented him with a cheque for £50, which had been raised by public subscription. This was a substantial sum, worth around £7,500 in purchasing power today. He was also presented with a chased gold ring.

Arthur responded by saying that whatever he had done for his old club he had done from the heart. He had always felt a special affection for Rodney Parade. He knew the exact spot where familiar faces would gather but, with due respect to the grandstand and enclosure, he confessed that his preference was for the "sixpenny side". "The remarks [there] were more unique and the shouts of encouragement more direct". Whilst living away, he had travelled many miles, sometimes overnight, to turn out for the "Mustard and Blackings" and Wales. He hoped to return once more and was dreading the coming of October with no rugby to play. However, he then enlarged on this thought with a concluding "joke" which could only be deeply offensive to a 21st-century audience. Reflecting the prevailing racist mind-set of Victorians towards colonised peoples, he concluded amidst laughter that he hoped that the black workers under his charge in the Caribbean would not have too bad a time of it because of his inclination to kick something.

1890-1

A week or so later, Arthur was on board a Royal Mail packet on his way to the West Indies where he would join his brothers to work on water supply and bridge building projects. This meant that, for the first time in eight years, there would be no shouts of support for Arthur Gould ringing around Rodney Parade. However, though "Monk" was absent in 1890-1, another Gould was beginning to excite the Newport faithful. It was during this season that Bert established himself as a regular 1st XV three-quarter, playing in all 27 fixtures in 1890-1 bar one. After sterling performances in two good victories over Cardiff, "Old Stager" declared that Bert's form had improved immensely over the season and suggested that he might well yet rival his famous brother. Another Gould was closing in on international honours.

Newport 1890-1. Back: J Webb, C Moggridge, H Day, T Pook, T Newcombe, T Harding; Middle: T England, J Hannam, T C Graham (captain), A Boucher, H Packer, H P Phillips; Front: T Downe, G Thomas, C J Thomas, Bert Gould, A Henshaw. (Courtesy of Kevin Jarvis at Newport RFC)

1891: Wales International Matches

Losing seven matches (four of which were against Swansea) out of 27, Newport had a reasonable season without Arthur, but for Wales it was another disappointing year. England gained quick revenge for Crown Flatt, winning 7-3 at Rodney Parade, scoring three tries and two conversions to one converted try. Wales collapsed In Edinburgh, where Scotland ran riot with seven tries, (only) one conversion, and two drop goals, winning 15-0. The season ended with the team squeaking a narrow 6-4 victory over Ireland at Stradey Park. Billy Bancroft was at his best that day. Not only did he drop a goal from half-way, but his conversion of David Samuel's try was the difference between the two sides. The match was also the first occasion on which brothers David and Evan James, the extraordinarily talented Swansea half-backs, played together for Wales.

5

Back in the "War Paint"

1891-2

Over six days in late September 1891, Buffalo Bill Cody and his Wild West Show were encamped in Cardiff, thrilling huge audiences of over 20,000 at the Sophia Gardens. During the same week, on the evening of Wednesday 23rd, another famous and popular showman arrived in Wales from the Americas. Perhaps Arthur had deliberately arranged his return from Barbados to coincide with the start of the new season. The *South Wales Daily News* certainly thought so and predicted that he would likely turn out for Newport three days later in their first home fixture.

This was probably expecting a bit *too* much even for Arthur. After all, he hadn't touched a rugby ball in over 17 months. Despite this, however, his passion for the game hadn't been diminished in the broiling conditions of the Caribbean. Even though he didn't play in Newport's victory over Devonport Albion, Arthur still managed to get himself involved by refereeing the match! What's more, as soon as the game was over, he headed to Cardiff to present himself as a delegate at the WFU AGM, held that evening at the Angel Hotel. As "200 Indians, Mexicans, Cowboys, Scouts, Buck Riders, Riflemen etc." whooped and took pot shots

CARDIFF SOPHIA GARDENS PARK
(by kind permission of the Most Hon. the Marquis of Bute.)

FIRST AND ONLY VISIT TO CARDIFF.
ONE WEEK ONLY.
COMMENCING MONDAY, SEPT. 21.

Return to England of the Original and Only

B UFFALO B ILL'S

(COLONEL W. F. CODY)

W ILD W EST.

Representation of Indian and Frontier Life.
200 INDIANS, MEXICANS, COWBOYS, SCOUTS,
BUCK RIDERS, RIFLEMEN, &c., in animated
Tableaux and Vivid Scenes.
VISIT THE PICTURESQUE INDIAN VILLAGE
AND FRONTIER CAMP.
The Most Colossal Amusement Enterprise that ever
visited Wales.
COL. W. F. CODY (BUFFALO BILL) WILL POSI-
TIVELY APPEAR AT EVERY PERFORMANCE.
For Six Days Only.
TWO PERFORMANCES DAILY, at 3 and 8 p.m.,
RAIN OR SHINE.
Doors Open at 1.30 and 6.30. PRICES, 1s, 2s, 3s, & 4s.
Nights Brilliantly Illuminated.
Tickets in advance.
Seats for 15,000 people. 5,000 One Shilling Seats.
GENERAL ADMISSION, ONE SHILLING.
Seats for all.
SATURDAY, SEPTEMBER 26, positively
Last Representation.   14587

Buffalo Bill's Wild West Show was in town the week Arthur arrived home from the West Indies. (Cardiff Times, 5 September 1891)

85

at each other just across the road, the AGM also had a battle on its hands. Some of the delegates were also on the warpath. The meeting was largely, though not entirely, divided on east-west lines and the main contention was Richard Mullock's financial management of the Union. Perhaps Arthur had been asked to attend to give moral support to Mullock, riding to the rescue over sharp-shooters from the west, as Bill Cody was also doing at that very moment. Mullock did manage to withstand the attack from the insurgents but announced that he would retire as secretary at the end of the season. An historic link with the origins of the game in Wales was about to be severed.

Much to everyone's relief, the *Western Mail* announced that Arthur had no intention of returning to the West Indies. He was "as brown as a berry" but otherwise looked unaltered. Because of the stifling heat, he said he hadn't been able to participate in any sport though he and Bob had done a great deal of riding there. How he otherwise kept himself fit though was not disclosed but reasonably fit he must have been because he was selected for Newport's next game against Wellington. As the *South Wales Daily News* put it, "A J Gould had decided to once more don the war paint". He would resume his partnership in the three-quarters with Bert who played in most of Newport's 33 fixtures in 1891-2. Bert and Arthur teamed up on 22 occasions. The youngster's confidence immediately benefitted from Arthur's presence, the *Star of Gwent* noting, "Well fed by his brother, Bert Gould was rarely seen to better advantage ... and ... showed great improvement on his previous week's form." And on that very same day, following a successful summer on the track, the latest in the family production line, Gus Gould, was playing his first game for the Newport 2nd XV.

Arthur's return heralded what was arguably the greatest period in Newport's history. During the late 1870s and early 1880s, they had been pre-eminent in Wales. However, over six seasons from 1891-2, they would become recognised as the leading club in Britain, losing only 13 fixtures – most by narrow margins – out of 170 played. Eleven of those reverses were against Welsh opposition: six times to Cardiff; twice to Swansea and Llanelli; and once to Penarth. Arthur wasn't even in the team for five of those 13 defeats. This six-year period included an invincible season in 1891-2; while no visiting club won at Rodney Parade between March 1891 and March 1893 and between March 1894 and February 1897. Arthur of course was at the centre of all this success.

But it wasn't all about Arthur. Besides the superb leadership of Tom Graham, the club had built up an extremely talented squad, full of internationals. During these six seasons, Newport forwards capped by Wales included Arthur Boucher, Harry Day, Jim Hannan, Harry Packer, Tom Pook, and Wallace Watts, as well as Tom Graham. In the backs, Bert Dauncey, Bert Gould, Llewellyn Lloyd, Fred Parfitt, Tom Pearson, Percy Phillips, Charlie Thomas and Llewelyn Thomas were also Welsh internationals. Throw "Monk" Gould into this formidable mix and it is no wonder that Newport dominated all-comers over those six seasons.

Judging by his form against Wellington, the *Star* thought that Arthur's time away had not affected him at all and his game was characterised by all his customary coolness and "trickiness". He had "always been a thorn in the side of Newport's south Wales rivals and this year he promises to prick very hard." He had lost none of his self-confidence, scoring a try and a trade-mark drop goal in an overwhelming 26-0 victory. Arthur was back. While the *South Wales Daily News* reckoned he hadn't *quite* matched his old form, he was easily the best three-quarter on the field. Both papers agreed that his greatest influence was as "director of the back division". For some time, Newport had been deploying four three-quarters and Arthur was now reconciled with the "Welsh system" too. "After a little coaching, the passes were given and taken at wonderful accuracy". According to the *Star*, "the combination of the homesters was superb. They passed generally with machine-like precision ... all the men appeared to have an almost perfect understanding." Arthur's return to Newport and together with Tom Graham's drilling of the forwards promised a very exciting season for the club.

The next match though would be a real test. The visitors were Swansea who had humbled Newport on four occasions the previous season. In Tom Graham's absence, Arthur took over the captaincy and he led them to a crucial victory by a try and a penalty goal to nil. The try came from a feed from Arthur, following one of his familiar breaks. His return to Newport had proved to be a "gain of immense value", according to the *South Wales Echo*. Under Arthur's direction, the backs had greatly improved, particularly in their passing and combination. Unfortunately, though, he suffered a kick on one of his shins, causing considerable swelling, so he missed the next two games. As Arthur began to get older, it's evident that he was starting to succumb to more injuries, though these were generally short lived.

Arthur returned against the Harlequins, who were utterly destroyed by the four three-quarter game and the passing of the backs. He "brought off several corkscrew runs" and scored twice as Newport ran out victors by seven tries to one (17-2). For one of his tries, "Monk" received "a pass and ran for the touch-line, to double away in another direction, shake off a couple of Quins and get over with the fifth notch of the game." How Arthur had returned to such a high level of skill and fitness so quickly, despite being out of the game for so long, is simply astonishing.

Such was his fame, now, that Arthur was still in demand by his old friends in London rugby. The following Saturday he joined Richmond in Yorkshire for a tough engagement with Bradford. There he suffered his first defeat of the season by 21 points to 4 in front of a 12,000 crowd. But he went straight back to Rodney Parade on the Monday, where Swinton were the next victims to fall to Newport by 19-0. During the second half, Arthur picked up a loose ball, went off on one of his runs, shook off two defenders, and then nonchalantly dropped a goal, "as cleanly as though it was the easiest thing possible."

1892: England v Wales

This year, the England international was held at the Rectory Field, Blackheath on 2 January and it attracted a substantial attendance for London of over 10,000. Arthur was restored to the captaincy while Bert was reserve three-quarter. Unfortunately, the 1,000 Welsh supporters, who travelled up by special trains, were to be disappointed. Crucially, both David and Evan James were indisposed and so were replaced at half-back by George Rowles of Penarth and Percy Phillips of Newport. Phillips' inclusion brought the Usksiders' representation up to six; while with Rowles and Dickie Garrett selected, it was the only occasion on which the "Seasiders" had more players in the Welsh team than their near neighbours Cardiff, who were represented only by Tom Pearson. The replacement half-backs, though, were a failure and were the main weakness in the side. Had Swansea's mercurial James brothers played, it could well have been an entirely different story.

Wales lost by 17 points (four tries and three conversions) to nil. This sounds like a real hammering and, dominated by northern players, England went on to take the Triple Crown this season. However, even the *Yorkshire Evening Post* conceded that, while the

Wales v England. 1892. Back: W Watts, J Deacon, F Mills, C B Nicholl, T C Graham, J Hannam; Middle: T Pearson, R Garrett, W McCutcheon, Arthur Gould (captain), R L Thomas, W Bancroft, A Boucher; Front: G Rowles, H P Phillips. (Courtesy of Swansea RFC Memorabilia CIC)

score-line implied "England had an easy win ... it was nothing of the sort". "Old Stager" agreed. It "was emphatically a game in which the score affords absolutely no fair indication of the relative merits of the teams".

The Welsh eight – with a hard core of Tom Graham, Arthur Boucher, Wallace Watts, and Jim Hannan from the all-conquering Newport pack – were inspired. The manner in which they held the English nine "was the source of some considerable comment". At fullback, Billy Bancroft had a faultless game. England spent much of the match repelling Welsh attacks but numerous scoring chances were thrown way. The three-quarters were unable to take advantage of any opportunities because of the indifferent play of the half-backs who would not, or could not, pass out. Of the three-quarters, Arthur, however, was "unquestionably the best ... playing with all his old coolness and skill ... [he] was the only man who showed up well, and simply covered himself with glory." The *Yorkshire Evening Post* thought the Welsh three-quarters tackled poorly, "with the exception of "Arthur Gould". "Goalpost" in the *South Wales Daily News* claimed that Arthur was easily best Welsh three-quarter and – bearing in mind that England included Dicky Lockwood, acknowledged as one of the finest players of the Victorian era – he added that "one might almost go further and say he was the best three-quarter on the field."

"Goalpost" had only one reservation. "A disposition to stray from his position was the solitary defect in his magnificent display of skill and resource." It was a criticism, however, picked up with much more venom by "Argus" in the rather less friendly Swansea-based *Cambrian* who accused "Monk" of playing to the crowd. "Gould's roving propensity, though making him prominent to the gallery, completely spoiled the chance of combination ... Gould should be spoken to by the committee on this point."

1892: Wales v Scotland

There were several changes in the Welsh XV to meet Scotland, including the return of the James brothers. Bert, however, remained as reserve. Those selected were forbidden from playing during the week before the match and each was requested to "do your best to turn up fit." Arthur complied with both instructions by refereeing Cardiff in their victory over Wakefield Trinity on the Monday.

Scotland visited St. Helen's for the first time on 6 February 1892, but the match is better remembered for an incident which took place immediately after the game. With six Swansea men in the Welsh team, a crowd of around 12,000 vociferous supporters came through the turnstiles and many were not at all pleased with what they witnessed.

Wales took the lead after Jim Hannan forced his way over, following a wheel, a technique practised with great success by the Newport pack. However, Scotland hit back with two tries and a conversion to take the match 7-2. David and Evan James were "beyond praise" while in the centre Arthur and Llanelli's Conway Rees attacked the Scottish line fiercely, but they were let down by their wings. *The Cambrian* thought Arthur was "in fine fettle." Bancroft uncharacteristically, though, had a poor game.

However, the referee, J R Hodgson, earned the ire of the crowd because of what were deemed to be his one-sided decisions throughout the match. While Scotland were awarded six free kicks, Wales received only one. There was particular anger when a mark claimed by Evan James was disallowed. On another occasion, the referee attempted to prevent Wales from charging a Scottish free kick and only relented after Arthur protested, reminding Hodgson that the laws of the game allowed them to do so.

Immediately after the final whistle, an infuriated mob tore onto the field, surrounded the referee and hustled him menacingly. One spectator then knocked him to the ground, just as Arthur and several other players rushed to his defence. As they tried to protect him, Arthur himself was struck on the jaw. The police then intervened and with great difficulty, given that the hostile crowd had now swollen enormously, they escorted Hodgson safely to the pavilion.

THE BROTHERS JAMES, SWANSEA.

In the opinion of Rev Frank Marshall, David and Evan James were the finest pair of half-backs in Wales who played regularly together. (The Welsh Athlete, 8 February 1892: Arthur Gould's scrapbook)

Eventually, the referee was whisked away to the Mackworth Hotel by cab. To ensure his further safety, he was accompanied by none other than Arthur. As Hodgson was a Middlesex County official, Arthur must have known him well. But in any case, this incident reveals the standing in which he was held, not to mention his personal courage, in that it was Arthur who was chosen to protect Hodgson.

It was a disgraceful incident. Hodgson was a late replacement and had experience of county and London club rugby but he was evidently not up to the task. Even so, there could be no justification for what had happened. "Old Stager" vented his shame. "For the first time in an International match on Welsh soil, we have seen a referee, a gentleman filling a responsible, and at all times unthankful post, not only hooted but actually subjected to the violence of the mob." The WFU had no authority at this time to close St. Helen's but, with such disturbances becoming more frequent in club games in Wales, the Union immediately adopted such powers and later acted on them.

Though the WFU passed a resolution regretting the attack, at the same time, they rather spoiled the full effect of this by requesting that in future the RFU appoint "competent men" to referee international matches. At least Arthur came out of the unfortunate episode well.

Since returning from overseas, Arthur had been devoting most of his spare time to playing, training and officiating, together with all the associated travelling. Even so, on the Monday after the Scottish international, he still fitted in a five hour meeting of the International Board in Manchester as one of the WFU's two representatives. The main business was a discussion on possible law changes, so delegating their current team captain was probably a shrewd move on the part of the WFU. He really was becoming a significant figure in the game.

Three days later, he was in the Newport team which despatched Llanelli in a mid-week fixture. They were without opponents on the Saturday, but it was not a day off for Arthur. He travelled to Richmond where he turned out for the London club for the last time, against Oxford University. Though the Dark Blues were victorious by 18 points to 0, according to *Sporting Life*, the Welsh captain was "by far the best player on the field". In the space of just two weeks, he had played for Wales, Newport (twice) and Richmond; as well as refereeing Cardiff and attending an International Board meeting.

1892: Ireland v Wales - Bert Wins His Cap

At last Bert received the confidence of the Welsh selectors and was picked on the wing to meet Ireland at Lansdowne Road on 5 March 1892. Following later withdrawals by Conway Rees and Billy McCutcheon, Bert was shifted to centre, while Norman Biggs and Fred Nicholls (Cardiff Quins) came in as replacement wings. With Cardiff experiencing their worst season to date, Biggs was their only representative: Cardiff Harlequins, however, did rather better with two, as Percy Bennett replaced an unavailable Tom Graham in the forwards. These changes meant that Arthur would have three new partners in the three-quarters. In the three internationals this season, he had to play alongside seven other three-quarters in all, from six different clubs.

In Dublin, Wales went down to their third defeat in the season, the first time they had ever suffered this ignominy. Ireland deserved their 9-0 victory. Apart from the excellent work of the James brothers at half-back, there was not much to be said for Wales. This time, the forwards were outclassed by the more powerful Irish pack. Bancroft was again poor, while at three-quarter there seemed to be a lack of understanding as chance after chance was lost. According to the *Western Mail* the wings were not a success, while Arthur "kicked well and showed some very tricky football but was not up to his usual standard". Bert played "a really hard-working game" but would have been much more effective on the wing. "His forte is not so much the tricky, dodgy play so exemplified by his brother, as his clever kicking and sharp determined rushes which take a lot of stopping."

There was a general feeling of frustration that, though Wales now had some of the best club teams in Britain, the national side was unable to transfer this superiority to the international arena. Critics recognised that it was the failure to apply the undoubtedly successful four three-quarter system properly. It was the lack of adequate co-ordination and combination at international level that was at fault.

Despite another disappointing result, the team "enjoyed a right good time" at the post-match dinner and one of the highlights of the evening was Arthur's rendition of the music hall comic song *Knocked 'em in the Old Kent Road*, no doubt delivered in a mock cockney accent picked up during his sojourn in the Metropolis. It became part of his regular repertoire.

A Bittersweet Memory

Joseph Gould wasn't at Rodney Parade on 9 April 1892 to witness his two sons' involvement in the ten-try hammering of Penarth. He was in the Midlands, making his rounds as a commercial traveller for a Birmingham firm of brass founders. He did, though, plan to be back home for the following Easter weekend to watch them play for the still undefeated Newport in their remaining two fixtures. However, the day after the Penarth game, the Gould family received the shocking news that Joseph had died suddenly of a heart attack in his hotel room in Northampton. Reporting his death, the *Western Mail* briefly described his business career in Newport but added, "it is, however, as an athlete and as a father of a stock of athletes that Mr. Gould was best known in the district."

Understandably, Arthur and Bert announced that they would not be available for Newport's last two crucial matches. However, despite their absence, on Easter Saturday, Newport continued their unbeaten run with a clear-cut five try victory over Aberavon. There was now a distinct nervousness at the club about the final match on Easter Monday against Salford. So the committee approached the brothers to ask them to reconsider. The press joined in too and suggested that, given Joseph's life-time commitment to sport and to the Newport Athletic Club in particular, he would not have wanted them to miss such a vital game. So in the end – and no doubt with the agreement of their mother and siblings – at the last moment, Arthur and Bert agreed to play. As they entered the field, they were greeted with a sympathetic ovation by the 8,000 crowd. The result was an overwhelming victory by five goals and five tries to nil. Newport had achieved an undefeated season, their first since 1878-9. But it must always have remained a bittersweet memory for the Goulds.

It was, though, without doubt an exceptional year for Newport and it prefigured the greatest period in the history of the club – six years of "great captains, great play and great success", according to the club historian, Jack Davis. Under Tom Graham's captaincy, of Newport's 33 matches in 1891-2, 29 were won and four drawn. They defeated both Cardiff and Penarth three times and recorded doubles over Swansea, Llanelli, Moseley, Gloucester, Exeter, and Salford. Only Swansea (twice), Cardiff and Old Merchant Taylors (when six players were on Wales duty) held them to a draw. They scored 72 goals and

The Invincibles. Newport 1891-2. Back: R Humphries, A F Hill, W Groves, J Osmond, A Henshaw, F Parfitt, T Pook, G Thomas; Middle: J Hannam, W Watts, Arthur Gould, T C Graham (captain), E Coulman, A Boucher; Front: H P Phillips, T England, C J Thomas, Bert Gould. Regular players absent here are F Dauncey and H Day. (Courtesy of Kevin Jarvis at Newport RFC)

95 tries conceding only a paltry three goals and five tries, so their line was crossed only eight times. The Goulds made a significant contribution to the success of the team. Bert played in all but three of Newport's fixtures and scored 14 tries. Despite missing ten games, Arthur easily topped the scoring with 31 tries and seven drop goals.

Arthur later explained the secret of Newport's success to the press:

> *We have no weak point, and have a pack of thoroughly clever forwards. Then our two halves know what passing means. And we have an excellent captain in Graham, and that is half the battle. They are very clever in picking up and passing amongst themselves. They go in for picking up and passing in preference to dribbling, and are almost as fast as three-quarters.*

He also described Newport's rather undemanding training regime, (though perhaps it was more rigorous than most clubs' efforts). Was Arthur deliberately downplaying how serious Newport took training here to avoid the accusation of being "too professional" in their approach?

> *It is a mistake to think we do a great deal of training. We only have one hour a week in the gymnasium, and our team do not touch a ball between football matches. Training is not compulsory – we bring no pressure to bear on the men, but if they were not up to form we should leave them out of the team. If they cannot exercise a certain amount of self-denial – give up a dance or some such thing – we should say, 'If you have not sufficient interest in the club to deny yourself, don't play, but make room for someone who can.' In the gymnasium we run about, use dumb-bells, and practice on the bars. The bars are excellent – they keep your limbs lissom, and your joints loose. I think a gymnasium the very best thing for a football team.*

The Best Football Team in the Country

The players were well rewarded for their achievement at a dinner held at the Albert Hall in the May. The 250 guests applauded enthusiastically as Lord Tredegar presented 19 team members, plus the regular touch judge, with inscribed gold watches, all paid for by public subscription. The event concluded with a few songs, one of which was performed by Arthur and another by William J Orders, a

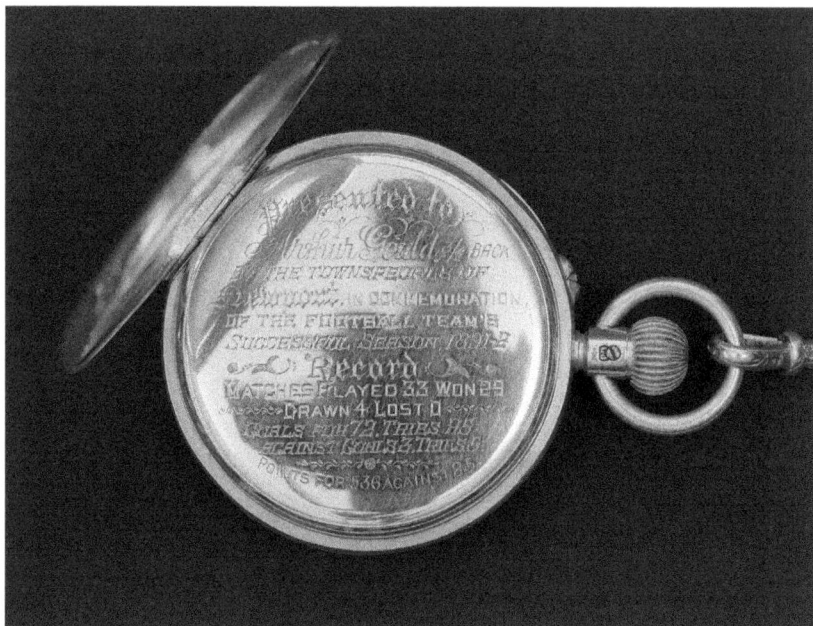

The gold watch inscribed with: "Presented to Arthur Gould ¾ Back by the Townspeople of Newport in Commemoration of the Football Team's Successful Season 1891-2". (Courtesy of Robert Gould)

committeeman who was to have a lasting influence on Arthur's life story just over three years later.

That wasn't the only recognition of Newport's achievements, however. A month later, the popular London periodical *Pearson's Weekly* published the result of their 1891-2 "Football Competition". This was an annual award which they made to, as they saw it, the best rugby or association team in the country. *Pearson's* appointed three judges to sift through all the records of a remarkable 725 clubs which had been nominated. The judges – none of whom was Welsh – were the editor of the London-based *Sportsman*, the editor of the Manchester-published *Athletic News* and the secretary of the Football League. Both the editors were unequivocal and had no hesitation in recommending Newport. One wrote, "playing so many first class matches without ... one defeat is almost unprecedented in the history of football". Perhaps unsurprisingly, the soccer official nominated Bury FC, despite their inferior record of four defeats in their 43 matches. *Pearson's*, though, decided that the prize should go to Newport, supporting their decision by acknowledging that this was actually against their interests, as it would cost them *more* to reward 15 rugby players than 11 footballers! "We agree with the editors of the *Sportsman* and *Athletic News* that this performance is simply marvellous and certainly more meritorious than any other club which entered the competition." The award was to comprise a £5 gift to each of the 15 leading players as well as the club secretary, costing *Pearson's* £80 in all.

A letter written shortly afterwards to *Pearson's Weekly* by Tom Graham demonstrates the strong ethos prevailing at the club under his captaincy. He pointed out that their success had depended on more than a bare 15 and so requested that the prize should be shared between the 19 leading players, each receiving £4. He also suggested that it would be fitting if this were used to purchase gold chains to accompany the watches received the previous May. *Pearson's* were happy to comply with these requests. So Arthur had another trophy for his cabinet. And he, together with eight of his Newport team-mates, would be collecting an even more prestigious award the following season.

Before then though there was another successful summer of athletics to enjoy. As usual, Arthur competed around the country winning cash prizes from Crediton to Crewe, and from local meetings in between like those organised by the NAC and Cardiff Harlequins. One of the highlights of his entire athletic career, though, occurred at the Midland Counties AAA championships at Aston in July, when he took both the 100 yards flat and the 120 yards hurdles titles. His winner's medals were attached to his new gold watch chain.

1892-3

Triple Crown Glory

The next season proved to be even more momentous for Arthur. Although Newport didn't quite manage to remain invincible, they still had an outstanding record; while in 1892-3 Wales at last fulfilled the potential promised by the growing ascendancy of their club game.

Tom Graham retained the captaincy of Newport, who suffered only three narrow defeats in 29 fixtures. Their wonderful record was eventually surrendered at the Arms Park well into the season on 11 February 1893, an easy but missed conversion being the only difference between the sides. This was Newport's first loss since going down to Devonport Albion while on tour almost two years earlier on 30 March 1891.

Judging by the match reports, Arthur was on fire this season. He was "again the prince of three-quarters" when Newport outclassed the Midlands champions, Coventry by 23-0. A couple of days later at Richmond, Arthur "played with brilliancy" as he collected five of Middlesex's eight tries against Surrey, winning 25-9. His role in Newport's 23-0 victory at Penarth on the following Saturday was a "superb one". Not content with enlivening the proceedings during the match, he also entertained the teams with a song at the post-match dinner. However, maybe he was overdoing it, as he had injured his leg earlier in the day.

After three missed games, he returned for the Cardiff match on 26 November. A close contest was anticipated, reflected by the huge crowd of 12,000 at Rodney Parade. According to *Athletic News*, even though a worried Newport committee had called a special three line whip to get Arthur into the XV, "the precautions were just a trifle unnecessary". Indeed they were, since Cardiff were slaughtered by six tries and four conversions to nil (26-0). "Old Stager" wrote that Arthur was" in splendid form; I have never, for that matter, seen him do better". He scored two of the tries, one of which was "the best thing of the match."

When Tom Graham's team arrived in Gloucester the week before Christmas, they were greeted with posters of the match announcing them as "The World's Champions". Gloucester gave them a testing time and the "Black and Ambers" only scrapped home by a single try to nil. However, the Welsh press were scathing about the bias of the referee who disallowed at least two tries, one by Arthur. After a splendid run, he grounded the ball near the posts but in an upright position. Bizarrely, the referee ruled that the ball should have been placed on its side and so refused to award the try! Though Arthur was justifiably nonplussed by this, he was nevertheless still "head and shoulders the best back on the field."

1893: Wales v England

Encouraged by the consistent form being shown by Newport, there was growing optimism this time about the England international. Arthur was again made captain, while seven other Newport men were in the team. In addition, Bert was named reserve. The match was scheduled for 7 January at the Arms Park but over Christmas the weather turned horrible. As temperatures dived, doubts began to be raised about whether the game could go ahead. The Cardiff club were naturally anxious that it should proceed, especially as the Arms Park had never hosted England before. So, with the onset of the freezing conditions, from Boxing Day onwards, the ground was protected with a covering of straw. The severe frost persisted. By Wednesday 4 January, "the park was as hard as a ship's biscuit, only more so" and, despite exercising some force with a knife, "Old Stager" was unable to penetrate the pitch by more than an inch or so.

What happened next, however, is a testament to the ingenuity and sheer determination of our Victorian forebears. The Cardiff committeeman, Bill Shepherd, is largely forgotten but he deserves a special place in the roll of Welsh rugby stalwarts because, without him, a famous chapter in the history of Welsh rugby would never have been written.

On the Thursday before the match, Shepherd carried out an experiment by setting fire to some straw and coal in a perforated bucket and this successfully thawed out the ground in the immediate vicinity. So he resolved to clear the pitch of straw, lay 30 boiler plates supported on bricks across the ground and place 500 coal-fired braziers (known as "devils") on top of and around the metal plates. The WFU readily agreed to the scheme and purchased the plates, bricks, buckets and coal as well as paying the wages of a large gang of labourers to attend the fires.

Shepherd's "devils" far outdid the most theatrical pyrotechnics which are now a necessary precursor to international match day at the Principality Stadium. In an age when artificial lighting barely touched the night-time darkness, the effect of hundreds of fires blazing in the town centre created a never to be forgotten scene which simply astounded those who witnessed it. The *London Morning Leader* has left us with a vivid impression of the dream-like vision which confronted them. It was a:

> *weird uncanny sight ... like a scene from Dante's Inferno ... Dozens of dark, ghoul-like figures were threading their way about the fires, heaping on fresh fuel, while the falling snow rendered the scene one of the most unique and romantic ever seen on a football field.*

"Like a scene from Dante's Inferno". A graphic depiction of the fire devils tackling the frozen pitch the night before the England game. At front centre, Bill Shepherd directs operations. (Evening Express, 7 January 1893)

"Old Stager" too was astonished. "The scene from Westgate Street is a most weird and interesting one. The ground seems literally one blaze of light. Scores of people are lining the walls watching the progress." "Welsh Athlete" recorded that the ground "was fairly ablaze ... the 500 fire buckets ... seen through the darkness and the haze of falling snow present a spectacle absolutely unique ... The stands ... appear weird and melancholy in the blaze of dancing flames."

As the players and officials arrived at the Angel, they too were naturally drawn to the night-time spectacle across the road. They all inspected the pitch and declared it playable, but RFU officials – perhaps sensibly – thought it better to wait until the morning, before they would give their consent to playing.

However, by match day, the "devils" had done their work: the game could go ahead. The fire buckets and plates were removed at noon. The pitch was then rolled and re-covered with straw which was cleared just before kick-off. Bill Shepherd (or "King of the Devils" as he became known) had been supervising throughout the previous day and night. He was later awarded a gold medal by the WFU for saving the match. And it was worth all the effort.

What followed on that January afternoon in 1893 was a game packed with incident, one of the most thrilling and sensational internationals of the era. Looking back on his career over ten years later, Arthur referred to it as the "day of the devilled ground" and remembered it as the most exciting game in which he had ever taken part. Despite the freezing cold, such was the level of anticipation that well over 15,000 spectators made their way to the Arms Park that day. A record gate of £800 was taken. The grandstand and the newly erected standing areas around the ground were packed. As the teams made their entrance, their scarlet and white jerseys created a stark contrast to the thick ranks of huddled spectators who formed a "black mass, unrelieved by the slightest vestige of colour." The Welsh players were in good match condition, according to Tom Graham. Asked about the large Newport contingent, he said they were all as "fit as fiddles", relying on their regular training regime of a good walk on Tuesdays followed by a session in the gymnasium on Thursdays.

Playing on a slippery pitch and into the teeth of a slicing, cold wind, Wales got off to a slow start. During an early English attack, the Welsh appealed for an offside and, instead of playing the whistle, they allowed the Blackheath forward, Fred Lohden, to cross for an unconverted corner try. The game was less than four minutes old and the visitors already had a two points lead. The nine English forwards definitely had the beating of their opponents during the first half and consequently the Welsh backs were given few opportunities to show their mettle. The English half-back Howard Marshall then scored from a scrum after he "waltzed through the defence" and this time the conversion was successful. It was now 7-0 to England. But the game wasn't over by a long way yet. In the last few minutes before half-time, Wales at last began to exert some control and Welsh prospects began to revive.

Shortly after the restart, however, Marshall wriggled over for his second try, though it was unconverted. England now led 9-0 and "hope all but fled" from the home fans. But in spite of everything, all was not lost just yet. After all, Wales did have the greatest player in the country in their ranks. The crucial move for Wales began well inside their own half. Some reports say it was Tom Graham who broke "in splendid style" from a scrummage, others suggest it was the Cambridge captain, "Boomer" Nicholl. Whoever it was, he passed to Jim Hannan following up and the powerful Newport forward crashed through his opponents. Reaching half-way, Hannan heard Arthur calling in support and sent him a well-judged pass. With a "phenomenal run from half way", Arthur corkscrewed across

Arthur on his way to scoring his crucial try with a "phenomenal run from halfway". (Aberystwyth Observer, 12 January 1893)

the pitch. He was faced by one of the few three-quarters of comparable ability, Dewsbury's brilliant Dicky Lockwood, but Arthur artfully evaded his tackle and he then dodged the fullback Edwin Field. As Arthur later modestly put it, "it was then a race for the line which ended in the ball being placed behind the posts." Billy Bancroft converted. Wales had suddenly reduced England's lead to 9-5 and they were right back in the game.

"Old Stager" reckoned this try was the turning point. "It was all up for Wales", but then "Gould's success infused new life into the home team and from then on they gave us a sample of their true form." Welsh spirits were definitely up now. As the English pack flagged, Wales were winning the game at forward. Within a few minutes of Arthur's try, "there was further cause for rejoicing, for a magnificent round of passing [which] completely beat the defence." It was a sensational move. From a scrum, Percy Phillips passed out to Arthur who made a break and then transferred to Conway Rees who, with a beautifully timed pass, put Norman Biggs away. The winger streaked down the touch line to score in the corner. Bancroft's conversion failed but Wales were now only two points behind at 9-7.

With a new energy, Wales were playing their own game now and were decidedly the more aggressive and dominant team. However, quite against the run of play, following a forward dribble downfield, Marshall managed to score his third try for England. Fortunately, the conversion was missed but England's stretched out their lead to four points again.

Wales did not give up and, using their dominance up front and their superior back play, they continued to attack fiercely. Then in the dying moments, with the tension stretched almost to breaking point, Arthur stepped up and took responsibility for winning the game. From a mid-field scrum near the English line, Phillips got the ball cleanly away and "gave a chance to Gould who took it in grand style."

Using all his speed and skill, Arthur bewildered the English defence, "sliding snake-like through the thickest throng" and scored another electrifying try under the posts. The drama continued, however: as the ball was placed for the conversion, it fell over and Bancroft missed! With only a few minutes to go, Wales were still behind, by two points.

However, there was to be one last twist in the story of this epic battle. Pressing hard, Wales were awarded a penalty, 25 yards out near the left touch-line. Bancroft decided not to risk a place-kick. Instead he drop-kicked a perfect goal to give Wales the lead for the first time by 12 points to 11. After the game, a story did the rounds that Arthur had instructed Billy to take a place-kick. However, concerned about the placed ball falling over again on the soft ground, Bancroft ignored his skipper. This tale has since become part of Welsh rugby folk lore but it has to be questioned. Shortly after the match, Arthur was tackled about it by the press and he strongly denied this account. Not only did Arthur state that he did *not* ask Bancroft to take a place kick, reported "Dromio", "but, knowing his strong point, he *asked* him to drop at goal". Arthur confirmed in another interview some years later that "the ball was given to Bancroft to drop". Having spoken to Bancroft, Arthur could not bear to watch the kick and he stood with his back to the posts until he heard the fullback exclaim, "It's there, Arthur!" A minute or so later, the match was over too. Some were unsure about the score, including several of the English team. Had they played under WFU laws, the tries would have earned three points, not two, and the final score would have been a 14-14 draw. But International Board laws applied: 12-11 to Wales.

The crowd reacted as only a Welsh one can. *Athletic News* was stunned by the post-match celebrations and reported that the home players were given a reception which had rarely been witnessed on any football field before. The scene at the finish simply beggared belief according to the *Sporting Chronicle*. The fans surrounded the players and Arthur was hoisted on to their shoulders to lead the procession to the Angel. Female admirers waved from windows and balconies along Westgate Street and Arthur was "cheered enthusiastically, for he was undoubtedly the hero of the match, as he had been of many others", declared "Argus" of *The Cambrian*. "Old Stager" described scenes that would be familiar to any 21st-century Welsh fan:

Later on every hotel bar along the main streets were blocked to the street doors, and everywhere football was the topic of conversation. The victory

The heroic victors in the freezing conditions at Cardiff. Wales v England 1893. Back: T C Graham, W Watts, J Hannam, F Mills, A F Hill, C B Nicholl; Middle: A Boucher, N Biggs, Arthur Gould (captain), W Bancroft, W McCutcheon; Front: J Conway Rees, H P Phillips, F Parfitt, H Day. (Courtesy of Swansea RFC Memorabilia CIC)

of Wales simply sent the population of Cardiff, plus the thousands of visitors, off their blessed chumps, and it will take some of us at least a week to get over the "enthusing" that went on.

Most of the press were in agreement about the match. Firstly, it was one of, if not the, most enthralling and exciting internationals ever witnessed.

Secondly, Wales had deserved to win, though some English critics thought that England had thrown it away. The *Pall Mall Gazette* even went so far as to suggest that, had Arthur being playing for them, England would have won comfortably since he would have scored at least six tries in the first half! "Dromio" agreed that England were distinctly superior in the first half, but Wales undoubtedly had the better of the play in the second. "Had the English made better use of their opportunities as the Welsh did later, victory would have been theirs." But the Welsh "players were in faultless condition ... whereas the English had not the staying power. Wales may thank the good training of its players for victory in a splendid game."

Thirdly, the game at last confirmed the effectiveness of four three-quarters. More than one RFU official, including Rowland Hill, admitted that it was responsible for the Welsh win. English columnists advised that their clubs would now have to seriously consider adopting the system. England would never face Wales again with only three three-quarters; and no English critic would ever dare describe four three-quarters again as the "Welsh abortion", as one had done only a couple of weeks earlier.

Finally, there was widespread recognition that, not only did Arthur play an inspirational captain's game, but that he was the obvious star of the match. "Arthur Gould was the shining light," (*Sporting Chronicle*). "To Arthur Gould Wales mainly owed their victory," (*The Morning*). "Gould, as usual was the life and soul of the Welsh team, and it is no exaggeration to state that he was far and away the best man on the field," (*The Sportsman*). "Arthur Gould ... played that dashing, resourceful, brilliant game which has so characterised him ... he was unquestionably the finest player on the field," (*South Wales Argus*).

The *Morning Leader* columnist succeeded in getting an interview with Arthur straight after the game, though the champagne he pressed on him was politely declined. Arthur put the victory down to superior combination and fitness. He believed that Wales had now proved that the four three-quarter system was the better one, adding "Welshmen keep themselves in strict training and the southern players as a rule do not." Asked how he felt after Marshall scored England's fourth try, he replied that from the beginning he had always thought Wales would win. He added that the slippery conditions favoured the heavier team and that on a dry ground Wales "would have done much better."

Arthur never represented the Lions but it is beyond any doubt that he would have done so had an official team been organised along modern lines during his time. After the match, "Welsh Athlete" spoke to one very prominent RFU committeeman who said that had they been selecting a team to tour Australia, the first back to be picked would be A J Gould, whom he regarded as the finest three-quarter playing.

That particular week also marked another milestone in Arthur Gould's life. Since returning from the West Indies, he had been taking on occasional contract jobs. There were suggestions that he had carried out some work at Rodney Parade and also that he might be appointed to a full-time position for the NAC. Such activities might have had implications for his amateur status but these stories were denied. In any case, on the Monday after the England match, the *Western Mail* reported that he was that day taking up a new post as a commercial traveller for Phillips and Sons, the Newport brewers and wine and spirit merchants. He would remain with his new employers until his death in 1919.

Arthur and Newport continued their winning ways before the forthcoming Scotland game. "Monk" dominated the Moseley game, dropping a goal and crossing for three tries, "all obtained after brilliant runs in his characteristic style". The quality of Newport's passing in their 29-3 victory thrilled Moseley supporters. Arthur's "passing was superb ... he was up to his best form ... and ... gave a brilliant display of the entire three-quarter game".

After Newport's 19-0 win over Blackheath, "Dromio" was almost lost for words in describing the Welsh captain's performance. "As for Arthur Gould, my vocabulary is nearly exhausted. The most brilliant, resourceful and versatile of players at all times, he fairly eclipsed himself ... once again he proved he has no equal as a scorer".

The 27-3 Penarth victory was played the Saturday before Scotland, but Arthur still managed to take part in a demanding game on the following Monday as well. It was a risk. He had been selected to play for Middlesex at Richmond against Yorkshire, in what was regarded as the likely decider of the County Championship. Tellingly, both sides fielded four three-quarters and some sources even claimed that Arthur had told Middlesex he wouldn't play in a three man line-up! He was partnered in the centre by Gregor MacGregor, who would play opposite him five days later in Scotland. Neither quartet functioned well, however. Arthur and Yorkshire's Dicky Lockwood were easily the best of the three-quarters and the latter must have been delighted to gain revenge over Arthur as Yorkshire easily defeated the Londoners 14-5. The Middlesex try, however, was magnificent and was started and finished by Arthur following a series of lightening passes. Rev Frank Marshall reckoned it was a breath-taking illustration of Arthur's cleverness and he declared it "the finest try that has ever been scored".

The match was the first time he had been on the losing side this season, while Yorkshire went on to retain the County Championship.

In an interview with Marshall shortly afterwards, Arthur confessed that "the Yorkshire forwards swamped ours ... we backs had not a chance. I should like to play behind the Yorkshire forwards". Commenting on Dicky Lockwood, he wistfully exclaimed, "What a player that man is! He is never properly fed in international matches. How I could feed him, if he and I were playing together behind the Yorkshire pack!"

1893: Scotland v Wales

Despite the stunning defeat of England, there were still calls for one or two changes in the Welsh XV. "Dromio", for instance, thought that Conway Rees had hung on to the ball too much and argued that replacing him with Bert Gould in the centre would strengthen the three-quarters, both in combination and individual play. To be fair to Conway Rees, not everyone agreed with this assessment, especially as he had fractured his collar bone quite early in the match and consequently had difficulty using his right arm throughout the game. A few months later, Arthur told Frank Marshall that he

The second leg of Wales' first Triple Crown. Wales v Scotland 1893. Back: N Biggs, W McCutcheon; Standing: T C Graham, F Mills, H Day, A F Hill, C B Nicholl, W Wilkins; Seated: A Boucher, W Watts, Arthur Gould (captain), J Hannam, Bert Gould, W Bancroft; Front: H P Phillips, F Parfitt. (Courtesy of Swansea RFC Memorabilia CIC)

thought Conway Rees was a better centre than Bert. What his brother made of this is not recorded. In any case, the selectors announced an unchanged XV to meet Scotland in February. However, Conway Rees' injury persisted and so in the end Bert did replace him, and consequently Newport's contingent increased to nine.

As usual, the travel arrangements for the Scotland international – arranged for 4 February – left no time for any pre-match practice. The team spent the day before the game on the train north. When they arrived in Edinburgh at 8.30pm, the players were greeted with an enthusiastic reception from a large crowd of Welsh students, who called for three cheers for Arthur when the captain appeared. Saturday morning was spent walking around the city, though presumably without Percy Phillips, who didn't arrive until 7am, having travelled overnight from Newport. They did things differently then. The weather was fine and the Raeburn Place pitch in good condition. About 10,000 spectators turned up. Always content to look down on the lower orders, "Old Stager" favourably compared the Edinburgh crowd to a typical Welsh one. He noticed in particular that the Scots were "essentially well-dressed." There were also more women present, he thought.

Up to now, the Welsh record against Scotland was poor, with only one narrow win in ten previous encounters and that was at home.

Bert Gould scores the first of Wales' three second-half tries against Scotland.
(Evening Express, 6 February 1893)

"Scotland has always been the hardest nut to crack", as "Welsh Athlete" put it. So no-one, including Arthur, was over-confident. However, as in the English match, Wales improved as the game wore on. There was no score at half-time but, in the second half, *Athletic News* reckoned "there was only one team in it". Wales scored three unconverted tries. This time the younger Gould got in on the act, while Norman Biggs and Billy McCutcheon also crossed. All three tries came from spectacular passing movements involving the three-quarters. For the third, Biggs obtained possession and passed to Bert. He gave to Arthur who set off on a run through the Scottish defence. Faced with only the fullback, Alexander Cameron to beat, "A J" drew him and then unselfishly passed to Billy McCutcheon who raced in unopposed. Billy Bancroft kicked a penalty and Wales triumphed by 9 points to nil.

The press were unanimous. Wales thoroughly deserved their win and the three-quarters played superbly together. There was a "let's talk about England" moment in the *Daily News* which declared, "though the Welshmen may [become] the champions, the great football contest of the year will still be England v Scotland." But there was no doubting the significance of the result. The *Edinburgh Evening News* acknowledged, "The Welsh back division fairly deluged the Scots with work in the second half ... at the finish the crowd were most enthusiastic in their praise for the visitors ... Scotland got thoroughly humiliated today." The *Daily Telegraph* thought the Welsh victory was so decisive that the question of their back formation was bound to come up for further consideration.

Bancroft excelled himself while, despite his lack of a decent night's sleep, Percy Phillips was prominent at half-back. But it was the three-quarters who came in for most praise. It was they who undoubtedly won the match. Significantly, *Athletic News* acknowledged that they had achieved a decisive triumph over the traditional three-man line-up.

Arthur was not at his *very* best, according to "Old Stager". But note the use of "very". He was still "streets ahead" of his opponents. On the other hand, the *News of the World*, with possibly a *little* exaggeration, wrote that "every run, every pass, everything in fact, in attack or defence was initiated by the Welsh captain." "Welsh Athlete" thought his display was "the cleverest, hardest and most self-sacrificing he has ever done."

Unsurprisingly, his most ardent admirer, "Dromio" was in absolutely no doubt about Arthur's contribution. He was "as usual" the most brilliant of the three-quarters. He took the ball perfectly, tackled with determination, kicked accurately and ran "with the old grace and cleverness ... For versatility, usefulness and judgement, "A J" took once more the place he has held for years – the first". Bert, too, he thought, had a grand game and more than justified his selection.

The dogged *Morning Leader* correspondent again managed to interview Arthur soon after the game. This time it took place over a cup of tea. Arthur admitted the result far exceeded his expectations. He attributed the win to the four three-quarters system but generously acknowledged that it was a team effort which also relied on "smart" half-backs and on eight forwards to provide them with sufficient ball. Asked if Welsh football was now in line with that of England and Scotland, he retorted with a self-assured smile that it was now a case of the other countries getting into line with Wales! Good old Arthur. The new formation, he confidently declared, was a thousand times more interesting to spectators and could revolutionise rugby. The "Welsh game", the four three-quarter system, was the game of the future, he correctly predicted.

The "Wales Day By Day" column in the *Western Mail* included a comment that February which casually illustrates the extent of Arthur's celebrity now. In a story about a man who had invented an appliance for getting jam out of a container, the writer joked, "Little boys will regard Mr William Rowland Deacon – *after Monk Gould* – the greatest man who ever lived".

Whatever highs the Newport nine experienced in Edinburgh, any lingering euphoria quickly disappeared in front of 12,000 at the Arms Park a week later. After remaining unbeaten for 23 months, Newport finally surrendered their proud record to their arch rivals. It was an extremely close result, 11-9. In the dying seconds, Arthur put Bert away to score under the posts. With the tension reaching excruciating levels, Tom England took the conversion to level the scores but missed and the record was gone. Newport had played poorly, though, and Cardiff deserved their triumph – perhaps too many players were still recovering from the previous week. Even Arthur was disappointing. He was too closely marked to get away very often, though he still managed to do "oceans of good work", admitted "Welsh Athlete". However, despite their enormous disappointment, the Newport XV took their defeat sportingly and graciously. There were no excuses and they accepted that they had been beaten fairly and squarely. The first to congratulate Tom Pearson, the Cardiff captain, was Arthur.

"Monk" was then on the losing side for the third time in two weeks against Devon in the County Championship. It was raining heavily, the Exeter ground was sodden, the backs were given few chances and a weakened Middlesex went down by 13 points to nil. Perhaps Arthur asked himself what on earth he was doing there, because it was his last appearance in Middlesex colours.

There was only one change in the Welsh team to meet Ireland

History has not always been kind to Richard Mullock. He deserves much credit for helping to establish both Newport RFC and Welsh international rugby. (F Marshall (1892), Football: The Rugby Union Game p.250)

at Stradey Park, with David Samuel of Swansea coming in at forward for Newport's Harry Day who was injured. The press announcement of the WFU selection meeting, though, included a brief and rather sad comment that the former WFU secretary, Richard Mullock had resigned from the Committee. This was a significant break with the past. Mullock had been the driving force at the birth of the Union and had even dipped into his own pockets to keep it afloat in the early years. Solely responsible for kick-starting Welsh international rugby, his departure from the game deserved rather more recognition than a couple of brusque lines in the Union's minutes.

1893: Wales v Ireland

The "Black and Ambers" had another good win the week before the international, making it four out of four against Swansea that season. Unfortunately, just before the final whistle, Arthur received a worrying injury to his left shoulder in a fall. It was a clearly a nasty one and he was in some pain as he was taken to Swansea Infirmary. It was confirmed there that no bones had been broken but he had suffered severe bruising. While taking his usual training run early in the week, Arthur did so with his left arm strapped up. Even on the Friday afternoon, he told a reporter that his shoulder wasn't quite right but that he intended to do his best to turn out against Ireland. Evidently, however, Arthur hadn't fully recovered by match day and he really wasn't fit to play.

Nearly 20,000 crammed into Stradey Park on 11 March 1893, a beautiful spring day, anticipating another exhilarating Welsh display. Yet they were to be disappointed and, given that Wales were on the verge of making history, the Welsh fans were reported as being unusually subdued throughout. The result was touch and go and Wales only scraped home by a single try to nothing. And it seems that Arthur's lack of match fitness was a primary cause of the Welsh under-achievement.

The Irish forwards gave the Welsh pack a hard time though their backs were unable to profit by this. Wales, on the other hand, were manifestly superior at fullback and half-back. However, it was the break-down in the combination of the home three-quarters which most shocked observers. Sad to say, it was Arthur who was mainly to blame for this. Badly hurt in a tackle early on, he made no fuss about it at the time but it had a marked effect on his play. Thereafter he was something of a passenger. He avoided both tackling and being tackled and, with one arm being practically useless, he was only able to give passes on one side. He later admitted that he was incapable of passing to McCutcheon. "Old Stager" thought Arthur had never performed so poorly and, as he deteriorated, this also affected the confidence of Bert. Given the shortcomings at centre, the wings Biggs and McCutcheon did remarkably well and both defended admirably.

Regardless of this handicap, there were occasional flashes of Welsh brilliance. The finest occurred in the first half, when Percy Phillips broke from the scrum, leaving both opposing half-backs in his wake. Selling a dummy, he then evaded the Irish centre and captain, Sam Lee and completed his run with a difficult but well-judged pass to Arthur. Despite his injury, "A J" managed to send the ball over the heads of the covering Irish forwards to Bert, who picked it up from his feet and sped in for a try. It was the only score of the match.

Though Arthur was in pain throughout, he never gave up. He contributed as best he could, even making the occasional good run.

Near the end of the second half, he was still involved in the play and, given the ball by "Boomer" Nicholl, he made a rapid dash for the line and apparently scored. Many journalists and players thought it was a fair try but it was not given. So too was Billy Bancroft's later penalty attempt, even though again many believed it was successful.

In the end, Arthur's decision to play did not lead to defeat. As a result, there were no recriminations. After all, winning the "Triple Crown" (though it wasn't called that yet) was an historic moment to celebrate. As "Welsh Athlete" put it, "March 11th will ever remain as a red letter day in the history of Welsh football." The WFU treasurer William Wilkins expressed his sympathy for Arthur not wanting to miss such an important occasion. Secretary Bill Gwynn suggested that the injury had cost Wales a handsome victory by two or three more tries. Neither, however, criticised him publicly for not dropping out. However, had Wales missed the chance of a first ever Triple Crown, there is no doubt that the knives would have been wielded. Arthur admitted to the press that he should not have played but added that he was "pressed to turn out." But "all's well that ends

A precious artefact of Welsh rugby history. One of only seventeen presented, Arthur Gould's 1893 Triple Crown medal. (Siân Prescott, courtesy of Robert Gould)

well", and Wales had finally shown at international level what her clubs had been ably demonstrating for some years now.

The 17 players who represented Wales in 1892-3 were later presented with a commemorative gold and enamel medal, with the three feathers in the centre, surrounded by shields with the emblems of the four countries. The words "Triple Victory" (note, not "Triple Crown") were highlighted on a scroll at the top. The name of the recipient was inscribed on the back. A parsimonious WFU had originally intended to present the players with just a team photograph, but a public outcry forced a change of plan.

"A Perfect Idol to the Populace of Newport"

As expected, Arthur missed Newport's next fixture with Cardiff. So he was not present on 18 March when his club surrendered their two year-old ground record by a mere sliver, 5 points to 3. The enforced rest worked, however, and the following week, a match-fit Arthur travelled to London where, from his time with Richmond, his popularity was undiminished. He was greeted with an ovation as he entered the Rectory Field, and at the conclusion of the game he was carried on the shoulders of an ecstatic crowd back to the pavilion. It was as though the London rugby fraternity now regarded him as one of their own. Blackheath v Newport was billed as the "battle of the giants" involving "the aristocrats of English and Welsh football". "W C S" in the *Illustrated Sporting and Dramatic News* described Newport as "the talk of the Football World [and are] looked upon as head and shoulders over any combination."

What should be acknowledged about the Newport team of this period is not just their match-winning record but also the *quality* of their play and the impact this had on the wider game. "W C S" claimed that over 14,000 were drawn to Blackheath. If correct, this was an enormous crowd for a London club match. The way Newport played was a revelation to the majority there who had not previously "been privileged to witness the four three-quarter game or the absolute perfection to which it has been brought ... the game will be stamped upon the memories of those who were fortunate to witness it as the finest exposition of football ever seen at the Rectory Field." This was praise indeed.

In one of their most outstanding displays ever, the match ended in Newport's favour by three goals and three tries (21) to two tries

(4). The now fully recovered Arthur was the pivot around which Newport's game turned. "Dromio" reckoned that "he did more brilliant and useful work than any back on the field" but he also recognised how important to the victory were his leadership skills. "He was the inspiration and controlling influence of the Newport back play and that play was great."

"W C S" referred to Arthur as "the pet of the team ... and a perfect idol to the populace of Newport." He thought few could boast a more brilliant career than Arthur, who had added a thorough mastery of the science of the game to his natural ability. With some prescience, he added, "his name will be handed down as one of the most skilful exponents of the three-quarter back play ever seen". "W C S" also provided another explanation for his widespread celebrity. Arthur's unpretentious and courteous manner "has won him the greatest esteem from all classes of footballers."

Despite having been hammered 36-6 at Rodney Parade over Christmas, Oldham inflicted the third and final defeat on the "Black and Ambers" in 1892-3 by 8 points to 5. They were the first northern club to adopt the four three-quarters system successfully after Billy McCutcheon joined them from Swansea. His stoic defence against the Newport attacks saved any number of tries, though the visitors were convinced that neither of Oldham's tries should have been awarded. The season ended though with an 8 -3 success in the first ever meeting with the Barbarians. Like many leading Welsh players of the time, Arthur never wore the famous black and white jersey, though he did come close a year later.

Newport's final tally for 1892-3 was: played 29, won 25, drawn 1, lost 3. The points totals of 540-48 provide a fuller story. Despite the three defeats, Newport were still regarded as the Welsh champion club with a record "unsurpassed in ... first class rugby football", according to "Old Stager". Arthur put their success down to their regular training sessions at the club gymnasium and to the captaincy of Tom Graham. "Our combination ... is as perfect as anything there as ever been seen." Bert played in every fixture while, Arthur had taken part in 24. Arthur also headed the try scorers with 37, a club record which still stands. "Old Stager" thought he had probably enjoyed his best ever season. He also made the point that Arthur's coaching of the backs and his untiring energy contributed greatly to the club's success.

To Rev Frank Marshall, he was now "the central figure in the football world": central in two senses, he explained. Firstly, as the

Newport 1892-3. Back: F Dauncey, F Parfitt, A Boucher, W Groves, H Day, Arthur Gould (captain); Middle: H Packer, W Watts, T C Graham, J Hannam, T Pook; Front: H P Phillips, T England, F W Cooper, Bert Gould. (South Wales Argus, 31 December 1892: Arthur Gould's scrapbook)

greatest centre that has ever played, and secondly, because of his key role in the extraordinary success of the Newport Club, and the remarkable achievements of the Welsh team this season. He thought it marvellous that despite his age, he was "all bone and sinew" and "still the most agile and dashing of players." And Marshall made that comparison which became all too common, "he can certainly claim to be the "W.G." [Grace] of the Rugby game".

As usual, the arrival of summer brought no rest for Arthur. He might have been forgiven for taking it easy but now athletics beckoned. He showed off his "clean style of jumping" in the 120 yards hurdles at meetings in Newport, Cardiff, Gloucester, Manchester and elsewhere around the country. These often attracted large crowds of sports-hungry Victorians of up to 10,000. He won frequently, even sometimes giving up a handicap of 20 yards or more. His confidence was high, because he again entered the 120 yards hurdles at the national AAA championships held in Northampton. The final was a close affair with the first three in contention until the last couple of hurdles. Repeating his 1887 AAA performance, Arthur was finally beaten into third place by a foot (30 centimetres). The winner was four times champion, Godfrey Shaw, who hadn't being playing international rugby three months earlier. As well as being arguably the best rugby player in the country, Arthur was also still one of Britain's leading sprint hurdlers. Had he concentrated exclusively on athletics, who knows what he might have achieved on the track?

Despite his hurdling successes, the talk in rugby circles that summer was about Arthur taking over the captaincy of Newport. However, despite looking forward to the forthcoming rugby season, Arthur had resigned himself that, if elected to lead the club, he would be without the support of his younger brother. In June 1893, Bert gave up the realistic prospect of adding to his three Welsh caps by sailing for the West Indies, where he was to work alongside Harry and Bob on Government construction projects.

6

"Captain Gould – Newport's Football King"

1893-4

"Monk" had a few more years of international rugby left in him yet. Marshall certainly thought so and, in a widely syndicated article in *Chums* in March 1893, he reckoned he still possessed:

> *the same bright, quick eye, the quickness and elasticity of movement, and the same vivacity which characterised his early days on the football field, whilst ... his powers show no diminution, and his play was never more taking and effective.*
>
> *His individuality in the game is most marked; not only is he the centre of the day as regards ability to feed his wings and keep the three-quarter line on the move, but his individual feats of today rival and excel those of his younger and presumably more active days.*
>
> *He seems as agile as ever, and likely to maintain his form for many seasons. In fact he is more likely to retire of his own free will than to be rejected by the Welsh Committee.*

Responding to Marshall, Arthur made it clear he wasn't thinking of retiring just yet. "I shall give up as soon as I feel my powers failing."

With Tom Graham standing down from the club captaincy after four wonderful seasons, there was only one serious candidate to replace him. And Arthur led Newport to yet another outstanding year. It was actually marginally better than the previous one, since they suffered the same number of defeats – only three – but won one more game. On the international stage, though, his performances did not always meet with widespread acclaim. There were some who, despite Marshall's predictions, now dared to wonder whether he was on the decline. Arthur was aware of this, as he told Marshall in a complaint that has resonated with Welsh internationals down the years:

At Newport they are always expecting me to do something extraordinary. I may be a bit off some days, and then I come in for a bit of slating. A football crowd is very enthusiastic, but very fickle. One week you may be the hero of the hour, and the next week be taunted with having gone off in your play, and with having thrown the match away by mistake.

Amongst the Newport faithful there was even one unseemly incident this season when a mob of fans rowdily questioned his commitment.

Newport started well and remained unbeaten until mid-November when Cardiff outscored them by 8 points to 3 at the Arms Park. They would not lose again for three months and again it was to the "Blue and Blacks". Between these two defeats, Arthur also had to contend with international confrontations with England and Scotland but there was to be no repeat of the previous season's Triple Crown.

The England game took place on 6 January, which followed hard on the heels of a demanding programme of Christmas club matches. After victories over Penarth, Rockcliff, the Barbarians and Watsonians, the international was Arthur's fifth game in two weeks. Given that he was possibly carrying an injury, there may have been questions about his match fitness on the day.

1894: England v Wales

Following a very heavy frost, the Birkenhead Park ground was rock hard. Arthur later said that he had been very doubtful that the game should have taken place at all, describing the pitch as "like a road". The authorities had adopted the WFU's strategy of the previous year and installed fire devils to soften the turf. But the weather was so unpromising that, despite 10,000 tickets having been sold, only 5,000 turned up. Most of the Welsh team were delayed several hours on their journey north on the Friday and so did not arrive at their Liverpool hotel until around 11pm.

Perhaps this contributed to the disaster which followed. *Sporting Life* commented, "the extraordinary way in which the Welshmen fell to pieces was an undoubted surprise to themselves." Not only were they well beaten at forward but, with England trying out four three-quarters for the first time, Wales were embarrassingly outplayed behind. There was only one side in it. England more than avenged their previous defeat at Cardiff by scoring four converted tries as well as a goal from a mark to win by 24 points to 3. It was a rout. To add to Arthur's humiliation, he did not have one of his best days at Birkenhead.

According to a chastened "Welsh Athlete", the three-quarters were woefully weak in both defence and attack. "Norman Biggs and Conway Rees were something awful. Gould was not much better and appeared thoroughly disgusted and disheartened at the manner in which several openings he had made were thrown away [by bad handling]". *The Sportsman* blamed the defeat on the "utter collapse of Gould, Conway Rees and Biggs" and thought they were in a "funk [because of] the state of the ground". In "Old Stager's" opinion, it was one of Arthur's weakest displays in a long time. "Not only did he pass wildly ... his tackling too was of the poorest". Opposite him, however, the England captain, Dicky Lockwood, "eclipsed himself", scoring a try and kicking three conversions. The *South Wales Daily Post* agreed that Arthur had given his worst ever international performance. "He failed to take the ball, showed poor judgement, and allowed Lockwood time after time to beat him."

It is not hard to account for this. It is evident that Arthur was not too happy about the playing conditions and, as he was to state later that season, at approaching 30, he *was* becoming more concerned about suffering serious injury. It seems too that he was now being troubled by a recurring knee problem, though whether this was bothering him on the day is not known. He had also recently badly injured his hand with a cut-throat razor whilst shaving and the wound had not fully healed by the time of the match.

One of the few contemporary players comparable to Arthur Gould, the brilliant Dicky Lockwood of Dewsbury, Yorkshire and England. (F Marshall (1892), Football: The Rugby Union Game p.444)

A week later, Arthur captained his club to a well-deserved revenge win over Cardiff by 9 points to nil. The youthful Cardiff replacement fullback made a sorry show. "Dromio" wrote that the youngster was nervous and made a number of bad errors; but he would later become much more generous in his praise of Gwyn Nicholls, the star who would later replace Arthur as the "Prince of Centres".

Newport's next task was dealing with Blackheath. Both sides had been beaten only once. The 12,000 who flocked to the Rectory Field were not disappointed. In a close and exciting contest, Newport achieved one of their finest victories by three tries (9) to one goal (5). The *London Star* pin-pointed the essential ingredient in Newport's consistent success. "Blackheath were fifteen men, Newport a team." As in the previous season, at the final whistle, the spectators crowded onto the field and lifted Arthur onto their shoulders and carried him to the pavilion. Amongst the throng was the former Newport and WFU secretary Richard Mullock, now resident in London. No doubt his face was wreathed in smiles of satisfaction as the former students demonstrated that they had now become the masters. After all, Mullock had arranged the initial meeting between the two clubs at Newport back in 1879, when Blackheath became the first ever team to defeat the "Black and Ambers". In a magnificent display of passing and running, Blackheath had run in 12 tries. It might have been a sobering defeat but it inspired a 15-year-old Arthur Gould who was in the huge crowd that day.

Although he refused to leave the field during the game, Arthur had severely wrenched his knee and so he decided to sit out Newport's next fixture against Llanelli in order to be fit for the Scotland game a week later. "Welsh Athlete" commented that even though he wasn't in the best of form, he was still the "prince of Welsh three-quarters" and Wales would sorely miss him.

1894: Wales v Scotland

Arthur's precaution was understandable. He was desperately keen not to have to withdraw from this particular international, as it was held on his home turf at Rodney Parade. However, Conway Rees and Biggs had been dropped and McCutcheon was unavailable, so "Monk" had to contend with a completely new three-quarter line-up. Tom Pearson (Cardiff) replaced McCutcheon outside Arthur on the right wing; while the new caps Dai Fitzgerald (Cardiff) at left centre and W Llewelyn Thomas (Newport and Oxford) made up the quartet.

Rodney Parade was a good venue for internationals but perhaps its geographic location was just a bit too far east. Only two more Wales matches would be held there, in 1897 and 1912. The *South*

Wales Daily Post recorded the lively atmosphere in the town before the kick-off, as upwards of 20,000 headed for the game:

> As the day wore on, and the excursions and special trains arrived with their thousands of excited passengers, as hundreds of Cardiffians arrived in wagonettes, traps and all manner ... of vehicles, the streets became more crowded, and discussion more heated, and the clamour more deafening.
> The eating-house keepers were doing a roaring business at a special tariff and the waitresses at the inns and hotels could scarcely keep pace with the demands, and altogether the tradesmen were reaping a rich harvest. Newport was wakened up in a manner which only occurs when it is honoured with an international match.

Six years earlier, Arthur had triumphed when Scotland had previously visited Rodney Parade. However, although Wales secured another impressive win, by 7 points to nil, this time Arthur wasn't the star of the game, by a long way. The man of the match was the new centre, Dai Fitzgerald, who scored both the try and the drop goal. Fitzgerald was an outstanding talent but was lost to Welsh rugby when he joined the Northern Union soon after. Wales thoroughly deserved their victory and could have won by more. However, the sporting press almost unanimously agreed that Arthur was disappointing and was

The scene at Rodney Parade, Newport during the Welsh victory over Scotland in 1894. (Evening Express, 5 February 1894)

not the player of old. He was criticised in particular for straying out of position and for not feeding Pearson on the wing. The *Manchester Guardian* even thought that he was finished as an international: "It is evident from his displays at Birkenhead and Newport that his light is waning and that he will have to recognise that fact."

In mitigation, he was still carrying a couple of injuries. It was reported that he would not play in Newport's next fixture against Liverpool because his knee was still troublesome and his hand wound still hadn't fully healed. However, yet another Gould was selected for the Liverpool match. "Gus Gould ... will be tried for the first time. He has all the dash and go for which his family have been famous." The 18-year-old Joseph Augustus Gould impressed Arthur who spoke generously about him to the press. "He is well built, he can sprint and will, I am positive, surpass me in time. Like myself, he took to sports from a kiddie".

Gus was good enough for international honours and was a Welsh reserve on four occasions. However, working as a commercial traveller, he led a nomadic rugby life, which took him around a number of English-based clubs. These included Stroud, Gloucester, Moseley, London Welsh and Portsmouth, while he also played representative rugby for Midland Counties and for Hampshire. This meant that, in all, he only ever had 18 outings for Newport between 1894 and 1901. As a consequence, he never came to the attention of the Welsh selectors frequently enough to be awarded a full cap. In the end, perhaps to keep an eye on his young brother, Arthur did partner him in the centre against Liverpool and they subsequently played together for most of the rest of the season. After the 13-0 victory, "Welsh Athlete" wrote of Gus, "The critics were much taken with him in the Liverpool match ... I suppose it runs in the blood."

Gus Gould (1875-1914) came very close to playing for Wales, having been selected as a Welsh reserve on four occasions. (Courtesy of the Gould family)

One game they particularly enjoyed together was the stunning 34-0 defeat of Bradford at home. Both scored tries and Arthur also kicked a drop goal and three conversions. "Old Stager" was impressed at the performance. "Great Shakes! How did Newport play on Saturday ... Arthur Gould was fleet of foot and clear of head, and played in a style that was a reminder of more palmy days." Another needle match with the "Blue and Blacks" at the Arms Park a week later attracted a vast crowd, estimated at 20,000. "Rarely, if ever, has an inter-club contest exercised so much interest", wrote "Old Stager". Newport were accustomed to appearing in front of very large crowds but, this time, they performed disappointingly and allowed Cardiff to inflict a defeat by two converted tries to nil and hence level up the four match series to two each. Unfortunately, this didn't go down well with some Newport supporters.

It is possible that Arthur had picked up on this and on other negative comments swirling about. Giving an interview to the *London Star*, he confirmed his withdrawal from the Welsh team to visit Ireland and also issued this *cri de coeur*, "Football is rather too prominent just now. Spectators take such an absorbing interest in the game that players have to undergo a terrible strain".

This interview was a lengthy one in which Arthur revealed more about himself than usual. Firstly, that injury. About three years previously, he had badly twisted his left leg, which resulted in "water on the knee, a nasty complaint liable to break out afresh". (This was probably ligament or cartilage damage). Lately, it had been troubling him a good deal. He admitted that he never went onto the rugby field now without dreading further injury and breakdown. Referring to the forthcoming Irish match, he said, "Under the circumstances, it is impossible for me to venture an international." So was this injury the explanation for his sudden loss of form this season?

Asked if his knee trouble might force him to retire, he replied somewhat despondently, "I can hardly say. It is horribly annoying for a fellow to fall back after he has done so much service. People refuse to understand that form cannot be sustained for ever." He does seem to have been seriously considering giving up both rugby and the track after this season and just concentrating on cricket, tennis and, as he put it, "such games".

Asked about his general fitness and conditioning, he revealed that his regime was not one which could be recommended to any serious 21st-century player. He attended the normal Newport gym practice just once a week. However, he was always walking and riding and "almost lived in the open air." He admitted he was a smoker – "not during the day, but every evening and night." He drank moderately but had never dieted in his life, not even for a track race. "As long as a man refrains from excess he is bound to keep in good form."

On the success of Newport, he commented with honesty: "By the bye, the four three-quarter system is generally credited to me, but that is wrong. Cardiff can claim the honour". Interestingly he added, "at first I was strenuously against it."

When it came to a question about professionalism in rugby, Arthur spoke out sharply. "I am afraid it is coming nearer and nearer but it will ruin the game to the same extent as Association. Money excites little of that local patriotism which obtains amongst our boys, who grow up and revel in the game for its own sake." It was payment for playing or inducements to move clubs to which he was opposed. He concluded by saying that he was strongly against professionalism in sport of any kind. In spite of these views, Arthur was later able to justify the acceptance of his testimonial; and it should be pointed out that he received many cash prizes during his running career. Over the years, the monetary total of these may well have amounted to a considerably large sum.

1894: Ireland v Wales

So Arthur missed the Irish international in Belfast on 10 March. Winning his first cap, Jack Elliott replaced him in the first all-Cardiff three-quarter line-up. Fitzgerald partnered Elliott in the centre with Pearson and Norman Biggs on the wings. The weather and ground conditions were very poor. On a dry day, Wales would probably have had no problem in winning but the Irishmen took the game by a penalty goal to nil and also achieved their first Triple Crown. Arthur, however, was not content just to sit at home resting his knee. On the same day, he refereed the Monmouthshire Cup Final, in which Machen Greys defeated Pontymister at Rodney Parade.

He was certainly fit again by the following Saturday. However, he was quite unprepared for what he had to face as he led his team onto Rodney Parade to do battle with Swansea. Throughout his career, Arthur was accustomed to being lionised by his many admirers, especially in his home town. This time, though, his and the Newport team's reception was very different. They were shocked to

Footballers Hooted.

SATURDAY'S SCENES ON THE USKSIDE GROUND.

An Unsportsmanlike Section of the Newport Crowd Hiss at the Town's Representatives.

Gamblers in the Rodney Parade crowd, who lost heavily on the earlier defeat by Cardiff, demonstrated their anger towards the Newport team. (Evening Express, 19 March 1894)

be confronted with a loud outburst of hooting, hissing and expletives from some of their own supporters on the "popular" side. There were also ironic cries of "good old Cardiff". "Old Stager" had never witnessed anything remotely like this. Following that defeat at the Arms Park, "sinister rumours" had been circulating that Newport had sold the game, an absurd and insulting notion, especially given that it was only their second defeat of the season. That any Newport side might throw a fixture against Cardiff of all teams is utterly unthinkable.

Swansea's *South Wales Daily Post* was appalled by the behaviour:

Gould, a man who has done more to earn the renown to the Newport fifteen than the rest put together, seemed to be the butt of the rough and objectionable ebullition and all his beautiful play was hailed with derision, whilst when he was temporarily injured, some of the crowd had the despicable meanness to laugh and cheer. It was a disgraceful attack on an old and brilliant warrior, and one which even a Yorkshire cup tie would not be guilty of.

The *Post* also admitted that Newport, fired up by the unwarranted hostility, handed Swansea a severe 17-0 thrashing in a "brilliant

126

exposition" of their game. "Gould showed that he has not lost all his cleverness and cunning, and gave one of his old-time exhibitions, certainly the best exhibition this season. He doubled, dodged, ran and passed in a marvellous manner, and proved that he is still the mainstay of his team."

Others agreed. "Old Stager" reckoned Newport gave one of their season's most spectacular displays. "Fast, open and brilliant, there was not a moment of dullness or monotony" and the inspiration for it all was Arthur, returning to "something like his old form." "Welsh Athlete" couldn't recollect him having a better game. With a metaphorical two-fingered salute to his critics in the crowd, Arthur scored a try and two conversions and then finally put Swansea to bed with a nonchalantly taken dropped goal.

"The Very First of Football Men"

Of course, it was only a small number of fans who had turned against him and it was widely assumed that the main culprits had been gamblers who had lost heavily on the Cardiff result. Arthur was still a hero to most, not least amongst his numerous female admirers. One had even composed a 48-line poem in high praise of *"Captain Gould … Newport's Football King"*. It wasn't Wordsworth but the sentiment was powerful enough for it to be published by the *South Wales Argus*. She ended her verse with:

> *So once more to Newport's "hero" – long may he live supreme,*
> *As **the very first of football men** the world has ever seen.*
> *And when, grown weary of glory he tranquilly stays at home,*
> *May he still be sung, by each football tongue, as **the greatest the world has known**.*

These lines recognise that Arthur could not go on for ever. However, a few days after the Swansea match, "Welsh Athlete" took issue with the pessimists who thought that Arthur was "played out". Far from it, he correctly predicted that "Gould still has three seasons, with ordinary luck of course, of first-class football left in him, probably more, and he will be very ill-advised if he loses the opportunity of establishing a record in international matches."

The following Saturday, Newport suffered a surprising defeat – their first at home for over a year – to Blackheath. Arthur's try and conversion and Gus Gould's two tries were not enough to match the London club's three goals, as they lost by 13 points to 11. Disappointing as the Blackheath outcome was, no team would win at Rodney Parade again for another three years.

There were victories in the club's final four matches, including a 3-0 away win at Salford where Newport attracted a 13,000 crowd. Gus scored the only try following "a lovely combination" with Arthur, who "did heaps of work being all over the field." An intriguing story later emerged in the *Evening Express* match report. This alleged that, while in Manchester, Arthur had received an invitation to join the Barbarians who were then on tour in the north. Though the status of the Barbarians at the time wasn't quite so elevated as it was to become, it is a great shame that Arthur had to turn down Percy Carpmael's invitation. Since he was always prepared to travel long distances for a game, no doubt had Arthur been given more notice, he would have been able to add Barbarian honours to his long list of achievements.

Newport finished off their official season with a 19-0 home romp over Llanelli. A week later, Arthur took a Newport XV to Northumberland to play an unofficial fixture against Rockcliff. They put on a thrilling display for the 8,000 spectators, winning by six tries and three conversions to nil. After such a successful season, Arthur at last let his team off the rope. At the match dinner, he remarked:

> I see all my men are enjoying themselves. I trust they will continue to do so, for I have no further use for them this season, therefore they may "go a buster", if they like, and good luck to them.

There is a suggestion here that during his captaincy, he was inclined to keep a firm lid on any excessive celebrations by his team.

The *Evening Express* referred to Arthur's contribution to Newport's fine season, in which only three games were lost. "After all that has been said about his falling away from his earliest and best form, A J easily heads the list of Newport scorers ... seventeen tries and eight dropped goals." He had played in 28 of the club's 31 fixtures.

Though he had now largely retired from the track, he spent the summer playing cricket for Newport and occasionally officiating at athletics meetings. A story made the rounds in several local newspapers at this time which, if true, reveals the expansive reach of Arthur's fame now. Apparently, a Welsh traveller in the interior

Newport 1893-4. Back: J Bowley, T Newcombe, T Pook, W Groves, T C Graham; Second Row: T England, H Day, W James, C J Thomas, W Watts, F Parfitt; Third Row: F Dauncey, A Boucher, Arthur Gould (captain), J Hannam, H Packer; Front: M Hannam, H P Phillips. (Courtesy of Kevin Jarvis at Newport RFC)

of Africa arrived at a "rough shanty" where some friends of his were living. The accommodation was very basic and "there was no attempt at elegance or comfort" apart, that is, from just *one* item of luxury – a photograph of the "Prince of Three-Quarters" himself!

1894-5

"Arthur Gould is a Marvel"

At Newport's annual meeting in May, the chairman Horace Lyne congratulated the club on its third successive season as unofficial Welsh champions. Predictably, Arthur was re-elected captain for the 1894-5 campaign. And it would prove to be an even more successful season than the previous one as, this time, out of 24 fixtures, there was only one defeat and that was away from Rodney Parade.

That single agonisingly narrow setback came early at Stradey Park in the club's fourth match. Llanelli won the bragging rights that season because they also held Newport to a 3-3 draw in the return fixture. However, overall, Newport could still claim to be the "champion" club, as Llanelli suffered four reverses during 1894-5. Though Cardiff also managed to force a draw in their first encounter with Newport, they then went on to lose the following three derbies. Arthur Gould's men also recorded doubles over Swansea, Gloucester, Blackheath, Coventry and Penarth; as well as victories over Huddersfield, Galashiels, Lansdowne, Salford and the Barbarians, amongst others.

Arthur turned 30 in the October. One *London Morning Leader* journalist wished "the prince of Rugby footballers and the joy of all Welshmen" many happy returns. "According to recent testimony ... this will be the last year of his brilliant career", but with his tongue very firmly in his cheek, the columnist added, "but then he told us the same thing only a season ago."

Despite his advancing years, Arthur started 1894-5 well and perhaps he was beginning to believe that he still had a few more seasons yet. His early form in the opening two matches was outstanding. Then at Llanelli, it was a simple missed conversion which cost Newport, who lost an intensely exciting and fast open game by 8 points to 6. Arthur, though, had "worked like a Trojan" in his efforts to save the match. The following week they were away again, this time at the Arms Park. Cardiff had enjoyed a good start to their season. They had taken Llanelli's ground record and, with the hope that Newport might at last be on the slide, most of the record crowd of 20,000 anticipated a Cardiff win. The local press claimed that no previous Welsh club game had generated such intense interest. If ever proof were needed of how popular rugby had become in late Victorian Wales, this was it. "Old Stager" described the scene:

> The meeting of Cardiff and Newport is always a great fight in Welsh football annals, and Saturday's match was no exception ... Even so early as 2 o'clock an unbroken stream of humanity was seen flowing towards the Cardiff Arms Park and for more than an hour and a half afterwards Westgate Street was thronged by a rapidly-moving mass making its way to the locale of the encounter ... No teams in the whole of the country may be relied upon for a superior exposition of the Rugby code than that almost invariably afforded by the Newport and Cardiff fifteens ... [and] never ... did the rivals play before such a huge crowd as that which filled the stands ... and swarmed around the ropes.

The forward-dominated game, though, did not live up to expectations. It had none of the thrilling passing moves of previous encounters. The Cardiff three-quarters were poor and Newport's quartet also lacked combination and relied mainly on kicking. Still, with a much weakened side, a no-score draw was a decent result for Newport and the team were even greeted by their fans on their return home.

A week later Swansea were swept aside 13-0 at Rodney Parade. "Dromio" was enthralled by Arthur's performance, which showed little sign of decline:

> *Arthur Gould is a marvel. With the exception that he is not so fast as he used to be, he seems to have lost none of his powers, and there certainly is not a man playing in Wales today who has the wonderful judgement he does, and his play on Saturday was a treat to see. His pretty breaking runs, his well-judged passes, and his marvellous kicking were the admiration of the spectators.*

These words confirm that Arthur still had some top class football left in him, despite what some critics had predicted. Besides, he still had his army of admirers. Dromio's *South Wales Argus* report was accompanied by yet another poem in his praise. Forty lines long, it concluded:

> *Where'er you go, whate'er you do,*
> *Search 'ere at 'ome or wander father*
> *There's none that can 'old a candle to*
> **Our own incomparable Arthur**

Injuries were dealt with in a fairly casual and rudimentary way in Victorian rugby. During the Swansea match, while attempting to stop a forward rush, Billy Bancroft fell on the ball and was left writhing in pain after receiving kicks to his thigh and ribs courtesy of the home pack. Arthur helped to carry his Wales team-mate off the field and laid him on an overcoat near the touch-line. After a while, Bancroft got up and tried to walk but collapsed in a faint. He was then carried to the pavilion and left on a table, where unspecified "restorative remedies were administered." He subsequently had to be taken to Newport Infirmary where he spent several nights and was visited there by Arthur and other Newport players during his recuperation.

This must have been a warning to "Monk". Inevitably, age was catching up with him, and injuries were taking an increasing toll. A week later, at home against Gloucester, he made one try by baffling his opponents before giving the crucial pass; and then scored himself after a remarkably clever piece of inter-passing with Bert Dauncey. However, it was Arthur's turn to be on the receiving end of "not entirely affectionate" attention, this time from Gloucester. According to "Welsh Athlete", he was felled after a rather violent collision with an opponent. It was initially thought he was just winded and he resumed play and even scored following this incident. However, it turned out that he had badly bruised his ribs and so he was forced to miss his team's next victory a week later over Coventry.

Soon after, Cardiff were again visitors to Rodney Parade, where another substantial crowd of 12,000 paid to watch. Both clubs drew support from their extensive hinterlands. "Dromio" noted that "a constant stream of hurrying people drifted from all parts of the town ... and as spectators passed over the Newport Bridge they saw trains laden with enthusiasts from the hills and Valleys passing into Newport Station. Cardiff, of course, brought a big contingent, and from many more distant quarters came followers".

Cardiff had been unbeaten until the previous week, when they went down to Penarth, so both sides had similar records. Unlike their previous meeting, "a better contested game" had seldom been seen at the Parade. Newport were leading a very close contest by a try to nil when Arthur put the game beyond Cardiff's reach with a beautifully directed left foot drop. "Dromio" regarded Arthur's quick thinking here as the clincher in the 7-0 victory:

> The dropped goal of Arthur Gould was as smart a bit of work as one could want to see – a quick pass [from Hannan], a sharp kick and the deed was done. It was another instance of the international captain's genius for seeing and taking a chance.

Injured during the East v West trial, Arthur was unable to take the field again for nearly a month. However, he made up for this over the Christmas holidays by playing three times in four days. On 27 December, in front of another enormous crowd, the "Black and Ambers" won handsomely against a strong Barbarian XV. "Dromio" reported that the 19-3 score-line was largely due to the superiority of the forwards, "unquestionably the finest pack that ever played". With

Newport 1894-5. Back: J Jenkins, T Pook, W Groves, J Hannam, A James, A Boucher, T Parsons, J Jenkins, T England, W L Thomas, G Thomas; Middle: T Saunders, Bert Gould, H Packer, Arthur Gould (captain), T Newcombe, W Watts, F Dauncey; Front: M Hannam, A R Williams, C J Thomas, F Parfitt. (Courtesy of Kevin Jarvis at Newport RFC)

the England international looming, he also happily testified that the Newport captain was in great form. "Arthur Gould played the best game he has this season. He seems to have recovered all his old pace, and for trickiness he still has no equal." There was, however, one man playing on the Barbarians wing who might claim to be at the very least Arthur's *sporting* equal. Not only did C B Fry later play both cricket and association football for England, in 1893 he matched the world long-jump record; and, but for an unfortunate leg injury, he would have won a rugby Blue at Oxford a few weeks before the Newport fixture.

1895: Wales v England

Then, on 5 January Arthur was off to Swansea to take on England, in yet another new centre partnership with the previously uncapped Owen Badger of Llanelli. The six Newport members of the Welsh XV must have been getting used to very large crowds now: there were upwards of 20,000 at St. Helen's. However, the *Western Mail* headlines tell the sorry story of the match:

Though Wales led twice, English pressure told and the visitors claimed victory by four tries and a conversion (14) to two tries (6). Wales were beaten where they least expected it: at forward. The half-backs, Selwyn Biggs (Cardiff) and Ben Davies (Llanelli) didn't work well together; while at fullback, Bancroft's "exhibition was of the sorriest description", according to "Welsh Athlete". The jury was out as far as Arthur was concerned. "Dromio" was largely supportive. He "played a fine game [and] without doing anything substantial played with fine judgement ... his passing was well judged, and he ran well, but was a little weak before the forward rushes." Much of the English press were generally in agreement. However, "Welsh Athlete" wrote that neither of the Welsh centres was satisfactory. "The Kelt" in the *South Wales Daily Post* thought Arthur's performance was only "so-so", occasionally showing his old brilliance, especially in attack, but sometimes passing wildly. He also criticised his tackling, as did others. WFU committee-man, William Wilkins, went so far to tell the press that he "never tackled a man". Slightly more measured was the *Morning Leader*'s assessment that Gould "did not collar well." "Welsh Athlete" summed up his tackling, "Gould we always look upon as being weak in this respect but what he lacks in this department he invariably makes up by his brilliant aggressive tactics." Arthur wasn't the only one criticised for poor defence and even he admitted to the press that tackling was the Welsh weak point. "Welsh Athlete's" comment that Arthur had *always* been a weak tackler, however, does not sit very well with the evidence of many match reports earlier in his career which praise his defensive qualities. That said, as he got older, it does seem that his tackling sometimes let him down.

There was little dispute that the better side had won. There was, however, a complaint about the final England score 20 minutes from the end which, had it not been awarded, *might* have given Wales a chance to save the match. At the time, the laws allowed a player tackled with the ball to call out "held" and a scrum would then be awarded. The England captain, Sammy Woods, was thought to have shouted "held" but then passed the ball out. The Welsh players stopped, waiting for the scrum but England carried on and Carey scored a soft try under the posts which was converted. As captain,

England won 14-6 at Swansea in 1895, but is that Arthur on the right, waiting to pounce? (Western Mail, 7 January 1895)

Arthur disputed the score but the referee replied that he hadn't heard Woods' call and so gave the try. One unnamed WFU official also grumbled to the press that "we never get a good referee in international matches." Some traditions go back a long way.

1895: Scotland v Wales

The conditions were decidedly bad in Edinburgh when the Welsh team arrived there for the next international. When the players and officials inspected the Raeburn Place ground, they found that a large area of the pitch was rock hard and quite unfit to play on. "Old Stager" also spotted numerous patches around the rest of the field which were frozen solid. With the biting cold weather continuing to deteriorate, the Welsh, perhaps mindful of how badly they had performed in similar conditions at Birkenhead a year earlier, were very reluctant to proceed. "Old Stager" claimed that Arthur was emphatic that Wales would not play on the pitch. The suggestion was then floated that the playing area be shortened by 20 yards. Some reports suggested this was Arthur's idea but the *Edinburgh Evening News* stated that "as it was, the compromise seemed to come *very reluctantly* from him and during the game he appeared to carry an ever-increasing grudge against those who had turned him out to play on such a ground." So the match did proceed on a much reduced pitch under rapidly worsening conditions, and "Old Stager" thought it an "extremely injudicious" decision to risk injury on so dangerous a ground. Given that the pitch had been unplayable for some time, the Scottish Union should really have postponed the game before Wales travelled.

Wales had made five changes, one being the replacement of W Llewelyn Thomas on the wing by the new cap Evan Lloyd of Llanelli. For much of the first half, though, the Welsh line-up was seriously disrupted after half-back Fred Parfitt was carried off having received several kicks to the head. What is often forgotten about the days before substitutions is that teams were further hampered by a loss of a player from having to re-arrange their line-up. Arthur had to call Boucher up from the forwards into the centre; move Badger to the wing; and tell Lloyd to take over at half-back. Arthur knew what he was doing and this actually worked better than expected. Boucher had played at centre quite a few times and was even Arthur's co-centre in the East Wales XV in the trial. If anything, too, his tackling stiffened up the defence of the Welsh three-quarters. Parfitt returned in the second half but must have still been affected by his head injury.

The *Post* thought Wales were unlucky not to win. Even the *Edinburgh Evening News* admitted it could have gone either way. The Scottish and the neutral press were disappointed that the visitors' three-quarter line hadn't fired as expected. The *News* reckoned this was because of their nervousness about the conditions. However, "Welsh Athlete" revealed that the Welsh quartet were given very few opportunities – "not more than half a dozen"- and in only one of those moves did they look like scoring when bad luck robbed them of a try. "Old Stager" accounted for the lack of Welsh attacking flair on the "palpably off-side tactics of the home centres". The winning Scottish score came in the second half from the charge down of a Bancroft clearance kick. James Gowans, the London Scottish wing, followed up smartly and somehow managed to squeeze through a phalanx of defenders near the goal line to touch down. What turned out to be the crucial conversion was successful. Soon after, Arthur made a scintillating break, passed to his wing Pearson, who passed back, leaving Arthur unmarked. As he raced towards the undefended line looking certain to score, he slipped on an icy patch and the chance of a try was gone. This wasn't the team's only misfortune. Because the pitch had been reduced at short notice, the new try line had to be marked out by tape. The Cardiff forward Frank Mills grounded the ball over the tape only for the referee to disallow it because he reckoned that the tape had moved, which raises the question: how were the players expected to determine the actual goal-line? However, Bancroft – who played well on the day – made up for his earlier mistake by dropping a beautiful goal from a mark but that was the end of the scoring. Scotland had won by 5 points to 4 and they went on to take their second Triple Crown.

Perhaps judging Arthur by his own superlative standards, some critics, like that of the *Edinburgh Evening News*, thought that, "though still dangerous [he] is not the man he was". *Sporting Life* too reckoned he "is failing" and, though admitting he did several "smart things", went on to criticise his tackling. Even "Old Stager" agreed that he wasn't at his best, but he still played a hard game and "showed once more his brilliant generalship". "Welsh Athlete" concurred. "Gould played with his head in all his old style". Had he been given more to do, the result might have been different. Unlike some reporters, "Old Stager" felt that Arthur and his wing Tom Pearson "offered a really sound defence and let nothing past them." Certainly, the Scottish three-quarters never broke through to score, even when Wales were reduced to 14.

The severe iron-bound frost across Britain continued, and several winnable fixtures on the Newport programme had to be cancelled. Consequently, it was a month before Arthur turned out again. The team had kept fit by training regularly at the club gymnasium. Though Gus Gould was away for most of the season, Bert had returned from the West Indies in late January and so was available for the match at St. Helen's. Reduced to 14 men after only a few minutes, Swansea still put up a stern fight and the "Black and Ambers" won by a solitary try from Boucher. Arthur had a mixed game. His old judgement and coolness had not deserted him, according to "Dromio" and "he was by a long way the best of the centres". But he fumbled, he was tackled in possession several times and had a kick charged down. Sadly, the game was scarred by an awful tragedy. It transpired that the injured Swansea player, Richard Burrows, had sustained a serious spinal injury in a loose scrum. He was left paralysed and died in hospital three weeks later. Bert Gould, who had been close to the incident was called as a witness at the inquest and testified that the cause of the injury was entirely accidental. The jury recorded a verdict of accidental death.

1895: Wales v Ireland

On 16 March it was time for the showdown with Ireland at the Arms Park. There were no titles at stake but naturally neither side wanted to sup from the "wooden spoon". There was intense interest for what was only the fifth international hosted in Cardiff. A record crowd of around 18-20,000 was claimed by some newspapers. The *South Wales Daily Post* went further and reckoned that the figure must have been closer to 25,000, after taking into account all those who managed to watch without paying. Spectators could be seen at the windows and on the roofs of surrounding buildings; in the trees on the river bank and behind the grandstand; on telegraph poles in Westgate Street; and even on top of a conveniently located pile of straw bales in the cricket field. Before kick-off, the Ferndale Brass Band entertained the crowd with a medley of Irish and Welsh airs. The Irish tunes were received more enthusiastically than the Welsh ones, except for *Hen Wlad Fy Nhadau*, which was taken up by the supporters "with great gusto". So ten years before the events prior to the New Zealand international, this match was possibly the first recorded occasion on which the strains of the Welsh National Anthem greeted the players because it was repeated as Arthur led his team onto the enclosure.

It was a keenly fought encounter with little between the teams, though "Dromio" and his fellow Welsh scribes believed Wales certainly deserved to win a match always full of incident. Ireland took the lead with an unconverted try by their forward Tom Crean, who would be awarded the Victoria Cross seven years later. However, Wales hit back with one of the greatest international tries ever witnessed up to that time.

The move involved six of the backs. The Welsh forwards won the ball from a loose scrum on their own 25 yard line. Llanelli's David Morgan picked up, made a show of running but passed to his half-back partner Ralph Sweet-Escott. He intimated that he was about to transfer to Arthur – always closely watched – but, causing confusion in the Irish ranks, he passed out wide instead to Llewelyn Thomas.

A splendidly detailed elevated view of a packed Cardiff Arms Park in 1895, when Wales defeated Ireland 5-3. (Evening Express, 18 March 1895)

The latter, who had replaced Evan Lloyd, then made a dash up field. As an Irish tackler approached Thomas, Arthur managed to get close. Coming at full pelt, he took a short pass and burst through. After drawing two Irish defenders, Arthur handed on to Owen Badger on the right. So far all the play had taken place in the Welsh half. Badger then successfully passed to Tom Pearson on the half-way line. The winger tore along the touchline "in magnificent style". Evading the tackle of Gardiner, his opposite number, by handing him off, he then swept around the fullback, Fulton, to ground the ball behind the post, "amid tumultuous cheering". Bancroft's successful conversion was enough to give Wales victory by 5 points to 3.

Of Pearson, "Dromio" wrote, "a man with less pace and strength would never have got through … one grand piece of combination, a grand run and a neat place-kick won the match." Talking to reporters afterwards, Arthur described the try rather dispassionately. It was just "a regular Welsh try, [scored] as a result of the ball passing all along the line."

Opinion about the captain's play this time was undivided. "Gould played as good a game as I have seen him play this year", wrote "Welsh Athlete" who reckoned his defence was sounder than usual. "Old Stager" agreed that "Arthur Gould was in one of his happiest veins". "Dromio" of course, was at his most effusive, brimming with delight at the Welsh captain's "sterling play".

Far from showing the last of his flagging powers, he came out brilliantly, showed not only splendid attacking powers, he defended most pluckily … again, he showed himself a master of the game, peerless in judgement and resource, and if Gould himself made no sensational run, he proved himself a model three-quarter.

It has often been said that he is not a defensive player – and there are times when he is not over-anxious to risk too much – but against Ireland he played as a fine defensive game as any man on the field, stopping forward rushes and tackling with the greatest determination. His play was worthy of his reputation: no more need be said.

He also raised the rumours that Arthur might be about to retire.

If this should be the last international in which he takes part – and who knows what the future may bring forth? – it will not be said of him, as it has of other famous men, that he played too long.

After the dinner at the Queen's Hotel, the players seem to have got on well. Some went to the theatre. The majority, though, were led by Arthur on what was euphemistically described as a "sight- seeing" tour of Cardiff which impressed one IRFU official. "A J Gould took a few of the 'bhoys' round the town and showed us several wrinkles [favourite haunts of local footballers]". A more sedate visit to Barry Docks had been arranged for the Sunday morning but, after a heavy night, most of the Irish party stayed in bed.

Just before they left the Queen's on the Monday morning, the Irish players and officials were surprisingly summoned to a special gathering. There they were presented with a box which had been left at the hotel with instructions for it to be given to the losing team. It was found to contain a large wooden spoon. The team took the joke well, and gave the "trophy" pride of place at the head of a procession of players as they made their way on the short journey to the station "amid much blowing of trumpets". By the time they reached their destination, this boisterous procession had grown from 20 to 200. Many more packed onto the platform to wish the Irishmen *bon voyage*.

Wales v Ireland 1895. Back: E B Holmes (referee), F Mills, E George, C B Nicholl, A Boucher, A M Jenkin, J Hannam; Middle: W Watts, H Packer, O Badger, Arthur Gould (captain), W Bancroft, T Pearson; Front: D Morgan, R Sweet Escott, W Llewelyn Thomas. (Courtesy of Swansea RFC Memorabilia CIC)

What subsequently happened to the trophy is unknown. So Wales had avoided ignominy of the "wooden spoon" and finished third in the championship.

Arthur suffered two defeats in the Welsh jersey this season, which was one more than when he wore the black and amber. To conclude Newport's season, there was a 6-0 win at the Rectory Field against Blackheath, which attracted 15-18,000. Cardiff were beaten twice in very tight matches: at home by 5-3 in front of 10,000, and away by 6-3 before a similar crowd. Crucially, Arthur was the try scorer in both games. Then he produced yet another memorable winning try against Salford at Rodney Parade, after intercepting in his own half. It was the only score. However, a cataclysm was about to strike the sport of rugby only a few months later with the creation of the Northern Union. This was the last fixture Newport ever had with a club which eventually joined what later became the Rugby League.

After the rugby was over, Arthur turned to cricket as usual, but he was always willing to give any sport a try. A few weeks into the close season, he captained a Newport rugby club VII in a special water-polo match, losing, perhaps predictably, to Newport Swimming Club by four goals to nil.

7

A Testimonial for a Football Prodigy

1895-6

After leading Newport for two seasons, in which only four fixtures out of 55 were lost, "Monk" decided it was time to relinquish the captaincy. This now passed to his fellow international, Arthur Boucher. "Welsh Athlete" wrote:

> The fact of Arthur Gould declining the captaincy ... suggests that the veteran is getting well on towards the close of his career. I don't suppose there will be a footballer in South Wales but that will regret the day when it does come. Unquestionably he is the finest exponent of the Rugby game Wales has ever produced. I might even say the Kingdom has produced. He should have a rare farewell when the time comes.

He cannot possibly have anticipated just how rare that farewell would very soon become.

As it happened, this *was* to be Arthur's last *full* season though, defying the gloomy predictions of some critics, there was no decline in form. Quite the opposite. During 1895-6, he produced some of his best rugby for several years.

Even though the inspirational Tom Graham had retired, under Boucher's leadership Newport still towered over the British club game. They sustained just two defeats – both away from home – in 26 outings. Arthur missed only three matches, and his exceptional form was again pivotal in the Usksiders' continuing success. It would, however, be the last season in which he played in the majority of Newport's games. But with Bert having returned home from the West Indies and Gus sometimes available, there were three occasions in 1895-6, when the brothers appeared together. Each time, Gus was Arthur's co-centre, while Bert featured at fullback. Bert played regularly for the club at the beginning of the season but he later fractured three ribs. Apart from a couple of reserve team matches, this put him out of the game for the rest of 1895-6.

By Newport's standards, the season didn't start too well. Of their first ten fixtures, two were lost and two drawn. Nevertheless, match reports continued to praise Arthur. In the 20-0 opener against Barnstaple, he dropped a goal and ran in two tries. "Athletic News" commented, "despite his years of service" he was "as clever and agile as ever". "Dromio" thought that, "he seems in great form at present ... it is really remarkable to think of him playing on years after his early contemporaries have become names only." There was more of the same from his greatest fan after the 35-0 pasting of Moseley. "Arthur Gould seems as buoyant and brilliant as ever. As was said of him the other day, he is *the prodigy of football.*" One of his runs ... was simply bewildering – he must have dodged some men two or three times" before giving a scoring pass to his wing Tom Pearson, who had transferred from Cardiff this season.

Then came a scoreless draw with Pearson's former club at Rodney Parade. "Old Stager" reckoned that, surprisingly, Newport were really stretched by their great adversaries. Even so, the Cardiff journalist acknowledged the "truly great generalship shown by Arthur Gould, whose play came very near to equalling him at his very best ... and [he] never tackled so frequently or so well". Newport's indifferent display was followed by one of their worst performances for some time, as Swansea grabbed an unexpected but well-deserved home victory by a try to nil. This was quite an achievement. It was Swansea's first success against Newport in six years of trying, having previously failed to overcome the "Black and Ambers" on 17 consecutive occasions. Arthur, though, "was never seen to better advantage. He played with wonderful spirit to save the game; his kicking was superb". Perhaps more telling than this opinion from the *South Wales Echo*, though, was that of Swansea's *South Wales Daily Post*:

> The feature of the game was the marvellous play of the two veterans Arthur Gould and Bancroft. Gould is playing in his best form and is unquestionably the best centre three-quarter in the four kingdoms today ... Arthur Gould, the evergreen, was head and shoulders better than any of the other three-quarters on the field, and he rarely worked harder than he did today.

His performances were mystifying the pundits. He crossed three times in an eight-try demolition of Gloucester and was, according to "Old Stager", the hero of the day. "People who allege that he is falling off ... should have seen him on this occasion. He was in the happiest of moods, dodging in and out of his men in his old style, and making beautiful openings." The visitors' quartet "were in rare form and simply delighted the spectators with their exceedingly clever work". The *Bristol Times* noted that over and over again they gave some capital exhibitions of passing, "in all of which Arthur Gould was the most conspicuous".

Such was the Welsh club's reputation now that they drew the largest crowd in many years to Cambridge University's ground. Expectations of a home victory were high. Not only were the Light Blues undefeated, they had not even conceded a single point. Some London journalists predicted that Newport were "in for a licking". They could not have been more wrong. The visitors "waltzed over" for four tries, two of which were converted to give them a resounding 16-0 victory. "Dromio" regarded it as Newport's finest achievement of the season. Arthur put on a masterful display for the undergraduates. He had "a great game ... in his best style" and was as fast as ever. "Welsh Athlete" wrote that Arthur and Tom Pearson "were in rare form, their passing, sprinting and all round play being superb".

It was not the last time that day, however, that Arthur demonstrated his fleetness of foot to escape a desperate situation. Later that evening in London, he was crossing the Strand with an old rugby pal from Blackheath. The traffic was heavy and, as they both tried to dodge their way through the constant flow of vehicles, his friend stumbled. Reacting quickly, Arthur jumped forward and just managed to pull him out of the way of a "heavily laden omnibus". According to one witness, he had put his own life at risk, just managing to escape the lethal wheels of the bus by only a hair's breadth. *The South Wales Daily News* reported his selflessness: "Plucky Save by Arthur Gould ... His act was an example of real bravery, and no-one but a man of his strength and agility could possibly have saved his friend and escaped with his life."

Then, at the Arms Park, Newport received their second (and last) defeat of the season. The ground was packed. Even for Cardiff v Newport, it was a huge attendance for a club match, estimated at anything between 17,000 and 20,000. The exhilarating atmosphere left the *South Wales Echo* awe-struck. "The very air seemed charged with electricity". Cardiff won a keen battle by the narrowest of margins, 6-5, two tries to a converted goal. They did most of the attacking and deserved their victory. "Welsh Athlete" made an interesting observation when he reported that the Cardiff quartet of Norman Biggs, Gwyn Nicholls, Jack Elliott and Viv Huzzey were collectively better in "combination" than their opponents. They may have displayed rather less sparkling individualism than Dauncey, Boucher, Gould and Pearson but they worked "more harmoniously together." Years

Arthur Gould's worthy successor as "Prince of Centres", Gwyn Nicholls. (C S Arthur, Cardiff Rugby Football Club History and Statistics 1876-1906, p.171)

later, in his superb *Rugby Recollections*, Townsend Collins ("Dromio") would sum up the difference between Gwyn Nicholls and Arthur Gould in a similar fashion. "While the latter was greater in individual skill, Gwyn Nicholls was superior as an exponent of the four three-quarter system".

The Usksiders' disappointment continued with a scoreless home draw with their previous season's nemesis, Llanelli. While the visitors never looked like scoring, Newport threw away plenty of chances, frustrated by the keen tacking of the Scarlets' three-quarters. Arthur though again played excellently, "running well, kicking grandly and tackling in fine spirit". Even "Dromio" was prepared to find fault when he thought necessary, however. He criticised Arthur's tendency to drive his wing, Tom Pearson, towards the touch-line before passing the ball. "A man like Pearson wants some room to move in."

From now on though, it was all success. There was only one blemish in Newport's last 16 fixtures of 1895-6, and that was a surprising 3-3 draw at Penarth in January, when Arthur wasn't present. For the 5-0 victory at Liverpool, he switched to left centre to partner Bert Dauncey. This was done to improve the winger's chances of selection for Wales, according to "Dromio". Arthur broke through time after time but the two struggled to combine well at first. However, their partnership quickly improved over the rest of the season.

Newport then came up against the undefeated Blackheath XV, who had recently claimed the scalp of Cardiff. The Londoners brought down an experienced side with seven English internationals, as well as Willie Cope who would play in the Welsh pack a few weeks later against Scotland. Newport fielded six internationals together with G Llewellyn Lloyd and Bert Dauncey who would win their Welsh caps this season.

In his account of the match, "Dromio" is lavish in its praise of his favourite club. It was a "glorious victory". No game so fast and vigorous had been seen at Rodney Parade for a long time and Newport were back to their old form, especially at forward. "It made one's blood dance", he gushed, "to hear the people shout as Newport bore down upon the Blackheath goal and when the first try was scored by Arthur Gould after a perfect piece of passing, there was hardly a man in the crowd who did not feel as happy as if he had found a five pound note". Arthur's try came in the first few minutes and involved some slick passing between Lloyd, Boucher, Arthur and Dauncey, who passed back to the veteran to enable him to score. Almost immediately afterwards, Arthur received the ball, evaded the England centre, Edward Baker, and gave a scoring pass to Bert Dauncey. At 6-3, Newport hung on to the end, and they could now reasonably claim to be the leading club in both countries.

Not for the first time, and certainly not for the last, "Dromio" was spellbound by his hero. "The palm must again be awarded to A J Gould who showed all his old skill and cunning, his wonderful grasp of a situation, and the same turn of speed as of yore. He was the mainspring of both the tries, and how a man, who has played so long, can present his form so marvellously, is to me an enigma. He looks as fit an athlete as when he used to compete for the hurdles championships."

In all the detailed press coverage of Arthur's on-field exploits, there is little which sheds light on his interior life. Yet one particular column does show that he possessed a genuine empathy for the welfare of those who were less fortunate than him. On Christmas Day, he left the comfort of his family celebrations to remember the destitute who were confined at the Newport Workhouse over the holiday. The *South*

Wales Daily News reported that during the afternoon, Arthur together with several other townsfolk organised a special concert for the benefit of the workhouse inhabitants. No doubt the programme included one of his celebrated turns. His presence was evidently warmly appreciated by the inmates. "Arthur Gould, of course, [came] in for a big share of favour." There was much more to Arthur than just a supreme talent for football.

Meanwhile, in Cardiff of all places, the audience at the *Grand Theatre* Christmas pantomime were enjoying a song dedicated to Arthur, the chorus of which was *Gould is the King of Football.* It was performed by the Principal

THE FOOTBALL KING,
MISS NELLY LAURAINE.

Wearing full rugby kit, Nelly Lauraine's rendering of "Gould is the King of Football" was "quite the song of the performance" in "Dick Whittington" at the Grand Theatre, Cardiff. (Evening Express, 23 January 1896)

Boy, Nellie Lauraine dressed as a rugby player. A magic lantern displayed images of other local rugby heroes, but it was Arthur's picture which had pride of place. One of the most popular features of the panto, "The Football King" was encored every night.

There can be little doubt about who was the people's choice in Wales.

1896: England v Wales

The Football King's next game was the big one, England at Blackheath. The aggressive and determined Owen Badger of Llanelli was picked to partner Arthur at centre again, while Badger's club captain Cliff Bowen was selected for the first time, on the wing. The experiment of partnering Bert Dauncey to help get him his cap had worked. Arthur of course retained the captaincy. "Old Stager" wrote of him before the match, "his play this season has often been characterised by much of his old time brilliancy ... he is still on his day one of the finest footballers in the Rugby world ... and has not failed in any important club engagement." Swansea's *South Wales Daily Post* was more succinct in its pre-match assessment. "A J Gould ... is one whom it will be well not to waste space on. The greatest three-quarter of the past decade, there is nothing fresh to be said about him."

The outlook in Wales was upbeat, particularly as England had been ravaged by the haemorrhage of the 22 clubs who had broken away to form the Northern Union the previous August. Nevertheless, England still managed to select ten men from northern clubs. The details of the match need not delay us. Wales suffered one of their worst defeats in the series since that first disaster in 1881. England ran in seven tries, only two of which were converted, to win 25-0. Losing Owen Badger with a broken collar-bone in the first 15 minutes sealed the Welshmen's fate, though the writing was already on the wall. With Boucher pulled out of the pack to replace Badger, the Welsh forwards, who were already struggling, were taken apart. They were so badly beaten that the backs received hardly any ball. According to "Old Stager", they were able to manage only a couple of attempts at back play in the whole game and Wales only made about half a dozen incursions into the English half. There was much criticism of the lax refereeing but the Welsh press uniformly acknowledged that the result was a fair one, even allowing for the loss of Badger. When interviewed afterwards, Arthur accepted that they would have lost, "Badger or no Badger". "Old Stager" stressed that no blame should be placed on Arthur for the defeat. "I would resist all attempts to out [him]. He was by no means the failure that may be imagined, and he put in several clever bits of play that were not equalled by the opposing centres." Remarkably, just as earlier in the season, even when his team was not doing well, Arthur still managed to stand out. "Welsh Athlete" thought that he had played a very hard game "and was really the best man on our side, but one cannot make bricks without straw". The English press agreed. *Athletic News* lamented that though he "stood out ... what was one man against so many?" *Sporting Life* declared that even though he was now a veteran, "he was still the right man in the right place and when meeting reverses, he never lost his head, and punted and tackled finely, as of yore."

1896: Wales v Scotland

Following one of their worst displays at Blackheath, Wales' next performance, against Scotland on 25 January at Cardiff Arms Park, proved to be one of their finest. Unsurprisingly there were six changes in the forwards, only one of which was forced because of an injury to Boucher. "Boomer" Nicholl and Harry Packer were retained. Fred Hutchinson (Neath) was brought back while, though it was a risk, five new caps were introduced into the pack: Jack Evans and William Morris (Llanelli), Willie Cope (Blackheath), "Barry" Davies (Cardiff) and Dai Evans (Penygraig). However, by far the most historically significant selection was that of Cardiff's Gwyn Nicholls as Arthur's partner at centre, replacing the injured Owen Badger. There were changes at half-back too with Selwyn Biggs and Fred Parfitt returning to the side. The rest of the backs, Bill Bancroft at fullback, and Bert Dauncey and Cliff Bowen on the wings all kept their places.

By participating in this game, Arthur equalled Scotland's William Maclagan's record of 25 international caps. Undoubtedly this added to the mounting enthusiasm for the game. Rather strangely though, the *South Wales Argus* described his achievement as "Arthur Gould's silver wedding in football".

Pre-match arrangements were very relaxed. The Welsh players were simply instructed to arrive at the Queen's Hotel no later than 12.30 for lunch at 12.45, a mere two hours before kick-off. The players, and in particular Arthur, must have been pestered by hordes of well-wishers throughout their various train journeys to Cardiff and during the short walk from the station to the Queen's. Among the medley of music performed to entertain the vast crowds at the Arms Park was a brand new tune composed in Arthur's honour, titled *Skipper Gould*.

The WFU reported that there had been an extraordinary demand for tickets and the attendance was later recorded at 20,000. These supporters had evidently not been deterred by the weather which had been atrocious. Fortunately, the rain had cleared by kick-off, but it had still left many pools of water on the pitch and these soon became a muddy quagmire, something all too familiar to regulars at the Arms Park. The Welsh backs, however, overcame both the treacherous conditions and the heavy, wet ball to mount a superb exhibition of running and passing. "Old Stager" reckoned that the high quality of the passing had seldom been witnessed in international rugby before.

This spine-tingling rugby, though, was the consequence of a combined effort. With the new forwards determined to impress, the Welsh pack quickly got on top of their opponents and they managed to provide their half-backs with plenty of ball to exploit. In both

At the International Match

We've all been there. "Five minutes before time". The crowd at the Arms Park during the Scottish international. (Evening Express, 25 January 1896)

attack and defence, Biggs and Parfitt proved to be "streets ahead" of the Scottish half-backs. *The Sportsman* thought they were the keystone of the Welsh victory, as "time after time they made beautiful openings" to feed the three-quarters, who invariably made good use of these opportunities. "Welsh Athlete" considered that the Welsh three-quarters also outclassed their opponents in every aspect of the game. *Athletic News* concurred:

> *Wales played their three-quarters for all they were worth ... how often the ball came out and was handled by the Welshmen can scarcely be counted ... it was a treat to see the ball flying about from hand to hand, and it was exhilarating to watch the active and accomplished three-quarters developing the movements initiated by Parfitt and Biggs.*

Even so, Wales still had a tough fight on their hands. As early as the sixth minute, George Campbell, who had partnered Arthur in the Middlesex XV, was just prevented from touching down by a desperate tackle from his old county team-mate. The sides were still tied no score at half-time but Wales eventually broke through with a splendidly executed effort in the fifth minute of the second half. Receiving the ball from his forwards, Biggs passed out to Gwyn Nicholls who beat two Scottish backs by dummying to Arthur and then transferring to Cliff Bowen who romped over in the corner. Bancroft's conversion attempt, with a ball which was now a "sodden lump of inflated leather", barely travelled "half a dozen yards." Ten minutes later, Wales struck again with the move of the match, and of the season. Again Biggs collected. The ball went swiftly through the hands of all four three-quarters. In possession a few yards out from the line, left wing Bert Dauncey found himself closely marked. However, both Scottish defenders made the mistake of going for him, fatally leaving Arthur unopposed. So Dauncey cleverly lobbed the ball back to Arthur over the heads of the two covering Scots and the skipper flew in for a breath-taking try. James Gowan, the Scottish centre who had had to withdraw from the team, said it "was the result of some of the best passing I have ever seen; in fact I would say I have never seen the veteran Welsh footballer in such form as today." This proved to be the last score, so Wales went on to take this thriller by 6 points to nil. No-one present that day could possibly have imagined that it would be a full three years before this particular fixture was resumed or that the cause of this serious falling-out would be Arthur Gould.

After the match, Arthur was overheard exclaiming delightedly, *"Cymru am byth!"* I don't know what it means, but I've been told to say it!" The players had to force their way through a delirious Westgate Street crowd towards the Queen's Hotel, though they were so plastered with mud that they were barely recognisable. As the *Athletic News* graphically put it, the Scottish fullback was the only man "who did not carry away a few hundred-weights of Cardiff real estate." The hotel was already hopelessly packed and the two teams had to struggle through the foyer to get upstairs to bathe and change. Arthur in particular was showered with congratulations by his many admirers. "Old Stager" could not recall ever seeing the veteran in a happier mood. "His ecstatic delight at the victory could be discerned by the most casual observer." Arthur then gave an impromptu interview to the waiting press. He said he was delighted with everyone's play but generously made a particular point of acknowledging the efforts of the forwards. He thought it a splendid game, under very trying conditions. "Why ... look at me ... I'm like

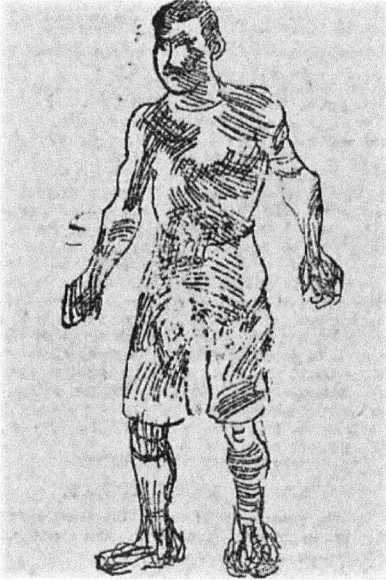

Arthur at the end of the match, covered in Cardiff real estate. (Evening Express, 25 January 1896)

a collier", he cried and, amid the hurrahs of the overjoyed throng, he bounded up the stairs to his room.

The press, and not just Welsh scribes, were virtually unanimous that, despite his age, Arthur had played a superlative game, one of his finest, according to some.

The Welsh skipper was the pivot ... the best man on the field. (Scottish Referee.)

Never did Monk Gould play a better game ... His tricky work took the spectators back several years ... Gould was quite the Gould of old, and all will know what that means. (Sporting Life).

If one man's play elicited more enthusiastic cheering than another's, it was that of ... Arthur Gould ... he was a tower of strength ... and while he was the most feared on the field ... his tackling and brilliant try proved him to be still the ablest centre three-quarter playing the game. ("Old Stager").

Gould was the hero of the match, and of all the games I have seen him play I never saw him to more advantage ... his tackling, too, a point on which he is not usually credited with being strong, was simply superb. Every time he got a man he bashed him down in no uncertain manner, while his generalship was simply perfect. ("Welsh Athlete").

Arthur Gould excelled himself. People who have convinced themselves that the best day is gone of this wonderful player should have seen him this afternoon. He was head and shoulders better than any other man on the field. He was brilliant. No other word can express it. (South Wales Daily Post).

Only seven months earlier, in June 1895, the *Daily Telegraph* had initiated a "National Testimonial Shilling Fund" for the iconic "Grand Old Man" of cricket, W G Grace. The scheme eventually raised £5,000. Even though Grace accepted this huge sum, as well as the proceeds from other testimonials, he was able to retain his amateur status.

A TALE WITHOUT WORDS.

Arthur Gould is compared with W G Grace, though while cricket handsomely rewards Grace, rugby opposes a testimonial for Arthur. (Evening News, 30 January 1897: Arthur Gould's scrapbook)

And though he had now reached 47 years of age, 1895 turned out to be Grace's cricketing "Golden Summer". The timing of this national campaign was highly significant. Arthur was often compared with "W G" and some believed that only Grace stood higher than him in the Victorian sporting public's favour. With Arthur now enjoying his rugby "golden winter", the *Daily Telegraph* appeal evidently struck a resounding chord with his many ardent devotees and admirers.

So, on the morning of Monday 27 January 1896, as readers scanned their copy of the *South Wales Daily News* before devouring the match accounts, some may not have been too surprised to spot in the eye-catching headlines:

Scotland v Wales - Brilliant Passing in a Quagmire
Welshmen Gain a Famous Victory
Testimonial to Arthur Gould

The third headline was a reference to a challenging suggestion raised by "Old Stager" in his column:

> *He is to the Rugby game what Dr. Grace is to the sister pastime. What do Welsh footballers say to the proposition that the veteran's inestimable services to the game, which is still growing in popularity in Wales, should be recognised in the form of the presentation to him of a national testimonial?*

And so began the controversy which was to rock the rugby world; and for which, sadly, Arthur Gould is probably best remembered by many today.

"Old Stager" wasn't the only journalist to suggest a testimonial. "Dromio" also proposed the idea in the *South Wales Argus*. "As Arthur Gould is as pre-eminent in football as W G Grace is in cricket, the footballing enthusiasts of Wales might recognise his services to the game ... by some national testimonial". No doubt the possibility of rewarding Arthur this way had been widely discussed in the Queen's Hotel and in other bars and pubs on the evening of the match. It had probably been gestating for some time within the Welsh rugby fraternity, especially given Arthur's current form this season. However, it appears that it was the *South Wales Daily News* which became the lead publication for promoting the scheme. It was to this newspaper that the public were invited to send their subscriptions and, just as in the *Daily Telegraph*, the names of the donors were regularly published in their columns. This is not especially surprising. If anything, the *South Wales Daily News* was an even more enthusiastic supporter of rugby than its principal rival, the *Western Mail*. After all, one of the proprietors was the former Cardiff player and WFU official, Alec Duncan who initially acted as treasurer of the Gould fund.

Only a day later, "Old Stager" declared his incredulity at the scale of the immediate response to the appeal, confessing that even he had quite underestimated Arthur's popularity. He quoted a letter he had received stating that "Mr Gould is now, and has been for many years, entitled to the style of champion "rugger" player of the world". On the very first day, £50 had been subscribed at the Cardiff Coal Exchange in less than an hour; while in Newport, William J Orders had raised another £50.

The Tuesday edition of *South Wales Daily News* contained the first of its regular lists of subscribers. There were over 100. They included a number of former rugby players, now prominent in the business community, like the Welsh internationals H J Simpson, J A Jones and T C Graham. Several well-known ship-owners, as well as D A Thomas, the Merthyr MP, were also amongst the very first to subscribe. Whilst the idea of promoting the scheme as a "shilling fund" was adopted to enable working men to contribute, many of the wealthier subscribers donated very much larger sums. The *South Wales Daily News* claimed that "all sorts and conditions favour the idea". All this makes it irrefutably clear that, from the outset, the testimonial was a national popular campaign and not, as is still sometimes claimed, a Welsh Football Union undertaking.

Excited by the overwhelming initial response, the *South Wales Daily News* enthused about

WALES V. SCOTLAND,

SATURDAY'S VICTORY.

TESTIMONIAL TO ARTHUR GOULD.

"OLD STAGER'S" SUGGESTION ADOPTED,

SPLENDID REPLY FROM CARDIFF DOCKS.

ALL SOUTH WALES SHILLINGS READY,

MR A. J. GOULD,

Headlines announce the proposal for a testimonial. (South Wales Daily News, 28 January 1896)

"prospects of an international tribute." If what was meant by this was that it would have the support of the English, Scottish and Irish Unions, however, this transpired to be hopelessly wrong.

The promoters decided to name the scheme the "Gould Testimonial Fund" and they arranged a public meeting in Newport on the following day. This was convened at the Talbot Hotel in Commercial Street, just a stone's throw from where Arthur had once lived above his father's workshop. There was a large attendance, including prominent members of the press and of the sporting and business community. William J Orders and Llewellyn J Phillips were invited to act as joint secretaries of the testimonial. A local ship-broker, Orders was very committed to sport in Newport. He captained the town's golf club in later years, and was an active member of the

William Orders, secretary to the Gould Testimonial Fund. (Weekly Mail, 20 February 1909)

Newport Athletic Club, having seconded Arthur's nomination for the captaincy of the rugby club in 1894. Phillips was a Newport solicitor and was also very involved in local sports. Many of the great and good of Welsh rugby and the press were then invited to join the executive committee. J R Stephens ("Old Stager") was thanked for his initiative. He replied that it was only necessary for someone "to strike the match to kindle the undoubted enthusiasm which had been manifested." He correctly predicted that the subscriptions would roll in from past and present players and from thousands of spectators who had witnessed Arthur's marvellous skills, both as a three-quarter and team captain. The reports make no mention of Arthur being present on the night and he may well have been avoiding any publicity by keeping out of the lime-light at this early stage.

One decision made at the meeting, though, may have hastened the gathering of the storm clouds. It was resolved to communicate immediately with the "various rugby unions, asking them to give formal consent to the presentation and to invite them to join in the general movement, so as to make the testimonial a truly national one". With hindsight, this was a somewhat naive aspiration.

The correspondence must have been despatched promptly because, just two days later, the RFU discussed the matter on the evening before the England v Ireland match in Leeds. The testimonial organisers' opening gambit had not been a sound one. To put it mildly, the RFU were not happy. The minutes of their meeting reveal that, on the assumption that the testimonial was to be a monetary one, they decided that they could not give it their support. Neither could they permit their clubs to subscribe. Ominously for the fund, the secretary was instructed to write to the WFU and the Newport club informing them that, if a monetary testimonial *were* given to "Mr Gould", the RFU would regard him as a professional.

However, from the very beginning, there was popular and widespread support for honouring Arthur in this way. Many newspapers enthusiastically endorsed the testimonial. For instance, *Sporting Life* called on all sportsmen "to weigh in their shillings", and contributions did pour in, not by any means all originating in Wales. Bristolians "weighed in", as did subscribers from Derby, Durham, Gloucester, Liverpool, Northumberland and even Spain and the Australian goldfields. By 4 February, the fund had reached over £210 and, not surprisingly perhaps for a Newport paper, the *South Wales Argus* had raised as much from subscribers as had their Cardiff-based rival spearheading the campaign. The *Barry Dock News*, *Bristol Mercury*, *Glamorgan Times*, *Gloucester Citizen*, *Newcastle Chronicle*, *Penarth Chronicle*, *Tenby Observer*, *South Wales Press*, *Sporting Life* and *The Sportsman* were also amongst the first newspapers to agree to accept subscriptions. Many others joined in later.

At their next scheduled meeting on 27 February, the WFU discussed the RFU's dismissive response with some disquiet. Doing their best to mollify the English Union, the WFU decided that they could no longer give the testimonial their blessing if it took the form of a monetary gift. However, the testimonial organisers then tried to get round the WFU's concerns about a "monetary" testimonial by coming up with an alternative use of the funds. Instead of giving Arthur cash, they suggested presenting him with the deeds of "Thornbury", the house which he was currently renting.

This solution worked. A month later on 26 March, the WFU agreed to sanction

This photograph of Arthur is dated March 1896 and was therefore taken during the "burning question" of the testimonial. He was then 31. (Arthur Gould's scrapbook)

a testimonial which would take the form of a gift of his house. At the same time, they now committed the Union to contributing "one thousand shillings" (£50) for this purpose. William Bromet, the Richmond captain and English international, had recently been presented with silver plate worth £50 on the occasion of – and, incidentally, a long time before – his marriage. Since members of the Richmond club and RFU officials were involved, and since the RFU had raised no objections, the Gould testimonial promoters were optimistic that the presentation of a house rather than cash would be acceptable to the RFU and the other Unions. Such confidence, however, was misplaced. Within days, the RFU wrote to inform the WFU that they considered the presentation of a house just as objectionable as a monetary gift.

With the testimonial dispute still rumbling on unresolved, Arthur shrewdly kept out of any controversy and carried on as normal in the hothouse of the domestic game. He featured in nine of Newport's remaining ten fixtures, all of which were victories. There was a particularly tough meeting at Stradey Park, billed as the match of the season. Not only were the home team undefeated in 21 contests but only two sides had so far managed to score against them. Moreover, Llanelli hadn't lost since the Penarth match a year earlier. Inevitably then, the town was in a ferment of excitement. The visit of Newport attracted 15,000 fans, the largest crowd at Stradey since the Welsh Triple Crown triumph there three years earlier. Unruffled by the vociferous crowd, the "Black and Ambers" withstood a spirited resistance to become the first side to score at Stradey all season. With two converted tries and a drop goal added by Arthur, the winning margin was 14-0. This was a turning in the road for Llanelli, who subsequently lost four more times, allowing Newport to capture the unofficial championship yet again. According to "Old Stager" though, the game was one of the finest exhibitions of fast and open rugby he had ever been privileged to witness. As for Arthur, "Dromio" noted that while he did not make any really clever runs, "he was continually doing something useful", including his tackling. His kicking to touch was cool, well-judged and effective; while his dropped goal under pressure "seemed simplicity itself but how few men could do it!" "Monk" was playing as well as ever. Returning to Newport that evening and still flushed by their success, Arthur and a few of the players decided to visit the Tredegar Hall to give support to the Newport gymnastics team who were engaged in a cup competition. As Arthur entered, the audience saluted him by whistling *See, the Conqu'ring Hero Comes!*

Arthur then scored three tries in a 39-8 drubbing of Liverpool. That evening – in the midst of the "burning question" of the testimonial – the 24 lines of verse in praise of Arthur called *Skipper Gould* first appeared in the *South Wales Echo*. A month later copies of the sheet music were selling for sixpence each. Few rugby players have ever been celebrated quite so devotedly.

Cardiff, who had already recorded a victory and a draw against the "Black and Ambers",

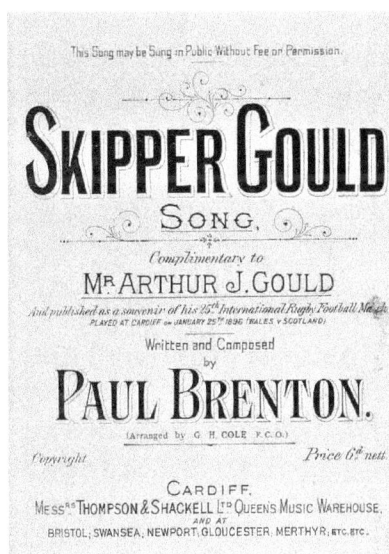

This Song may be Sung in Public Without Fee or Permission.

SKIPPER GOULD

SONG,

Complimentary to

MR ARTHUR J. GOULD

And published as a souvenir of his 25th International Rugby Football Match PLAYED AT CARDIFF on JANUARY 25TH 1896 (WALES v SCOTLAND)

Written and Composed
by

PAUL BRENTON.

(Arranged by G. H. COLE F.C.O.)

Copyright   *Price 6^d nett.*

CARDIFF.
MESS^{RS} THOMPSON & SHACKELL L^{TD} QUEEN'S MUSIC WAREHOUSE,
AND AT
BRISTOL; SWANSEA; NEWPORT, GLOUCESTER. MERTHYR; ETC. ETC.

Produced as a souvenir to celebrate Arthur winning his 25th cap in January 1896, the sheet music for Skipper Gould could be purchased for sixpence. (Courtesy of Robert Gould)

were next up in front of 12,000 spectators at Rodney Parade. Defeat for Boucher's team here would have given Cardiff an unassailable lead in the annual four match series. Inevitably, it was close. The visitors were leading by a point, when Gwyn Nicholls was forced to leave the field for a while. Newport took advantage and scored a further eight points in his absence to give them an 11-4 victory and level the series. "Dromio" reported that Arthur played a consistently good all-round game throughout.

Newport then maintained their unbeaten record at the Rectory Field, winning 10-0, though "Dromio" thought Blackheath were lucky not to concede more. It was estimated that Arthur and his team-mates had attracted 10,000 supporters to the match, some of whom were keen to get a look at the Welshman who was at the centre of a growing controversy. He did not let them down, making some of his characteristic weaving runs, kicking admirably and generally performing well all-round.

There was no let-up in the programme, since the next opponents were Swansea who had taken Newport's undefeated record earlier in the season. Despite the return of the James brothers at half-back, Newport gained revenge by 6 points to nil, with Arthur crossing for both tries. In the first half, he took a long pass slung out by Boucher from a line-out, and raced across the field to place the ball while being hotly pursued. A few moments later, he was over the line again. Receiving from Lloyd, he then "made one of those short tortuous runs which paralyse the defence, and left Bancroft standing. One did not know where he was going."

1896: Ireland v Wales

Well everyone *did* know he was soon going to break the record for international caps. This happened at Lansdowne Road on 14 March 1896. Congratulating him on this achievement, Dublin's *Evening Herald* declared that Arthur had "always been a perfect terror to the opposition [and] has done more damage to Ireland than any other Welshmen by his splendid play." Adding to the sense of occasion, whoever took the spoils in this match would secure the International Championship. Despite this prospect, and even with 100 Welsh fans making the trip, the attendance was disappointing. Perhaps the dreadful weather over the previous two weeks had put many off, though it had improved by kick-off. The pitch, however, was in a very soft and sticky state and, as Arthur commented pre-match to the press, this was not ideal for the Welsh attack and he would have preferred dry conditions.

"Monk" received a fine ovation as he led his team out. According to "Old Stager", the band played *Hen Wlad fy Nhadau* as they filed onto the field, though other match reports refer to *Men of Harlech*, the more traditional tune then adopted at these events. Someone may have misheard. In response to the band's rendition of *St Patrick's Day* during the entrance of the Irish XV, "Boomer" Nicholl led the Welsh players in an Irish jig, which fortunately went down well with the spectators.

Despite the concern for the conditions, the game turned out to be a magnificent affair "brimful of high-class football." *Freeman's Journal* reckoned it was the finest exhibition of football ever seen in Ireland. "Dromio" had seldom seen a more brilliant or faster game. The Irish press were in unison that Ireland just deserved their victory by two tries and a conversion to a dropped goal (8-4); but "Dromio" thought Wales had been distinctly unlucky and other Welsh journalists agreed. On one occasion, Gwyn Nicholls was actually over the line when he passed to Arthur who was held up or in touch

– the accounts vary. There were a few mutterings about some of the refereeing decisions. Two infringements were missed in the lead-up to the second Irish try. Cliff Bowen touched down behind the posts, only to be brought back for a marginal forward pass. Late in the game, Arthur returned a kick which was then touched in flight by an Irishman. The ball was gathered up-field by a Welsh forward with a clear run to the line and a potentially match-winning try. However, he was penalised for what "Dromio" termed an "alleged" off-side. The only score Wales managed was an exquisite dropped goal courtesy of the master.

Wales had the best of it up to half-time when the score remained at nil-all. The Welsh pack scrummaged well but were outplayed in the loose and crucially a couple of forwards ran out of steam in the second half. The three-quarters played a brilliant passing game but "never had a halfpenny's worth of luck", wrote "Dromio". *The Sportsman* thought that the passing of the Welsh backs was "beyond comparison" and that Arthur was the best of the three-quarters. The *Dublin Daily Express* went further. "Gould ... was conspicuously the best of the team. His passing, running, tackling and kicking were beyond praise." As for *Freeman's Journal*, the Welsh three-quarters could not be given too much praise. "A finer quartet never played ... but ... Gould once again carried off the palm, and his efforts were simply close to grand." So Arthur may not have celebrated breaking the record for caps with another Championship title but, incredibly, the veteran demonstrated that he was still at the top of his game. He was a truly exceptional footballer.

This was acknowledged by the *Dublin Evening Telegraph*. "It has been fairly said that what Grace is to cricket, Gould is to football". Referring to his remarkable longevity at the highest level of the game, the *Telegraph* perceptively remarked that there would have been boys at the match who had "not seen the light of day when the prince of three-quarters played his first international". Asked to account for his extraordinary form over such a long period, Arthur coolly responded, "of course, it is exceptional, but I feel no change myself and still keep going on." Questioned about his training regime, he again confirmed just how astonishingly relaxed were attitudes to match preparation then. He explained that he didn't believe in strict training. He thought that a man might train to win one particular event but if he persisted it would "tell on him" and he could "never last at it." For himself, he relied on doing just what he pleased within reason. He admitted that he wasn't a teetotaller and that he smoked. "In fact, I live just as I ordinarily would, and I take as much exercise as I can."

Evidently, it wasn't only in Wales that Arthur had plenty of admirers. After the match dinner, the Welsh players went out on the town where they were engulfed by huge crowds. Trying to get away from the attention, Arthur led his team to Corless's, a well-known pub mentioned by James Joyce in *The Dubliners*. This was of no avail, however, as they were quickly spotted by over 100 students from nearby Trinity College. Such was Arthur's fame, they attempted to parade him around the city to celebrate his achievements and his record international appearances. However, he shrewdly and quickly avoided this embarrassment by delivering a short speech, "as modest as it was tactful and appropriate". Back at the team's hotel, the students continued to gather outside, shouting "until they were hoarse".

The following Saturday, there was an immense turn-out – reckoned to be 25,000 strong – at the Arms Park for the game which would decide the unofficial Welsh championship. The ground conditions at "the celebrated mud patch" were awful, with pools of water and grassless sludge covering the pitch. Despite the traditional rivalry and needle between the two groups of supporters, Arthur was given a warm reception by the crowd, reflecting the general rugby public's affection for him. Newport secured a decidedly clear victory by 8 points to nil to take the four match rubber and the Welsh club title. "Dromio" thought that, for once, the three-quarters were rather disappointing. Even so, according to "Old Stager", Arthur was by far and away the best of the visiting backs. He "wound up a really pretty piece of play by planting the ball between the uprights"; while he had a hand in Newport's second try by chipping ahead, as he was being tackled, for Llewelyn Lloyd to collect and run in unopposed.

On Easter Saturday, the Northumberland champions, Rockcliff were back at Rodney Parade. It was another win for Newport, by 9 points to nil. Though "Dromio" criticised the team for not running up a heavy score in the second half, "Monk" was beyond reproach. He "played a dashing and resourceful game. He made several runs and gave Dauncey passes galore. His dropped goal was perfect and his tackling was excellent." Before kick-off, the large crowd had been entertained by the town band and one of their selections was particularly well received – the recently composed song, *Skipper*

Gould. During the evening, both teams attended a musical concert in the town, where *Skipper Gould* was again performed. According to the *Star of Gwent*, this "raised a great deal of enthusiasm, the Newport team joining in with the chorus to great effect. The individual referred to was, of course, the object of every eye, and cheers were given at the conclusion of each verse."

"It would be difficult to imagine a more brilliant finish to the season" was how "Dromio" summed up the final game against the Barbarians on Easter Monday. Despite the morning kick off, 10,000 witnessed the events. Rugby in Wales was never more popular. On the same day, 12,000 fans were at the Arms Park to watch Cardiff meet Swinton; while 20,000 turned up at St. Helen's for the Swansea v Llanelli derby. Newport triumphed 24-6 with a six try spectacular, their highest score against the Barbarians in their five meetings. Scoring one of the tries, Arthur was in his most outstanding form and evaded his opponents "like an eel". Reviewing Newport's season, "Welsh Athlete" had nothing but praise of the veteran. "Arthur Gould ... still stands easily in first place. His play during the past season has been equal to any of his previous efforts, his judgement is as good as ever, while his defensive powers have shown a marked improvement." Though Tom Pearson headed the 1896-7 try scorers with 20, Arthur was second on 16 and he contributed five drop goals, as well.

Even though Newport's season was over, Arthur's wasn't. A couple of weeks after Easter, together with three of his club-mates, he turned out for the Keynsham club at the Recreation Ground against a Bath XV. How and why this invitation came about is not known. Arthur stamped his mark on it, all the same. He dropped a magnificent goal from almost half-way. Then, following Bath's kick-off at the restart, Arthur fielded the ball, made some ground and dropped another long range goal from the touchline. His enthusiasm for other sport, too, remained undiminished. In late April, he was elected as one of the two Eastern District representatives of the South Wales and Monmouthshire Amateur Athletic Association.

It was now commonplace for Arthur to be referred to as the "Prince of Three-Quarters" but in May 1896 one churchman raised him to an even more exalted station. In Wales at this time, there were many preachers who held that playing football was the way of the devil but the Reverend J H Jones saw things rather differently. Writing to the *Church Times* about the condition of the Church in Wales, he rejoiced at the tremendous growth in athleticism in Wales and suggested that

A BACKYARD QUARREL.

"A Backyard Quarrel". England, Scotland and Ireland argue with Wales over Arthur's right to accept the testimonial. (Evening News, 27 February 1897: Arthur Gould's scrapbook)

it was the most helpful sign of better things to come. In conclusion, he wrote that "football is making straight the way of the Kingdom of Heaven and A J Gould is our Baptist!"

He wasn't *everyone's* favourite at that moment, however. The International Board was now gunning for him and on 9 May they convened a special meeting to discuss the proposition that "the giving of a house is tantamount to giving a monetary testimonial". The WFU's delegates, Walter Rees and William Wilkins, requested that the Board give some direction as to how the proceeds of the fund might be dealt with. The response was that the gift of a house would be an act of professionalism and its receipt would not only make Arthur Gould a professional but, rather absurdly, all the subscribers too! The Board directed that the testimonial should only take the form of a gift of £100 worth of silver plate, with the balance being handed over to charity in Arthur Gould's name.

This arrogant demand was then considered by an exasperated WFU committee on 30 May. Arthur was enjoying himself playing cricket for Newport against Cardiff that day, as the committee resolved to request that the International Board receive a deputation from the WFU to discuss the issue further. This eventually took place on 29 August, but the other Unions were resolute. The WFU next met on Saturday 19 September, immediately prior to the Union's AGM. Describing his and Bill Phillips' experience at the International Board meeting, James Livingston reported that the representatives of the other three Unions were quite adamant: the testimonial should *only* be given in accordance with their previously stated wishes. They were very determined on this and it was evident that, if the WFU persisted, there would be no international matches with Wales next season. The dispute was getting serious now and the WFU committee's resolve wavered. In view of the "difficulties which have arisen with the International Board", Livingston proposed that the WFU withdraw its sanction of the Gould testimonial, and this was carried. It was also agreed to withdraw the Union's £50 contribution to the fund.

Perhaps understandably fearful of a hostile reaction from the member clubs, the WFU's weak-willed decision to rescind their sanction of the testimonial fund was not immediately disclosed at the AGM, and the press only heard about it several days later. "Welsh Athlete" angrily wrote that their action was an extraordinary one and that the whole issue had been "badly bungled". He acknowledged though that there had been no mincing of words by the International Board. "The Welsh Union were led to understand in no uncertain manner what would be the outcome if matters did not go the way the Board wanted them to."

Arthur, though, may have got wind of what was happening before everyone else.

8

The Testimonial Comes Home

1896-7

The new season was just getting underway when a sensational story broke, though perhaps it was not a totally surprising one. Arthur had been expected to play in a pre-season practice match at Rodney Parade which took place on the very same Saturday on which the WFU general committee had convened to discuss the consequences of their meeting with the International Board. However, the previous evening, he had called on the Newport captain, Arthur Boucher, to inform him that he had decided to give up the game. In an interview with the *South Wales Argus*, he denied that he was retiring just so that he could receive the testimonial. He was adamant that he

"An Irreparable Loss". A bizarre depiction of the effect of Arthur's retirement on Newport RFC. (Evening Express, 21 September 1896: Arthur Gould's scrapbook – Note the handwriting in the top right-hand corner)

wouldn't accept it if there were any conditions which might prevent him from playing for Newport's reserve or veterans teams, or from refereeing, or from attending matches. "I will not have the thing on that account".

"Welsh Athlete" summed up the views of many on the decision:

> It seems strange to commence a football season in Wales without being able to reckon upon the services of Arthur Gould. For many years now he has been the central figure, not only of the famous Newport Club, but also of Welsh football generally ... his announcement that he will not be available during the current season comes as a sort of thunderclap.

It seems appropriate that the impact of the retirement of a player, who 14 years earlier had burst onto the scene like a storm, should be described in a similarly dramatic way. However, the announcement eventually turned out to be more of a damp squib than a thunderclap.

Naturally, over the next few days the press was full of the story. *The Graphic* of London went so far as to maintain that, in its way, it was "as great an event as the eventual retirement of W G Grace"; adding that not even Grace had done more for cricket than "the superb footballer" had done for rugby. More than anyone, Arthur Gould was responsible for keeping Newport "at the very head of Rugby Union clubs". Continuing the comparison with Grace, *The Graphic* also made a valid point for the time that a 32-year-old footballer is "more of a phenomenon" than a cricketer at 50.

Sporting Life reckoned that, since Arthur's form during the previous season had been as good as any "even in his remarkable career", it had been widely assumed that he would continue in 1896-7. However, as Arthur explained in his interview with the paper, he did not want to let Newport down by being a failure. Though he had so far escaped serious injury, he was growing increasingly worried about the risk of this as he got older. Arthur also took the opportunity to vent some of his feelings about the increasing pressures demanded of leading players by fickle-hearted followers. "These days a man has to play very much in the eye of the public ... in South Wales where the game is so popular, the public are becoming more exacting. They have come to think that the game exists for them, and they are prompt to express their disapproval if a man does not play at his best." If his form were to suffer, he didn't want to overhear hurtful remarks from supporters like, "Why doesn't that old crock retire?" *Sporting Life*

THE PASSING OF ARTHUR.

"The Passing of Arthur." Both a play on words on Arthur's footballing skills, and an allusion to Tennyson's famous Arthurian poem "Idylls of the King." (Evening News, 26 September 1896: Arthur Gould's scrapbook)

sympathised. "The public have short memories and a football crowd has little gratitude and doubtless he does well to retire before he does show signs of diminished prowess."

Bert Leaves for South Africa

Arthur may have announced that he was finishing, but Bert kept up the Gould presence at Newport, taking part in their opening five fixtures. However, the 16-3 victory over Blackheath on 31 October 1896 was his swansong for the "Usksiders". After 111 1st XV games, the Gould wanderlust had got the better of him. A couple of weeks later, he sailed for South Africa to take up a post with a mining company. He didn't give up his rugby there, of course. He captained the Wanderers club in Johannesburg and represented Transvaal in 1897, later joining the King William's Town Pirates. When the

Anglo-Boer War later broke out, Bert enlisted and was wounded in the knee in 1900.

However, any concerns Arthur may have had about playing again proved to be very short-lived. He had promised Boucher that he was always willing to help the club out should they ever need him. And the call soon came, only five weeks into his "retirement", when Tom Pearson was forced to drop out. Of their six games so far, Newport had lost only once – to Penarth – but they were expecting a difficult encounter at home against Swansea. We can sympathise with the visitors if they felt any sinking feeling as they saw the old warrior, who had tormented them so often in the past, in the Newport line-up. If so, it was justified. He scored the solitary try, displaying yet "another example of [his] splendid judgement". "Arthur played a capital game and seems to have lost none of his form", wrote a delighted "Dromio". Having received a warm welcome from the home supporters on his return, he apparently sent them wild with delight with his winning score. "Welsh Athlete" reckoned that he had lost little, if any, of his pace. There was no evidence that the powers of "the old crock" were diminishing yet.

In the meantime, subscriptions continued to pour into the testimonial fund. Then, shortly after Arthur's return to the game, the WFU received a demand from the International Board that they must inform them of what had become of the matter. They had obviously gathered that he was playing again. The WFU replied that, as agreed, they had withheld giving their sanction to the testimonial *and* had withdrawn their promised subscription. Gould had also intimated that he would not accept the testimonial if it were to affect his amateur status. The Union were evidently keen to demonstrate that they were keeping the testimonial fund at arm's length. "It's nothing to do with us. What more could we do?" was the implication.

Irrespective of all the rugby politics, the veteran's playing days were not over yet. He was persuaded to fill another vacancy in the next match at Oxford. Newport deservedly won 12-0 and it was Arthur who drew the first blood. Baffling a ring of converging opponents, he shook off a half-tackle and dropped a perfectly placed, long range goal. "Dromio" was so thrilled by his performance that he issued a plea for him to return to the game fulltime. "To Arthur Gould, all are inclined to sing *Will ye no come back again?* – *and remain*, for his play still reveals the inspiration of genius and there is not a centre even now who is his equal." The *London Morning Leader* thought that

Arthur's East Wales v West Wales trial cap, 1896. (Courtesy of Robert Gould)

"Gould still stands out as the trickiest player breathing. His running was as strong and swift as ever."

"Dromio" had his wish granted because Arthur took his old place in the Newport line-up yet again for the home clash with Cardiff. It was the second success this season for the "Mustard and Blackings" over their rivals, a 14-0 victory. Arthur was, declared "Dromio", "the bright particular star ... for not only did he drop two fine goals, but he showed his dash, pace and resource worthy of his reputation". Cajoling the Welsh selectors into doing their duty, he proclaimed that he had no doubt that on this form Arthur was now a certainty for the forthcoming international against England. Moreover, in his three games this season, he had shown that he was "as well fitted to captain Wales as ever".

Even "Dromio" seemed astonished by Arthur's comeback. "A marvel he always has been, but it is more marvellous than ever that he should emerge from his retirement to play with such brilliancy ... He seems as fast as he has ever been ... while he shows as much dash as a spirited youngster of twenty ... If Arthur Gould does not play ... for Wales, the team will be without the finest player in the country. So, far from being played out, he is showing marvellous dash and resources."

1897: Wales v England

Few were surprised, then, when he and Gwyn Nicholls were named as the centre pairing for the England match arranged for early in the New Year. Arthur also retained the captaincy. It wasn't so much "Arthur is back" as "Arthur never went away." Meanwhile, his splendid club form continued. "Dromio" reported that in the 18-0 triumph over Cambridge, he was reminded of "Monk" of "the days of old." When the Barbarians were beaten 16-0 at Christmas, he displayed his old audacity and self-confidence, dodging through his opponents to touch down for what "Dromio" reckoned was one of his finest ever tries – and he had seen a few.

The sun may have been setting on Arthur's career, but it was turning out to be a spectacular sunset. By taking part in the England match at Rodney Parade on 9 January 1897, Arthur stretched out his international appearances record to 27. This was also the 25th time that he played centre for Wales, a record which Arthur held until 1980, when Steve Fenwick became the most capped Welsh international centre. Furthermore, the England game was the 18th time Arthur captained Wales – and 97 years would pass before Ieuan Evans bettered this in a World Cup qualifier against Portugal. To this day, only eight men have captained Wales more often. However, though few anticipated it at the time, this was to be his very last cap. Events were now fast unfolding which would rob him of the chance of winning more.

The international was the 14th meeting in a series which the English had unquestionably dominated so far. Wales had only managed two wins and in both cases by a narrow one-point margin – at Dewsbury in 1890 and at Cardiff in 1893. However, Rodney Parade in 1897 would witness the first distinctly clear-cut Welsh victory over the old enemy.

As usual, the January weather was foul. It had rained practically all week and, on the morning of the match, heavy showers drenched the pitch. Just before kick-off, the rain had turned to a fine hail, accompanied by a cold and strong wind. Even so, 15,000 fans still crammed into the ground. There were fears that the wet and mud would restrict Wales from playing to their strengths, now universally described as "the Welsh game". In a memorable observation, "Welsh Athlete" feared that it was:

improbable that the Welsh backs ... would be able to do a little of what is their forte – that of swift, sharp, low passing, which seems as easy to "crack" local players as it is pleasing to the eye of the spectator, and which is so difficult for the premier backs in the three sister countries to acquire.

Despite the anxiety over the conditions, and the over-confidence of the English press, the night before the game, Arthur had predicted – correctly as it turned out – that Wales would "do better in the mud" than their opponents. In the end, it was the supremacy of the Welsh forwards which won the day. Their success is often said to have been the result of the decision to select "Rhondda forwards". The term was really a loose euphemism for any working-class players. Only four were Rhondda clubmen: Jack Evans and Dick Hellings of Llwynypia, and Jack Rapps and Dai Evans of Penygraig. Of the others, Fred Cornish played for Cardiff and Bill Morris for Llanelli; while Newport's Arthur Boucher and Harry Packer weren't working-class. Incidentally, four of the pack, Boucher, Cornish, Hellings and Packer, had all been born in England. Even though this match may have marked a new approach in the selection of Welsh forwards, of the eight, only Cornish and Hellings played for Wales again.

The *London Morning Leader* was certain that "the Rhondda forwards won the match", giving Wales what they always needed: "tenacity, strength and dash in the pack." He summed up, "Wales can always win behind; on Saturday she won everywhere". Rev Frank Marshall in *Athletic News* agreed that Wales thoroughly deserved their win, conceding that "the Taffies [*oh dear*] ... knew how to pass – Englishmen are yet novices at the game." England were outplayed, admitted "Old Ebor" of the *Yorkshire Post* though what struck him most was the remarkable agility of the Welsh players and their ability to adapt to the muddy conditions.

Bristol's *Western Daily Press* placed Welsh rugby on the highest of pedestals. "South Wales ... players have brought Rugby football to perfection ... The interest taken in football in Wales is very remarkable, as no other sport flourishes in the principality, but the gallant little country may be assured that there are thousands of Englishmen who envy them their team and the fine football they can often see." And we should not need to remind ourselves of Arthur Gould's contribution to the creation of that "very remarkable interest."

The programme from Arthur's final game for Wales. (Courtesy of Graham Sully)

Wales missed several scoring chances before registering their first points. Gwyn Nicholls would have been in but for a slip in the mud. Arthur failed with an easy penalty attempt; and then debutant half-back, Dan Jones of Aberavon, fell on the ball under the posts but, for reasons no-one understood, his try was disallowed. However, the pressure was building and a minute later Pearson went over "to thunderous rounds of applause". This came from a wonderful opening by Selwyn Biggs, who passed to Gwyn Nicholls. He and Arthur broke through the English defence and Pearson eventually went over in the corner. For the pressmen uncomfortably huddled against the rain and wind at their pitch-side table, the details of the later stages of this move were a blur. "There were some further exchanges in the far corner but we could not see them", "Welsh Athlete" confessed frankly. Bancroft missed a difficult conversion. The English were now beginning to look beaten. A forward dribble took the ball over the English line and Boucher was first up and fell on it. Bancroft's conversion attempt again failed. So Wales were 6-0 up but the game was still not yet safe.

"Old Stager" noticed that, at this critical stage, it was Arthur who held the ship steady when a lack of concentration might have allowed England right back into the game. "The grand general-ship of Gould was never more potent. He was, in three words, here, there and everywhere, playing a magnificent defensive game, of which even his most inspiring admirers thought him unequal to, and his example had a most inspiring effect." With no further scoring until late in the game, the crowd's excitement had reached fever pitch. There were only ten minutes left when, as the forwards mounted an attack inside the English 25, a pass was thrown out to Arthur. Unfortunately, though, it went to ground before he could take it. "Old Stager" recorded what happened next. "The prince of strategists" quickly realised the risk of attempting to pick up with two English defenders fast bearing down on him. So instead, he deftly flicked the ball by foot towards Dan Jones who collected near the line and rushed in under the posts. Bancroft added the points, "evoking a scene of indescribable enthusiasm and delight." At 11-0 down, there could be no coming back for England now. It was the third time Arthur had

Arthur's last international. Wales v Scotland. 1897. Back: W Morris, R Hellings, Jack Evans, Dai Evans, J Rapps, F Cornish, H Packer, H Bowen (WFU); Middle: T Pearson, W Bancroft, Arthur Gould, A Boucher, G Nicholls; Front: C Bowen, Dan Jones, S Biggs. (Courtesy of Swansea RFC Memorabilia CIC)

played at Rodney Parade for Wales and he had been on the winning side on each occasion.

After the game, the English captain and half-back, Ernest Taylor complained about the state of the ground. "It was not good to play on." One of his forwards, Wilfred Stoddart, agreed that the pitch wasn't fit. Maybe, but the Welsh players evidently managed to cope. The centre Edward Baker laid the blame for their defeat squarely on the English forwards whom he described as badly beaten. "We backs never had the ball passed out to us at all." Arthur expressed disappointment with the wet conditions but thought that had it been fine Wales would have won by more. He was delighted with the way the forwards worked, and reckoned they were the best pack ever fielded by Wales.

"The Old War Horse"

The Welsh backs were praised for their handling despite the greasy ball. The impressive play of Nicholls and Pearson was particularly commented on. There was some criticism of Arthur for opting to take and miss a drop goal at the early penalty, instead of offering it to Bancroft to place kick. He also failed with a couple of later drop goal attempts, when he might more usefully have passed. Though perhaps not rising to the heights of some of his recent games, Arthur still played well and worked hard throughout. His touch kicking was excellent and his defence was better than "Welsh Athlete" could remember. On one of the few occasions when the opposition backs attempted to attack, not only did "Monk" stop the move but he drove Baker back yards, a feat "eliciting a thunderous applause". "Who ... in that vast crowd ... would have credited the old war horse with such phenomenal strength?" mused "Old Stager".

The Welsh selectors immediately named an unchanged team for the next international three weeks later on 30 January in Edinburgh. The Scots announced their XV shortly afterwards. So everyone was expecting the match to go ahead as normal. Then, with only a week to go, a bombshell landed. Rumours had begun to spread from Newport that the Scottish Union were on the warpath. The Scottish secretary, James Aikman Smith was renowned for his uncompromising views on amateurism. The Scots now announced that they regarded Arthur as a professional and would therefore refuse to play Wales if he were included in the XV.

Just five days before the international, on Monday 25 January, the International Board called an urgent meeting in London. The newly appointed Welsh secretary, Walter Rees, had received an astonishing demand from the Board that he must obtain a formal written statement from Arthur repudiating the testimonial. This high-handed ultimatum also included two questions which the Scottish Football Union insisted that the WFU delegates should answer at the meeting. Firstly, what was to be done with the money? Secondly, if Arthur were to accept the money or a gift "in a form objectionable to the Board", what did the WFU plan to do about it? Since neither of these Scottish questions had emanated from the International Board, the WFU regarded them as impertinent and naturally refused to comply. Horace Lyne and Bill Phillips faced a confrontational reception in London, where even the WFU's good faith was called into question. In response to the Board's antagonism, the two not only fiercely defended the WFU but also disputed the right of the Board to interfere in the testimonial at all. They were able to do so by pointing to a crucial secondary clause in Bye-law 5 of the International Board's rules which stated that the Board *"shall have no power to interfere with the game as played within the limits of different Unions"*.

Eventually, this acrimonious meeting passed two startling resolutions, proposed by J Aikman Smith (SFU) and seconded by G Rowland Hill (RFU):

> 1. *That the gift of a testimonial in money or kind in opposition to the suggestion of the Board is on the part of the givers or Mr. Gould, an act of professionalism.*
> 2. *That the keeping of the fund in hand with the possible intention of presenting a testimonial, in opposition to the suggestion of the Board, on Mr. Gould's retirement, is also an act of professionalism.*

Naturally, the Welsh delegates were left with little choice but to dissent from both resolutions. There was no prospect of the Scottish match going ahead now.

Beyond the infighting within the rugby world, even popular entertainers were closely following what was, after all, a major sporting controversy. That very week, Austin Rudd, one of Britain's leading comedians, was on stage at the Newport Empire. During his act, he performed one of his well-known comic songs called *Red Light!*

Danger! This he cleverly adapted to include some lines criticising the Board and suggesting that Scotland and Ireland were in a "funk" about playing against Wales with Arthur in the line-up:

> *Both Scotland and Ireland seem*
> *To see with Arthur in the team*
> *Red Light! Danger! ...*
> *There's danger on the line*

Lyne and Phillips hot-footed it back from London with the news of the other Unions' intransigence. The WFU regarded the Board's resolutions as completely unacceptable. It helped that they had the support of much of the press, and not just in Wales. The idea that *everyone* who had contributed would be guilty of professionalism was widely considered risible. In any case, the Board had not explained *how* the WFU were expected to deal with a fund committee over which they had no control and with the vast number of subscribers who were completely unknown to them. In desperation, the general committee met the following day, Tuesday 26 January, in Cardiff. However, the International Board's latest resolutions had only served to stiffen the WFU's resolve. This time, they produced an indignant response to what was perceived as the interfering high-handedness of the other Unions.

Six resolutions were passed and these were immediately despatched to the International Board. In summary, the WFU's arguments were:

> *1 The International Board had not been formed to deal with professionalism but with the laws of playing the game.*
> *2 Since the Board had made no rules relating to professionalism, any questions of professionalism could only be dealt with under the rules of the relevant Union.*
> *3 Neither the subscribers to the testimonial nor Arthur Gould had broken any rules relating to professionalism made by the Welsh Union.*
> *4 Without admitting the Board's right to interfere, the WFU had complied with the views of the Board by withholding their sanction of the testimonial in any form other than that indicated by the Board; and the WFU therefore felt that they could do nothing further in the matter.*
> *5 Even if the WFU accepted the Board's latest two resolutions, they had no power to implement them, since they had no control over the funds, which were in the hands of a committee independent of the Union.*

"Throwing Down the Gauntlet." The WFU defy the International Board, while "Dame Wales" gives her support. (Evening Express, 28 January 1897: Arthur Gould's scrapbook)

> 6 *The WFU were willing for the Board to make rules on professionalism, provided they were agreed by all four unions, and were not applied retrospectively.*

There was widespread praise for this unequivocal response from the Welsh Union. An outraged "Old Stager" claimed that the British sporting press had never been *so* unanimous as they were in their condemnation of the International Board's "ill-advised and precipitate action" against the testimonial. He also pointed out that the organisers had never consulted Arthur about the timing of the presentation, nor had they even asked him about which form of gift he would prefer.

Despite the increasing acrimony, the WFU were still hopeful, naively perhaps, that the Scottish and Irish internationals might yet go ahead before the end of the season. So they asked for another urgent meeting with the Board, which took place on 20 February in Edinburgh. Predictably, though, Lyne and Phillips had another wasted journey. It was deadlock. So the WFU general committee convened two days later and this time took a very firm stand. This was a turning point in the dispute. As the *Evening Express* headlines exclaimed: "The Football Crisis Reaches A Culminating Point. International Rupture Now Complete." The Welsh Football Union had crossed their Rubicon. They now unanimously resolved:

> *That in consequence of the resolutions passed at the International Board meetings on January 25th and February 20th 1897, this Union regrets it finds itself obliged to withdraw from the International Board.*

Support for this bold but risky move was strong throughout Wales, where it was believed that the Union had been left with no other course of action. At last, "a smack of stiffness in the back", "Welsh Athlete" rejoiced, though he regretted that the Union had not gone further and instructed member clubs to cancel "all existing engagements with English organisations." This point did not go unheeded. Meanwhile, Newport immediately announced their resignation from their long-standing membership of the RFU.

Arthur informed the press that there was no truth in the rumour that he was about to retire. He admitted that he would have to miss a few games because he had badly injured his knee in the game against Cardiff held on 13 February. Amidst all the turmoil, though, he wasn't going just yet.

That Cardiff v Newport match had been the 34th and last time that Arthur took part in this particular fixture. The game proved to be a memorable one, but for the wrong reasons. It was contested vigorously but in good spirit. Unfortunately, though, the home club's 13-6 defeat upset an unruly section of the 15,000 strong Arms Park crowd. As the experienced English international referee, George Harnett, was leaving the field, he was physically attacked by a large and threatening mob of spectators from whom he had to be shielded, first by Cardiff players and officials and then by the police. For his protection, he was hurried to the nearby police station, and only later was Harnett able to make his way safely to the Queens Hotel, again with a police posse, and finally to the railway station. Arthur had witnessed similar unpleasant scenes

Cardiff v. Newport

In the aftermath of Newport's victory at the Arms Park, Cardiff supporters sportingly applaud the referee, George Harnett. (Evening Express, 12 February 1897)

before, of course, particularly after the Scotland match at Swansea in 1892 when he himself had received a blow while defending the referee. Following those events at St. Helen's, the WFU had given themselves powers to close grounds for such shameful behaviour. As a consequence, the Arms Park was controversially suspended for five weeks.

The nasty knee injury which Arthur received proved to be rather more serious than was realised at the time. He played only three more games for Newport that season and thereafter only on four future occasions. As a consequence, he missed the home contest with Llanelli who became the first club to win at Rodney Parade in three years. In all, Newport were only defeated in four matches out of 27 in 1896-7 and Arthur was absent on each occasion.

While he was recuperating, in late February, the WFU sent the other Unions a powerful response, setting out a closely argued justification of their case. Recognising that public opinion was shifting strongly in their favour, a printed version of this was also shrewdly despatched to the press who gave it widespread publicity. William Orders then wrote to the Welsh Union, confirming that he had arranged the presentation of the testimonial for Easter Monday.

To clarify their position, on 17 March, the WFU then made three significant resolutions. These were:

> *1 That since the gift of the testimonial did not breach any of the Union's laws relating to professionalism, the committee resolved to revert to their original decision of subscribing £50 to the fund.*
>
> *2 That since the testimonial was of a "national character", the committee would now sanction it, provided it was given in a way approved by the Union.*
>
> *3 That clubs and individuals would be free to subscribe, so long as the Union's laws on professionalism were not breached.*

Additionally, in a clear warning shot across the bows of the opposition, the committee further resolved to alter the Union's bye-laws to prohibit Welsh clubs, "if thought necessary", from playing against clubs of any other Unions. Implementing such a provision could have serious consequences for those clubs with close Welsh ties. That season, for example, a third of Gloucester's fixtures involved Cardiff, Llanelli, Newport, Penarth and Swansea.

A fortnight later on 1 April, the general committee confirmed that the gift of a house would not breach their rules. At last, 14 months after the testimonial was first launched, the way was now open for the organisers to finalise the purchase of "Thornbury", Arthur's home.

Late in the season, Arthur travelled to the Rectory Field to take on his old adversaries, Blackheath, one last time. He had always been a popular visitor there but, this time, the welcome he received was quite exceptional. Several English newspapers employed the same expression that he received a

"Thornbury", Clytha Park, Newport. (South Wales Echo, 20 April 1897)

"right royal reception" from the spectators, who realised that in all probability it was the last time they would witness Arthur's magic. And he did his best to give them something to remember. According to an *Evening Express* report, he "played a wonderfully good game, dodging and turning in the style so familiarly his own, and which nonplussed more than once the best players of every country." Newport won 11-0 and Arthur delighted the crowd by crossing for one of the tries. "With one of his bewildering twists", he avoided the tackle of the English international winger, Ernest Fookes, who was left sprawling on the ground as Arthur touched down. Given that this fixture took place under the most controversial of circumstances, the Blackheath supporters' welcome sent an unambiguous message to the International Board. It was clear that the Board's position on the testimonial was far from universally accepted, even within English club rugby's establishment. And you couldn't get much more establishment than Blackheath Football Club. Arthur may well have been anxious to turn out as a special thanks to Percy Carpmael, the secretary of Blackheath and founder of the Barbarians. A month earlier, shortly after Wales had withdrawn from the Board, Carpmael had sent a widely published letter to the press supporting Arthur and strongly disagreeing with the International Board. He argued that the WFU should be free to manage their own internal affairs and, importantly, that Arthur should be allowed to accept the gift of a house. It must have made a gratifying read.

Easter Monday 19 April 1897 was a very special day in the life of Arthur Gould. As he entered the field against Rockcliff for what was expected to be the very last time, he was given a very warm reception by the crowd, its relatively small size of 8,000 explained by the morning kick-off. Arthur put his side into the lead with the very last of his many drop goals for Newport, who secured their 22nd victory of the season by 13 points to 4. However, even though Arthur had an important event to attend later, he still found time to officiate at an athletics meeting at Rodney Parade in the afternoon.

During a magnificent banquet held in his honour that evening, Arthur was finally presented with the deeds of "Thornbury". His home town had been buzzing all day. "Newport was alive from early morning until late at night", "The Keeper" of the *Daily Mail* enthused. There was only "one topic to name in every man's mouth and, as a matter of course, in every woman's ... Arthur Gould! Arthur Gould!"

Over 250 guests packed into the banqueting room in Newport's Albert Hall. It was an all-male affair, so the ladies, including Arthur's biggest fans, his mother Elizabeth and his sister Effie, had to make do with a crowded balcony. The room had been specially decorated and, from the balcony rail, images of Arthur and "Thornbury" looked down upon the proceedings. The guests included, amongst others, D A Thomas MP; the Mayor of Newport; local councillors; prominent townsmen; representatives of the WFU and leading Welsh clubs; and Newport and Rockcliff players and officials. Even the Argentine consul bought a ticket. "Old Stager" referred to the celebration as a unique event which, he predicted, would live long in the memory.

Speaker after speaker voiced support for the Welsh Football Union's firm stand. They also acknowledged Arthur's lifelong sportsmanship. The main address was given by the WFU President, Sir John T D Llewelyn. He first spoke warmly of his friendship with Arthur's father, Joseph, who had done as much for Newport cricket, he believed, as his worthy son had done for football. He went on to say that he was delighted that subscriptions had come, not just from Wales and the rest of the Kingdom, but also from as far away America, Australia and Africa. Referring to the testimonial, he believed that it was "surely a misappropriation of words, a misuse of the term professionalism to apply it to Arthur Gould." He concluded

Richard Mullock's elaborately decorated and inscribed Illuminated Address. (Siân Prescott, courtesy of Robert Gould)

One of the illustrations in the Illuminated Address which depicts Arthur in the act of kicking during a match against Scotland. (Siân Prescott, courtesy of Robert Gould)

by saying he spoke for the whole of Wales in wishing Arthur many years of prosperity.

William Orders then read the words recorded in an elaborately illuminated address, which had been bound in leather. This has had been beautifully crafted, illustrated and inscribed by the former secretary of Newport and the WFU, Richard Mullock, who knew Arthur well, of course. It was his last ever contribution to Welsh rugby. The address read:

National Testimonial presented to ARTHUR J. GOULD – the Prince of Threequarters – At a Complimentary Banquet held at the Royal Albert Hall Newport, on Easter Monday, April 19th 1897, This Illuminated Address, together with the Title Deeds of "Thornbury", Clytha Park, Newport, were presented to him in commemoration of his brilliant success as an all round Athlete, in recognition of his valuable services to Rugby Football, and of his extraordinary powers as a player, He has taken part in more International Contests than any other player since the formation of the Rugby game.

Signed on behalf of the Subscribers, John T D Llewelyn, W J Orders, Llewellyn J Phillips

As J T D Llewelyn formally presented Arthur with the address and the title deeds, a prolonged and loud cheering broke out in the Hall. It was minutes before silence could be restored and only then after the band had struck up *See, the Conqu'ring Hero Comes!* This famous chorus was almost becoming his signature tune.

Accepting the testimonial, Arthur modestly responded that he didn't think he deserved the great honour which had been bestowed on him. Whatever he had done for rugby, he had always done from the heart, whether playing for Wales or for "the dear old club". Then, for the first time, he expressed his own opinion on the dispute. And who can blame Arthur for revealing his satisfaction at the outcome of this unpleasant controversy? Perhaps surprisingly after all that had been said and done, he spoke in a generous spirit about the members of the International Board. They were all personal friends, he declared. What they did, they did so honestly and in the belief that their actions were in the best interests of the sport. But the Welsh Union were right and the International Board wrong. He did wonder now, though, what they thought, having seen the overwhelming response throughout the country. It was a matter of great pleasure to know that his amateur status had been so staunchly supported by the Welsh Union, backed up by the whole of the Welsh public and press and most of the English public and press too. He trusted that the Rockcliff club would suffer no penalty for supporting him and concluded by apologising for causing "no end of worry" to so many during the past season.

It was an outsider, "The Keeper" who summed up the experience of being present at one of the most extraordinary events in Welsh rugby history. "As to the feeling that ran through the whole evening's oration, there could be no doubt, and that was the enthusiastic support of the position taken up by the Welsh Union, and *the whole-souled worship of the hero of the day.*"

After such a physically and emotionally charged day, Arthur might have been forgiven for taking some time off. But not a bit of it. The very next morning, he accompanied the Rockcliff players to their final tour fixture at Bristol, where he was the referee. There Arthur "met a splendid reception when he came on the ground." At the match dinner, his health was toasted, coupled with the remark

The Testimonial to Arthur Gould

GOT IT AT LAST.

"Got It At Last". A cartoon that speaks for itself. (Evening Express, 1 April 1897: Arthur Gould's scrapbook)

that he had done more for rugby than any other player. "Some minutes elapsed before the cheers had subsided sufficiently to allow Mr Gould to speak" and it is revealing that on this occasion it was *English* admirers who were doing the cheering. He responded with his customary charm, confessing that he had a warm affection for the Bristol club, of which he was proud to call himself a member. This went down very well.

With Arthur announcing his retirement from international rugby, the way was now open for him to stand for election to the WFU. At the AGM in Cardiff on 4 September 1897, he was nominated for one of the three East District positions. Basking in the affection shown towards him throughout the country, it was perhaps inevitable that he headed the poll, even pushing the experienced committeemen, W M (Billy) Douglas of Cardiff and A J Davies of Cardiff Harlequins and Glamorgan County, into second and third place. Arthur remained a WFU committee member for the rest of his life.

"One of the Happiest, Most Pleasant, and Popular Things"

The RFU committee had several times debated whether they should ban their clubs from playing against Arthur now that, in their eyes, he had been professionalised. However, they had held back from voting for it. Coming so soon after the loss of so many clubs to the Northern Union, there was clearly a great worry that any break with the Welsh might irreparably damage the game. Welsh clubs were now amongst the strongest in the land, playing attractive rugby and drawing large crowds to English grounds. There must have been a fear that the RFU's obstinacy might isolate the Welsh and eventually force them into the welcoming arms of the Northern Union. There was even speculation that some English clubs with regular Welsh contacts might be tempted to side with the Welsh if such a split occurred. However, whether realistically many would have isolated themselves in such a way is a matter for debate. As for the Welsh Union throwing in their lot with the Northern Union, there was not a universal appetite for this in Wales at the time. Whilst some *were* sympathetic to "broken time" payments, Cardiff and Newport, for instance, were reported to be "dead against" the idea. So, such a move might have even resulted in a disastrous split within the Welsh game, with some clubs joining with the Northern Union and others remaining "loyal". Association football was just beginning to put down roots in south Wales in the later 1890s, and any such division at this time might have even been catastrophic for the Welsh game. However, had the RFU and International Board remained resolute for several years, who is to say what the consequences might have been? The lack of cross-border and international fixtures might well have motivated the WFU into joining forces with the Northern Union. And had they done so, the future of rugby football would have been very different.

However, perhaps fearful of such unintended consequences, just in time, the RFU had seen the *Red Light! Danger!* signal ahead and slammed on the brakes. They now adopted a remarkably pragmatic and equivocal approach. Collectively gritting their teeth, in August 1897, the committee decided to place the following resolution before the Annual General Meeting of the RFU:

That Mr A J Gould having accepted a testimonial in a form that the Committee of the Rugby Union has decided to be an act of professionalism, nevertheless under the exceptional circumstances in this case, this Meeting recommends the Committee to allow him to play against Clubs under their management.

This resolution was eventually put to the RFU's AGM on 16 September 1897. There was a lively discussion before the vote, which revealed some startling differences of opinion, even among the members of the RFU committee, three of whom opposed the motion. The WFU came in for some harsh words. "Why should Wales be pandered to?" Arthur too was personally blamed for the crisis. However, others took his side. Percy Carpmael was one, arguing that it was wrong to punish Gould since he had not broken any of the laws of the Welsh Union. The referee, George Harnett, demonstrated that he held no lingering resentment against the Welsh, despite his rough handling by the Arms Park crowd seven months earlier. Amidst laughter, he remarked that he was in favour of Gould having his testimonial, as he would have been a fool not to have taken it. However, the risk of casting the Welsh Union into the wilderness with the consequent loss of international and, importantly, club fixtures had a sobering

"Resting Upon His Laurels." After a tumultuous year, Arthur relaxes at last with the local paper's football pages. (South Wales Argus, 21 April 1897: Arthur Gould's scrapbook)

effect on the assembled delegates. "On a show of hands" the resolution "was carried by a large majority" and this decision was greeted by a loud cheering. Presumably many of those cheering the loudest were the relieved representatives of those clubs which enjoyed regular contact with the Welsh. There is no doubt that this was a major climb down. "Stigma removed from the recipient", was the way the *South Wales Daily News* put it.

Asked by "Old Stager" for his response to the RFU's act of "forgiveness" Arthur said that, of course, he was glad it has been done. However, obviously feeling somewhat frustrated by it all, he remarked that it was a pity it hadn't happened a year earlier as it would have saved "all the bother". He repeated his earlier generous acknowledgement that he believed the RFU had acted in what they considered to be the best interest of the sport. However, he was evidently rattled by RFU secretary Rowland Hill's comment that proposing the resolution had been one of the most unpleasant duties he had ever performed. "I don't see how it can be unpleasant to noble minds to confess you're in the wrong and to make restitution ... from my point of view, I think it one of the happiest, most pleasant, and popular things he ever did."

9

Extra Time

1897-8

"Positively His Last Appearance?"

Arthur had at last officially given up international and regular club rugby. At first, though, he found it difficult to escape his past and he could not quite come to terms with never playing again. For a few more years yet, he would play the occasional match. Even after finally hanging up his well-worn boots, he never completely severed his ties with the game. It cannot have been easy for a sportsman of such stature to fashion a new life which was anything like as fulfilling as his former one.

He repeated his promise to help Newport out if needed and, in his first year of retirement proper, his services were indeed called upon three times, all at Rodney Parade. Even before those games took place, however, Arthur acted rather provocatively when he accepted an invitation to turn out for another club in 1897-8. Arthur was no fool, and he must have realised that playing for an *English* club would surely stir up trouble. Perhaps this was unwise, even arrogant, but it seems almost like an act of defiance: he was not a professional, so why should he not do as he pleased?

So, at Christmas, he was back in Bristol but this time guesting for the club whose members had been so supportive during the "Gould Affair". He claimed to have been a Bristol member for five years and was happy to accept the offer of a game. And he was a great success, scoring all of Bristol's points – two tries and a drop goal – against Old Edwardians. "The Keeper" of the *Daily Mail* wrote that there was no mistaking the warmth of welcome he received from the Bristol crowd, many of whom attended solely to see him play. Despite being his first game of the season, his form was "simply wonderful" and he seemed to have lost none of his speed. The match may have resulted in victory but it caused ructions at the RFU and there were repercussions for Arthur. At their next meeting on 10 January 1898, the RFU got their retaliation in by banning Arthur from playing for *any* English clubs in future.

For some time now, the WFU had been pressing the International Board for re-admission. This was finally approved on 17 February 1898. As a condition, the WFU agreed that "A J Gould be not available for international matches." In some quarters, this was seen as a capitulation by Wales. "The Keeper", in particular, was especially critical of the WFU, "who, vowing that they would never consent, consented to sacrifice the man who had done more than any other to make Welsh football what it is." However, this ignored the fact that Arthur had previously announced his retirement from international rugby, so it really wasn't a major *volte-face*. Following

THE INTERNATIONAL MUDDLE.

Wales to England, Scotland, and Ireland: "Will you play us again?" Chorus: "Yes, if you leave that bad boy Gould out."

Wales: "Will you play us again?" England, Scotland and Ireland: "Yes, if you leave that bad boy Gould out". Meanwhile Arthur admires the model house in the toyshop window. (Football Sun, 15 January 1898: Arthur Gould's scrapbook - Note the handwriting above the cutting)

re-admission to the Board, Wales hurriedly arranged fixtures with Ireland (in March) and England (in April) but Scotland declined to travel to Wales and so the two teams did not meet again until the following season. But the Gould controversy was finally over.

Meanwhile, Arthur had returned to the Newport team in late January 1898 in a 28-0 runaway win over the Monmouthshire League XV. He still demonstrated a good deal of his "old-time dash", scoring a try and conversion, his last ever points for his club. "Argus" of Swansea's *Cambrian* thought Arthur "displayed his old cunning and agility" but likened him to a leading operatic tenor of the day. "Is the Prince of Welsh three-quarters vying with Sims Reeves in the frequency of "positively his last appearance?" He was evidently beginning to irritate "Argus". Back in Newport colours in March for the Gloucester game – another thrashing by 24-0 – he did "yeoman service", according to "Welsh Athlete." However, "Argus" carped that Gould "seems determined to give the Welsh Rugby Union as much trouble as possible. His friends have served him well but it cannot be said that he has served his friends well over the dispute with the English Rugby Union."

"Monk" always seems to have enjoyed teasing the media. After quizzing him about rumours that he might play against Cardiff, "Old Stager" revealed an intriguing insight into Arthur's personality. "He is such a facetious sort of chap, his "yes" might just as well mean "no" and vice versa." However, this time, "no" meant "no" and Arthur didn't play. Cardiff won 18-0 and, in so doing, inflicted a humiliating clean sweep of four victories in a season for the first time.

Arthur played his last ever game at Rodney Parade for Newport on 9 April 1898. This was against Rockcliff but there was no fairy-tale ending. Newport lost by 5 points to 3. It wasn't, though, his last game for the club nor was it his last match at Rodney Parade.

1898-9

The RFU minutes for 17 December 1898 contain a curious entry. The secretary had received correspondence from Racing Club de France asking for the committee's views on "Mr Gould taking a team to Paris". The RFU's predictable response was that such a match would be "in opposition to the wishes of the Committee". Was this Arthur and did he intend to play? In the event, no visit to Paris by an A J Gould XV seems to have been arranged.

It was a Gloucester match crowd who were privileged to be present at his 231st and final appearance for Newport on 11 March 1899.[1] As he trotted out at Kingsholm, it had been an astonishing 16 years and four months since he had made that dramatic debut back in 1882. How many team-mates had he played alongside in that period?

Newport were badly short of backs and in their desperation they were forced to borrow three-quarters from Pill Harriers and Pontymister. But pressing Arthur into service too was "a hazardous experiment" in the opinion of *Sporting Life,* and they were right. This was a game too far. Not only did Newport lose 11-0, but Arthur struggled badly against a powerful Gloucester team, who had previously beaten Cardiff, Swansea and Llanelli. Age had caught up with him at last and, playing in an unfamiliar line-up, Arthur had the worst game of his career. He frequently dropped passes, fumbling on one occasion when he should otherwise have scored. A poor pass from Arthur led to a Gloucester try, while even his drop goal attempts were disastrous. All the press agreed that he was a failure but *The Cambrian*'s "Argus" really lashed out this time:

> I consider that Gould acted indiscreetly, to say the least of it, in turning out ... He has been the cause of enough unpleasantness already, and if he does not know how to keep his place, the Welsh Rugby Union should take him in hand. He should not be allowed to do just as he likes.

This feels unnecessarily harsh and critical. Newport *were* desperate and surely it was the club who were primarily at fault – if indeed there were any fault – in asking him to play. Why shouldn't he do just as he liked? After all, he was not banned from playing for his club.

Though Arthur had played his last game for the official Newport 1st XV, he had one more match in black and amber for what was virtually a full strength team. The day after the club's final fixture of 1898-9, a strong Club XV travelled down to the South Coast to take on Portsmouth. Ten of the 1st XV who had played the previous day were in the team alongside Arthur. The Newport XV took Portsmouth's ground record, winning 22-5, though the result does not feature in Newport's official records. We might wonder what

1   Newport RFC: http://www.blackandambers.co.uk

Gus Gould in Portsmouth colours. (Courtesy of Richard Tyrrell and Portsmouth RFC)

"Argus" of *The Cambrian* made of *Sporting Life*'s account of the match, which identified Arthur as one of best players on the field. Now resident on the South Coast, Gus Gould – who had arranged the fixture – played against Arthur for Portsmouth. Just a few months afterwards, while running as "Joseph Gould" and representing Portsmouth Harriers, Gus remarkably matched Arthur's earlier success in the national AAA Championships by finishing third in the 120 yards hurdles.

1899-1900

Newport had an open date on 3 February 1900, so the vacancy was filled with an unofficial match against an "Old Players" XV which was full of former internationals. The veterans made a game of it, holding a strong Newport team to a draw, one try apiece. At left centre, Arthur was reported to have "looked dangerous" for the Old Players at times and was unlucky not to succeed with a drop goal attempt. His youngest brother, Wyatt had begun playing for Newport this season but unfortunately was not in the team that day. Neither was Gus, who had a couple of games for his home town club in 1899-1900 but was otherwise still a regular at Portsmouth.

As it happens, Gus was enjoying a very good season and had been particularly impressive at centre for Hampshire in the English County Championship. In their 24-0 defeat of Eastern Counties, he scored a hat trick of tries and initiated the other three. He also kicked three conversions. The *Evening Express* was impressed. "The lion's share of the honours fell to Gus Gould, who played in a superb fashion and was almost wholly responsible for so complete a success ... [he] was quite the hero of the match." Although playing almost entirely outside Wales, it was performances such as this which earned him selection as reserve centre against Ireland in the March. Victory in Belfast resulted in Wales' second Triple Crown and heralded the beginning of the first "Golden Era", 12 seasons of unprecedented success.

Marriage and Family

To the dismay of many of his female admirers, Arthur married in the autumn. His bride was Lilian Augusta Smith, the third daughter of the late Samuel Smith, who had been a corn merchant in Newport and had resided in Clytha Park, near "Thornbury". The wedding took place on 25 October 1900 in Bristol, where Lilian's widowed mother now lived. Wyatt was Arthur's best man. The couple spent their honeymoon in Paris and then returned to "Thornbury", where they later brought up four children: Lilian Mary (born 1901), Dorothy Josephine (born 1903), Gwendoline (born 1905) and Arthur Jack (born 1909). Arthur's youngest daughter would follow in her father's sporting international footsteps by representing Wales, at lacrosse, in the 1920s.

A delightful family photograph: Lilian, Jo, Jack, Arthur, Mary, and "Goog" (Gwendoline), the future lacrosse international, sitting on her father's knee. (Courtesy of the Gould family)

1900-01 to 1909-10

Even though he was now married, Arthur could not resist the temptation of pulling on his boots for one final match. So, on 2 March 1901, a full 18 and a half years after his first game for Newport at Rodney Parade, he was there again, representing the "Old Players" against Newport. This time it was an official fixture which Newport won 9-0 and is recorded as such in the club records for 1900-1. Arthur, who was now well over 36, seems to have had a quiet game. With someone as competitive as Arthur Gould, it would be risky to suggest that he never played again. It is quite possible that he took part in later charity or minor matches which simply did not receive much publicity. Nevertheless, this game does almost certainly mark the moment when the curtain came down on his dazzling career.

Gus, Wyatt and Bert

Again both Gus and Wyatt only had a couple of games for Newport this season and so neither played against their illustrious brother in this fixture. Bert, on the other hand, happened to be briefly home on leave from the Anglo-Boer War and had just had a successful run out for the Reserves against Cardiff. So a week later, he was selected to partner Arthur in the centre for the Veterans. It must have been an emotional experience for the brothers, knowing that it was their last game together. The following week, Bert returned to South Africa where was he was serving as a lieutenant in Brabant's Horse, a light cavalry contingent raised in the colony in 1899.

Gus had three games for Newport in 1900-01, his last being against Swansea in the February. In addition to Portsmouth, he also played for London Welsh this season, and was again selected reserve for Wales at centre or wing for all three internationals. During the week before the England game, there were rumours that Gwyn Nicholls might be unable to play and, if so, Gus would replace him. But Nicholls didn't withdraw and, sadly, despite getting so close and being reserve four times, Gus never won a full Welsh cap. Just a month after Wales beat Ireland in the March, "Gus Gould of Newport *and other teams*", as the *Western Mail* succinctly put it, sailed for South Africa to join the Cape Mounted Police. He later saw action in the Anglo-Boer War serving with the Queenstown Rifle Volunteers. Gus continued to play rugby in South Africa for the Uitenhage Swifts club and was in the Combined Port Elizabeth XV which lost 13-0 to the British Lions in August 1903.

Though Wyatt had been occasionally selected at three-quarter for Newport since 1899, he and Gus never played together for the club. In fact, Wyatt never appeared in the same Newport line-up with any of his brothers. So with Arthur's final retirement and with Bert and Gus both leaving for South Africa, suddenly, Wyatt found himself the last to uphold the reputation of the Gould brothers at Rodney Parade.

Wyatt played 71 times for the 1st XV at centre or wing over the eight seasons between 1899-00 and 1906-7, though his last game for a Newport XV took place as late as 1910. Illness and serious injury prevented him from playing more often and may well have cost him a Welsh cap. Even in his year of captaincy, 1905-6, he could only manage a handful of games for Newport and unfortunately he was forced to relinquish the leadership to the great Welsh international forward, Charlie Pritchard. Only in 1902-3 did he complete a full season, when he missed just one of Newport's 33 fixtures, only two of which ended in defeat. His reward for his consistency that year

Newport 1902-3. Back: G Thomas, J C Jenkins, C M Pritchard, Wyatt Gould, G Boots, S Adams, A G Brown, C C Pritchard, H Packer; Middle: G Spillane, G E Lewis, T Pearson, G Llewellyn Lloyd (captain), J Hodges, G H Thomas, J E C Partridge; Front: C L Williams, D J Boots, E Thomas, J Hillman. (Courtesy of Kevin Jarvis at Newport RFC)

was his selection as reserve left centre for Wales against England in January 1903.

Any prospects of a Welsh cap the following season, however, were cruelly dashed. Wyatt took part in all of Newport's opening 11 fixtures in 1903-4 and was then invited to play at right centre for the Possibles in the Welsh trial at Tredegar on 9 December. With snow on the ground, the pitch was in a dangerous condition. Unfortunately, in a collision with Cardiff's Bert Winfield, he suffered a serious thigh injury which was so bad that he had to remain in bed for several weeks. He didn't play for Newport again for almost two years. Effectively, this accident put an end to his promising rugby career and he subsequently played for Newport on only seven more occasions.

He missed the whole of 1904-5 and so, for the first season in the 28 years since 1875-6, no member of the Gould family featured in the Newport team lists. Though he was elected captain for 1905-6, after only four games, he was forced to stand down because of health problems combined with a worrying knee injury. Over six feet in height, Wyatt was tall and rangy and some thought that he was not quite robust enough. According to the *Evening Express*, "he has ... done a service to the team, and a useful thing for his own physique, in standing down for a time, until he sufficiently recovers ... it is a great pity [because] ... the beginning of the season ... appeared to be so full of brighter promise".

This meant that he missed out on the honour of captaining his club against New Zealand, a game in which Newport pushed the visitors close before going down 6-3. The following season was Wyatt's last for the 1st XV. He played just twice in two victories: on the wing at Gloucester and at centre a week later at Rodney Parade against Exeter. The date of this last fixture was 1 December 1906, almost 31 years after Harry had made his 1st XV debut on 20 January 1876. Wyatt then announced to the press that he intended to retire from rugby. No doubt, he wanted to concentrate on his blossoming athletics career. He did, however, represent his club just once more three years later in Newport Reserves' 7-0 victory at Penylan on 12 March 1910. The *Evening Express* reported that Wyatt, "after a long retirement, donned the black and amber again ... and showed that inherent quality of being a good sprinter." The following April, he took part in a Newport Married v Singles charity match but hopes that he might return full time in 1910-11 were finally quashed when he announced that he had definitely decided not to play again. Thirty-four years after it had begun, the Gould brothers' remarkable era at Newport was finally over.[2]

Wyatt was an extremely gifted all-round sportsman, especially on the track. Shortly after being picked reserve for Wales, he was acclaimed by the athletics correspondent of the *Evening News*, Arthur Manning, himself a recent AAA and Welsh AAA champion. Asked whom he considered to be the best all-round athlete in Wales in 1903, he opted for Wyatt. Not only was he a brilliant three-quarter, Manning pronounced, but he was one of the best hurdlers in "England", a sound sprinter on the flat, a "splendid swimmer, jumper and gymnast", and was good at cricket and billiards. "I do not know anyone who can lay claim to being his equal."

Olympic athlete, Wyatt Gould (1879-1960), captained Newport and was a reserve for Wales. (Courtesy of the Gould family)

As a track athlete, Wyatt was superb. The leading hurdler in Wales during the first decade of the 20th century, he won the Welsh 120 yards hurdles unofficial championship in 1901, and the official championships of 1902, 1903, 1905 and 1909, missing out in 1904 and 1906 because of rugby injuries. The year 1903 was a particularly outstanding one. Not only was Wyatt selected reserve for Wales and was the Welsh hurdles champion but he also matched Arthur's and Gus' achievement in the national AAA 120 yards hurdles. Like them he placed third, an astonishing record for the rugby playing brothers. In 1908, Wyatt became an Olympian, representing Great Britain at the London Olympics. Though it was not his best event, he qualified for the semi-final of the 400 metres

---

2   However, in 1994-5, yet another of Joseph and Elizabeth Gould's descendants, Wyatt's great-grandson Ian Harvey played briefly in the centre for Newport.

hurdles in front of 40,000 spectators at the White City. Perhaps Arthur was amongst them.

Wyatt was employed as a docks official in Newport, Cardiff and London. In 1932 he was appointed manager of the Great Western Railway docks at Plymouth. The last surviving Gould brother, he outlived Arthur by 40 years, and passed away in Plymouth in 1960 aged 80.

Arthur with the Whistle

Even as a player, Arthur had been happy to officiate when needed but, after retiring, he took up refereeing seriously for quite some time. Still a very popular celebrity, in the early years, his presence at a ground could significantly improve attendances, much to the delight of club treasurers. Precisely because he was such an attraction, he was frequently invited to referee around the country. Match reports often refer to his being warmly welcomed onto the field by spectators.

On some occasions, a special post-match dinner might be held in his honour. One was arranged, for example, in October 1897, significantly just weeks after the RFU decision to accept the testimonial. This was following the Plymouth v Exeter match, which had been attended by a "splendid" crowd of 5,000. Even today, when some referees are celebrities in their own right, it is unlikely that their mere presence on the pitch would boost attendance figures. The *Western Morning News*, however, was rather dismissive both of the Plymouth club for making "a show of Arthur Gould" and of the fans who turned up, curious just to get a look at him. "He exhibits no extraordinary ability as a referee ... no better or no worse than the majority of official referees ... as may be seen almost every week at any first class match."

It is true that Arthur was not regarded as good a referee as he was a three-quarter. In December 1901, the *Evening Express* was of the opinion that, though he was one of the greatest players, "he is one of the weakest referees". In a recent Llanelli v Cardiff match – which the latter won – he frequently missed forward passes and offside infringements, though he was not biased to either side, the *Express* conceded. However, when he took charge of Penygraig's game with the Australian tourists in October 1908, the journal *The Referee* thought Arthur had been far too lenient of the "flagrant breaches of the rules committed by Penygraig".

Plymouth Rugby Club, Home Park, Oct. 2-97

PLYMOUTH V EXETER.

ONE PENNY.   **OFFICIAL CARD.**   ONE PENNY.

PLYMOUTH.

Back: W. Churchill

Three-quarter Backs;

F. Crosse   T. Mills   W. Beasley   M. Sturt

Half Backs:

V. Bartlett   F. Smails

Forwards:

T. H. Thomas (Capt.)   W. L. Martin   J. Masters   G. Tucker
C. J. Lent   C. Coles   R. Chaplin   W. Williams

EXETER.

Forwards:

Browning   Powell   Lucas   Rowe
Ashton   Chislett   Edwards   Mortimore

Half Backs.

Labbett   Vosper

Three-quarter Backs:

Chapman   Hutchings   Reed   Hannaford

Back: Hitt

Referee- Mr. A. J. GOULD, Newport, Wales.

Any alterations made at the last moment are unavoidable, but such changes if
occurring will be found posted in the Stand and Grounds.

Plymouth v Exeter match programme, 2 October 1897. Note that the referee's name is given greater prominence than those of the players. (Arthur Gould's scrapbook)

Some went further. After Cardiff scraped home against Bristol in October 1902, the *Bristol Magpie* claimed that Arthur had admitted to the Bristol players that he hadn't awarded them a vital try because he was afraid of the crowd. "A J was a grand player, but he is a dashed poor referee as is well known in South Wales." However, this does sound rather like sour grapes – after all, would any referee seriously make such an admission to the losing side?

Others though were even more critical. Admittedly, there may have been some East-West bias at work since the game involved

Neath at the Arms Park, but in October 1899, "Argus" of Swansea's *Cambrian* seethed:

> *I have never entertained a high opinion of Mr A J Gould as a referee. He is weak, erratic, dogmatic and ill-informed all in one. On Saturday many of his decisions unjustly handicapped the visitors who deserved to win.*

Perhaps it is just as well that Arthur didn't have social media to contend with.

Even as a referee, Arthur was not far from controversy. There was, for instance, the notorious Glamorgan League final between Mountain Ash and the Rhondda club, Llwynypia, in May 1895, played in front of 5,000 fervent supporters at Pontypridd. With only a few minutes to go, Llwynypia were leading by a goal and a try to a try. A line-out was called near the Llwynypia goal-line and from this a Mountain Ash forward barged over for a try which was quickly converted. Arthur allowed both scores but Llwynypia immediately protested that, though the throw-in was theirs, it had been incorrectly taken by Mountain Ash. Arthur had been unsighted so he asked the Mountain Ash touch-judge which side had thrown in and was told it was Llwynypia. This was vehemently contested by the Rhondda players, so Arthur asked the Mountain Ash half-backs who had taken the throw-in. One of them admitted he had done so. With that, Arthur disallowed the try and conversion and ordered another line-out. There was no further score and so Llwynypia were declared the winners.

Some match reports claim that Arthur was then surrounded by a threatening mob of "upwards of a thousand" and that he had to be rescued by police and players. Arthur, though, denied that he had been threatened. The supporters had merely gathered round curious to know why the try had not been allowed, he claimed!

There were official protests from Mountain Ash, of course, who argued that the referee should not have changed his decision. The matter was raised at the WFU Executive Committee and they agreed with Mountain Ash and so over-ruled Arthur. However, they also described the action of the Mountain Ash touch-judge as "reprehensible", which was a weak and inadequate response given that he appeared to have cheated. The match was therefore declared a draw. As it happened, perhaps justifiably, Llwynypia won the replay by 8 points to 7 but with a different referee.

It does seem that, though the letter of the law was applied by the WFU, in terms of natural justice, Arthur was in the right, given that he had been misled by the Mountain Ash touch-judge, who had utterly failed in his basic duty, to put it very mildly. Although Arthur refused to be drawn by the press on the particular circumstances, he did, in principle, justify a referee changing his decision where there was a "palpable mistake".

Arthur refereed at all levels – charity, club, cup final, county, trial and tour matches – apart from one. In his time, a number of former international players like Billy Douglas, Harry Bowen, Tom Williams and Gwyn Nicholls, not to mention several fellow WFU officials, were invited to take charge of international games, but this was an honour which never came Arthur's way. The nearest he got was running the line for Wales. Perhaps he was judged simply not good enough. Alternatively, following the "Gould Controversy", maybe it was just one step too far for some officials. However, when he refereed the County Championship match between Gloucestershire and Devon in October 1897, both the touch judges were RFU officials. One was the current RFU President, R S Whalley, who had sat in judgement on "the Gould Case" many times. Just a few weeks earlier, Arthur's testimonial had been cleared by the RFU, so perhaps all was now forgiven. But, if so, unfortunately it was not for long. Only two months later, Arthur lobbed that hand grenade at officialdom by turning out for Bristol on Boxing Day 1897. Not only did a furious RFU retaliate by forbidding him from playing for English clubs, in March 1898 they went further and banned Arthur from refereeing in England. With that decision, any prospect, however slight, of his taking charge in an international disappeared.

Besides refereeing, Arthur remained closely involved with rugby as a WFU official until his untimely death in 1919. Though he had stopped playing just before the full flowering of the Welsh international game in the first decade of the 20th century, he still had a part to play in the first "Golden Era" as a team selector. Probably his proudest moment during that period of unparalleled success came after the 3-0 victory over New Zealand in December 1905. Writing in the *Daily Mail*, he had predicted that Wales stood a good chance of winning because he judged them to be different from any team the All Blacks had so far met. When Wales scored towards the end of the first half, he exclaimed to all around, "I knew that Teddy [Morgan] would beat them; he is the fastest football sprinter in the world!" At half-time, he was seen at the press table, waving his hat in the air and excitedly yelling that "the New Zealanders have the pace but they cannot pass like Welshmen!" After the match, Arthur wrote in the *Mail,* "what a game it was! Such excitement had never before been witnessed in the Principality ... the victory was well earned." However, with an understandable nod to his own playing days, he could not resist the temptation of adding that the Welsh team of the "last dozen seasons" would have beaten them. In addition, Arthur was not above using his position as a journalist to defend himself as a selector. He was "particularly pleased", he wrote, that despite "all the uncomplimentary things said about the selection committee", they had been proved absolutely right in their decisions!

A Sportsman Still ...

Arthur thrived on activity, and sport was integral to his life. So just because he had retired didn't mean that he gave up other forms of competition. He had been playing cricket for Newport since he was 14 and he continued to do so, well after he had packed in rugby. He also held the post of cricket club secretary for a number of years and represented Monmouthshire CCC regularly, including taking part in their matches in the Minor County Championship after they had joined in 1901.

Arthur's speed was a useful asset at the wicket as "Old Stager" revealed in 1897:

> The veteran footballer is no particular genius with the bat, but he gets runs on the smallest provocation. And won't he make his partner sprint too. A soft hit just sending the ball a dozen yards in the slips Gould gets a run off, counting (and rarely mistaking) his chance of getting to the other wicket before the fielder can reach the ball and throw it in.

The 1925 history of Newport Athletic Club makes several references to Arthur's cricketing skills. He "took cricket, like all his sport, seriously. He was not a born cricketer, but got to be quite a good defensive bat purely by perseverence, and his quickness in running between the wickets, and his fielding at cover point made him worth his place in the side". As evidence of Arthur's agility when fielding, the history mentions a drawn match with Guy's Hospital in 1892 in which he took five catches. He won the club average bat in 1901 and

Newport Cricket Club Veterans, 1914. A somewhat older looking Arthur is seated second from the left. (Arthur Gould's scrapbook)

1903. Arthur played cricket right up to the First World War, though the Newport Veterans team photograph shows that by 1914 he had aged visibly.

During the winter months, when his refereeing commitments allowed, Arthur took up hockey, usually for Newport's 2nd XI or Newport Thursdays. He was also an active playing member of Newport Golf Club and represented Newport at tennis too. He was even adept at table tennis and billiards. Such was his competitive nature, he was only too happy to give any sport a go. Many years earlier, he had even played soccer. In 1894, when asked his opinion of "association", he responded by saying that he had played the game when he was in London. He "found it very agreeable but there is not one half of the excitement".

... and Still a Celebrity

Because of Arthur's undiminished popularity with the public, he was asked to take part in a major cultural celebration of Wales held in Cardiff at Sophia Gardens over two weeks during the summer of 1909. This was the "Welsh National Pageant" involving a huge cast of over 5,000 participants who re-enacted dramatic moments in the history of Wales. Many of the leading characters were played by members of the *crachach*, the Welsh establishment. Though unaccustomed to being selected as a reserve, for the pageant Arthur was required to understudy "Mr Morgan Williams, St Donat's Castle" as Llywelyn the

Great. It cannot have been a co-incidence that the "Prince of Three-Quarters" was invited to portray (albeit as standby) arguably the greatest of the independent Welsh princes. Despite being understudy to his "social superior", press coverage confirms that the substitute did get on the field on at least one occasion. Arthur's scene was set in 1215 and depicted Llywelyn Fawr negotiating with the Marcher Lords as he strengthened his control over of much of Wales. At the climax, those playing the Marcher Lords were required to exclaim *"Cymru am byth!"* Presumably, given his confession of his ignorance of the Welsh language after the 1896 Scotland game, the pageant organisers had made sure that Arthur now knew what this meant. Llywelyn ruled much of Wales for over 40 years, so there couldn't have been a more appropriate celebrity to represent him than the person who had reigned over the sporting and even cultural life of Wales for so long. Although it was 12 years since he had last pulled on the Welsh jersey, he would still have been one of the most recognised faces amongst the throng of performers, including those "of high social status". A photograph exists of him, or what is said to be him, looking a little uncomfortable in his costume of chainmail and surcoat.

The Prince of Centres poses in costume as "Llywelyn the Great", Prince of Wales, at the Welsh National Pageant. (Evening Express, 6 August 1909)

Just over six months later, in March 1910, Arthur took on a much more onerous public duty, when he was summoned for jury service at the Monmouth Assizes. This was no ordinary trial though, as he found himself acting as a juror on one of the most notorious murder cases of the period. The defendant had been charged with brutally murdering an elderly couple after he had broken into their cottage in Bassaleg to steal their savings. The evidence presented against him was overwhelming and the jury took only 15 minutes to reach their verdict.

Significantly, the jurors had elected Arthur foreman, so it fell to him to make the grim announcement to the court that the jury had found the defendant guilty. The convicted prisoner was hanged a month later.

Arthur was back in court again two years later, at least nominally, first as a defendant and then as an appellant. This was an unusual but important case. The plaintiff was Frederick Skrine who had been in the crowd for the Wales match against Ireland in 1911 and who claimed £1,000 damages from the WFU for negligence. During this crucial and successful Triple Crown match, a record 40,000 supporters squeezed into the Arms Park and there were several serious accidents as a consequence. One of the injured was Skrine, who broke a kneecap after being thrown forward by the pressure of the crowd when a barrier collapsed. While some newspapers listed all the WFU committee as defendants with "A J Gould" as the first named, others simply referred to the case as "Skrine v Gould"! The jury found for the plaintiff with £300 damages. An appeal by the WFU was dismissed. Presumably, in order to maximise public interest, Arthur's fame was the reason why the press gave him precedence over all of the other committeemen.

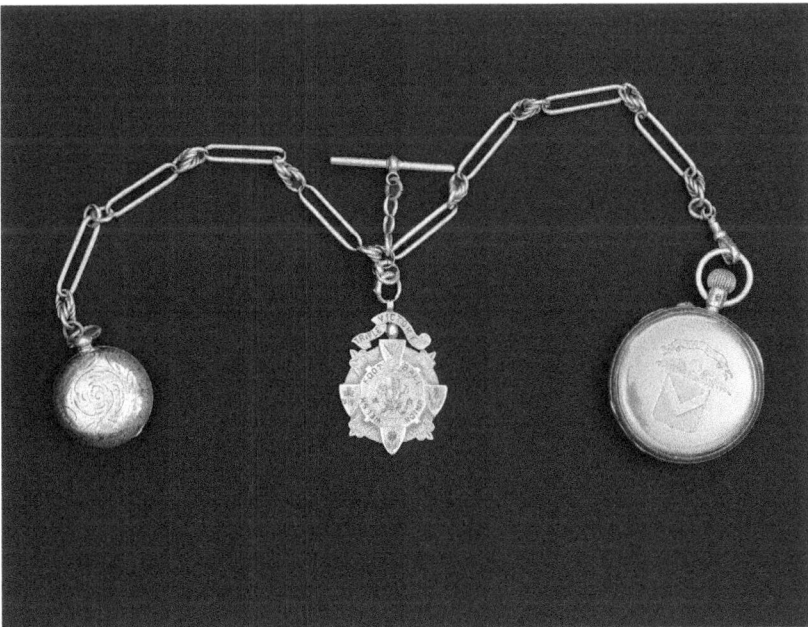

The gold watch, Triple Crown medal and fob chain which Arthur lost but was found and returned by an admirer. (Courtesy of Robert Gould)

His must have been the most recognised face in and about Newport. The stories that he was often followed around by groups of admiring youngsters, even after retirement, are probably not apocryphal. On one occasion, whilst in the street, he unknowingly dropped his 1892 Newport gold watch with the Triple Crown medal attached to the fob chain. He returned home only to discover that this precious souvenir of his past was missing. Arthur was obviously devastated but there soon came was a knock at the front door of "Thornbury". A passer-by had found the treasured watch, recognised its provenance, knew where its owner lived and, despite its monetary value, returned it, to the great relief of all the family.

Arthur Gould was an undoubted celebrity of Victorian and Edwardian Britain. And, as with any modern celebrity, his image was widely publicised and would have been familiar to many, not just those in the football bubble. As David Smith and Gareth Williams elegantly explained in *Fields of Praise,* "his exploits were recorded in countless pen portraits, his handsomely chiselled features and lithe form as familiar to sportsmen and even to mere newspaper readers as the portly fame of the best known Englishmen of the day, W G Grace." The comparison with Grace is a valid one. "Monk" was sometimes depicted in cartoons dealing, not just with particular matches, but also with key moments in his career, such as the "Gould Controversy" or his retirement; and several of these have been used in this and other accounts of his life. Occasionally, his familiar moustachioed face was enough to represent a rugby player in comic or satirical cartoons.

His image could also be found on the shield-shaped "Baines" football cards commonly worn by fans in their lapels. These were very popular at the time and remain so with collectors to this day. Some cards with "Play Up Newport" or "Play Up Wales" used Arthur's image to portray the archetypal club or international player. In addition, enterprising photographers would produce images of leading players or teams for purchase by the public. For example, one Cardiff firm in 1904 had a stock of over 400 photographs of past and present players for sale. These were available for as little as two pence each. Arthur's portraits were particularly popular with the public. A much reproduced favourite image, still sought after today, is the cabinet card photograph taken by Siedle Brothers of Newport, with the handsome Gould in the famous seated pose, balancing a ball on his hip and looking out at the camera with an air of supreme confidence. [See page ix]

What Welsh supporters were wearing in their lapels in 1893: a Baines card, featuring "A J Gould, Newport". (Arthur Gould's scrapbook)

A typical newspaper pen portrait of Arthur. This was published around the time of his first announcement that he intended to retire. (Evening Express, 28 September 1896)

Even in the 21st century, this particular image continues to inspire. Skinner's Brewery in Cornwall recently produced a beer pump clip displaying a representation of a rugby player who is clearly based on this familiar image of Arthur. Unfortunately, however, the designer committed the unforgiveable sin of dressing Arthur in an *English* jersey! Another version of the clip shows him in a modern British Lions jersey, still an anachronism but at least the colour is red.

Some commercial printers sold post-cards with sketches of Arthur. Remarkably, one example showing him running with the ball was used to promote the sales of a Belgian chocolate manufacturer! It is unlikely that Arthur received any royalties for this, even if he ever knew about it. However, he presumably *was* paid for one early rugby example of celebrity endorsement. This was a promotion for Fry's cocoa which appeared in newspapers across the country during the 1900s. In the advert, he proclaimed, "I have found it a capital drink after a hard game or practice. It is a most Effective Strengthening." Arthur was still advertising Fry's cocoa and milk chocolate in 1909, though by then he was joined by Gwyn Nicholls, C B Fry and the English soccer international William Wedlock.

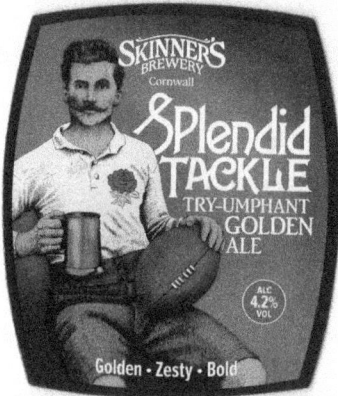

*With an Oxfordshire-born father, Arthur was eligible to play for England, but **this** never happened! (Courtesy of Dick Tyson)*

Also, Arthur never played for the Lions, though he was certainly good enough! (Courtesy of Dick Tyson)

Even during his playing career, businesses would cleverly associate themselves with his name without Arthur being directly party to any endorsement. In the programme for his final international at Newport

Together with other sporting stars of the era, Arthur was happy to put his name to this advertisement for Fry's cocoa and chocolate. (Athletic News, 11 October 1909)

in 1897, for instance, one local coal merchant's advertisement eye-catchingly led with, "We cannot all be A J's and drop goals".

Because of his celebrity, his opinions were still highly valued. So "A J" was able to supplement his income with regular columns in newspapers, journals and magazines across the country. These were not just confined to match reports. He often contributed well-written articles on a variety of subjects, such as how to play the game, match tactics, great exponents of rugby and memorable games of the past. He sometimes reported on cricket too. Like any celebrity, his views were still manifestly worthy of attention, well after he retired.

"The Greatest Three Quarter Who Ever Donned a Shirt"

In the years leading up to the First World War, Arthur suffered several close family bereavements. In October 1909, his mother Elizabeth passed away aged 69. Then, only four years later, there came an appalling double blow from South Africa. In December 1913, Arthur learned that Bert had succumbed to pneumonia. Just three months later there was further distressing news. Gus too had died of the same infection. They had both been working at the same gold mine in Germiston, Gauteng (Transvaal), Bert on the surface and Gus as an underground official. They were buried near each other in the local cemetery.

With the outbreak of war in August 1914, Arthur's involvement in rugby finally came to an end. The WFU immediately suspended all fixtures for the duration, and official rugby did not return until the autumn of 1919. There was limited work for committee members to do, therefore, for the next five years. They met very occasionally throughout the war but Arthur's last recorded attendance at a general committee meeting was in November 1915. He was absent from the subsequent ten meetings held up to the end of 1918.

Then, reporting the meeting held at the Queen's Hotel in Cardiff on 22 January 1919, the WFU minutes starkly record:

> *Vote of Condolence. A vote of condolence was passed with the Relatives of the late Mr A Gould and the late Mr Geo Bowen.*

George Bowen had played for Wales twice in the 1880s and had also served on the WFU committee. However, considering the massive

We CANNOT ALL *– BE –* **A.J's**

AND

Drop Goals

BUT

We CAN ALL

Drop A POSTCARD

TO

POST ⚬ CARD

D. E. HOWELL,
3 WOODLAND ROAD,
MAINDEE,
NEWPORT.

If we require a load of the very
Best House Coal at a
Moderate Price.

Bright Fires make Happy Homes.

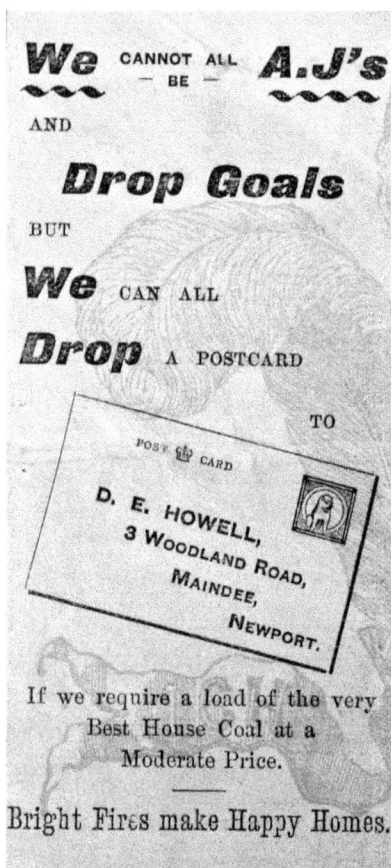

A Newport business cleverly uses Arthur's fame to promote their services in the Wales v England match programme, 1897. (Courtesy of Graham Sully)

impact which Arthur had on the Welsh game, both on and off the field, the brevity of this reference to his death comes as something of a shock. There was only one further comment. A couple of weeks later, the minutes reveal that a letter was read from Arthur's widow, Lilian, thanking the committee for their vote of condolence. And that was it.

On Thursday 2 January 1919, Arthur had gone into work as usual at the offices of Phillips and Sons Brewery in Station Street, Newport, where he was now employed as a cashier. Suddenly, at around 1.15pm, a colleague in a nearby office heard him cry out, "Billy, I've done something". He immediately rushed to his aid and was distressed to find Arthur bleeding profusely from the mouth, having apparently ruptured a blood vessel. A visitor to the office then accompanied Arthur the few hundred yards to his home. Medical assistance was summoned to "Thornbury" but, tragically, before his doctor was able to attend, the greatest player of the age had died of the haemorrhage. He was only 54.

According to the *Western Mail*, though Arthur's hair had whitened, he had shown no outward sign of illness. Townsend Collins, who knew him better, however, did comment that that he had aged greatly in recent years. There can be little doubt that the long, grim years of anxiety, deprivation and loss during the Great War had taken their toll on the physical and psychological well-being of a whole generation.

Even in a society inured by four wretched years of war, his death at such an early age sent shock waves through the rugby world and beyond. Townsend Collins wrote that the news of his loss came as a great surprise to all. That deep sense of shock was evident in newspaper columns, not just in Wales, but throughout the rest of the country. There was a widespread perception that Arthur Gould's death marked the passing of a sporting era.

Arthur in his 50s. (Illustrated Sporting and Dramatic News, 11 January 1919)

The funeral service was held on 6 January 1919 at St. John the Baptist where he had worshipped and where he had acted as a churchwarden's assistant for some years. It was said to be one of the largest funerals ever seen in Wales, involving huge numbers of players, team-mates, officials and admirers from the general public. His four children were present as was his brother Wyatt. The lesson was read by the Reverend Alfred Mathews who had been a half-back in the Welsh team alongside Arthur against Scotland 33 years earlier. At the conclusion of the service, he was laid to rest in the nearby St Woolos cemetery where his grave is still marked to this day by a large Celtic cross.

Not long after his death, a campaign was launched to commemorate his life by endowing a hospital bed in his name. The driving force behind this was his long-time admirer Townsend Collins, who became secretary of the Arthur Gould Memorial Fund. This was opened in September 1920 and by December 1922 it had raised £1,525, sufficient to endow a bed at the Royal Gwent Hospital in Newport. With the country in the grip of a severe post-war depression, it had not been an easy task. However, the support from across the rugby diaspora was heartening and demonstrated the enormous affection in which Arthur was still held by the wider public. Donations flowed in from China, Egypt, Palestine, the Gold Coast (Ghana), Nyasaland (Malawi) and the USA, and from the rugby clubs of Antwerp, Bristol, Gloucester, Richmond, Watsonians and the Middlesex County RFU, and many others. The Welsh Football Union gave £100. Clubs around Wales donated gate money, like the £117 receipts from a Neath v Aberavon match, whilst Newport RFC raised £439 in April 1921 from a special fixture arranged with Cardiff.

The bed was endowed at the Royal Gwent Hospital in 1923 and above it a brass plate was fixed bearing the inscription:

To the Memory of Arthur Gould, - Greatest of Rugby Football Players, - Captain of Newport, Captain of Wales, - the Mainstay in their Invincible Seasons of Richmond (1886-7), Middlesex (1887-8), Newport (1891-2), and Wales (1992-3), - This Bed is Dedicated by Admirers in Five Continents.

The *Gloucestershire Echo* reflected the sentiment throughout the whole game when it declared:

If ever a footballer deserved a memorial, "Monkey" Gould did, for he was the greatest three-quarter who ever donned a shirt.

A classic portrait of the Prince of Centres. (Sporting Sketches, 15 February 1896: Arthur Gould's scrapbook)

Afterword

As the first real international celebrity of Welsh rugby, Arthur Gould was the torch-bearer for so many of the all-time greats who followed. In Wales, a select group of truly outstanding players are frequently referred to by just their first name. Simply mention "Gareth," "Bleddyn", "Gerald" or "Barry" and everyone knows who they are. There is an underlying implication that, despite their fame, they are one of us, familiar and approachable members of the family, which in a sense they are. "Arthur" was one of these.

Wales was the land of his birth but not of all of his fathers. However, though both his father and maternal grandmother were English, Arthur always regarded himself as Welsh. After all, it was

One of us - familiar and approachable. While admirers gaze dumbstruck at their hero, according to the caption, a porter encourages the Bishop to speak to Arthur, adding "he'll let you." (Evening Express, 22 January 1898)

Newport which had nurtured him as a player and he never forgot this. He was certainly intensely proud of, and committed to, his home town club. Perhaps just occasionally he mused what might have been had he played behind a Yorkshire pack or for England, but he never ever regretted playing for Newport and Wales.

It would be hard to overestimate Arthur's impact on rugby in Newport. He played for the "Black and Ambers" 231 times between November 1882 and March 1899 and, to this day, he still holds the club record for most tries (159). He was central in helping to establish Newport as one of Britain's elite clubs and was a towering presence in the team's extraordinary successes of the 1890s. Arthur took part in nearly 80% of Newport's fixtures during the six seasons from 1891-2 to 1896-7 when they were the foremost power in British club rugby. According to the club's historian, Jack Davis (quoting "Dromio"), this was "without doubt the greatest period in the history of Newport". There was the invincible season in 1891-2, when Newport were acknowledged as the finest team of either football code in the kingdom. There was also a two-year ground record from March 1891 to March 1893, followed by a three-year period unbeaten at home between March 1894 and February 1897. Newport were the "talk of the football world" and "looked upon as head and shoulders over any combination" in the 1890s, claimed one London journalist. Arthur was integral to all this.

Arthur's illustrious career not only spanned most of the last two decades of the 19th century but two eras of rugby as well. Though this was not a period of great international success for Wales, it was nevertheless a time of lasting consequence for the future of Welsh rugby. Coming late to the international table, it took some years for Wales to catch up, but at the domestic level matters moved much more swiftly. In the very early 1880s when Arthur started playing, interest in the game in Wales was only beginning to emerge, but by the mid-1880s it was growing markedly. As local newspapers attest, by the 1890s it had become by far the most popular sport in south Wales, with very many hundreds of teams and many thousands of supporters regularly attending club matches.[1] And so intense had this interest grown, that Welsh clubs, exploiting

---

1   In 1895-6, for instance, there were over 230 teams of all kinds in the Cardiff area alone. Gwyn Prescott, *This Rugby spellbound People*, (Cardiff, 2015), pp.107 and 238-241.

their four three-quarter system so effectively, came to dominate the British club scene, well before the 20th century. Now it would be misleading to suggest that Arthur Gould was alone responsible for this. He was even initially reluctant to accept the superiority of four three-quarters, though he changed his mind by the 1890s and became one of the system's greatest exponents. There were, of course, many outstanding and dazzling players of the period who all helped to create the vibrancy of pre-First World War Welsh rugby. However, Arthur's contribution to the remarkable popularity of the game in Wales was both a lengthy and a substantial one. There is no doubt that his mere presence on the field could increase the number of supporters paying at the gates. There is also no doubt that, when he was on form – which was often – his scintillating displays created many new converts to rugby, both spectators and players alike. And with a reputation which went far beyond the regular, predominantly working-class, fans, Arthur Gould gave the sport a cultural status in Wales which transcended that of a mere game.

Moreover, it wasn't just in Wales that he was a celebrity. Beyond his homeland, too, he was widely considered to be the finest three-quarter of the 19th century and one of the greatest players of all time. As *Fields of Praise* aptly puts it, Arthur was "the first to go beyond local fame, regional renown, even national recognition, to earn both meanings of the word an 'international'."

One of the reasons for the nation's shared pride in Arthur's genius was the confidence which he inspired in Welsh rugby and its adherents. After all, he helped to put Wales on the rugby map. Those administrators and journalists who had initially looked down condescendingly on Welsh aspirations to be accepted as equals were now forced to sit up and take note. His lightning speed, elusive running, superb handling, accurate kicking and

"The Laurel of Fame": a sketch dated 9 February 1897. (Arthur Gould's scrapbook)

his intuitive "feel" for the game set him apart. There had been other Welsh stars of course who were every bit as good as leading players elsewhere, but none was quite like Arthur. His longevity and fame transcended them all. If Welsh rugby was capable of producing a player of such stature – the finest player in the land, perhaps the greatest so far seen – then what was to stop Wales producing the finest international team? Arthur's legacy to the Welsh public was to instil a lasting pride and growing confidence in what their own distinct version of rugby football was now capable of achieving.

His experience of international rugby was not characterised by prolonged success. He was only on the winning side in ten of his record 27 matches for Wales and he only played in one Triple Crown team. However, it is better to view his time in an international jersey as a period when Welsh rugby was laying down the foundations of success. Only three years after his international retirement, Wales entered their first "Golden Era", when six Triple Crowns were won over 12 seasons and when New Zealand were defeated in what was regarded as the unofficial world championship. Arthur heralded what was to come in this period of unprecedented achievement in which he also contributed his expertise more directly as a WFU selector.

The "Gould Affair" demonstrated just how far the Welsh Football Union was willing to venture in fending off intimidation from the other Unions in defence of their own independence. Withdrawing from the International Board, with the consequent loss of international fixtures, involved very serious risks, but that they were prepared to go to such lengths reveals the increasing self-confidence of the Welsh Union. What was involved, of course, was very much more than just protecting the interests of a popular and celebrated favourite son. But we have to wonder whether any other

Rugby's First Superstar. (Arthur Gould's scrapbook)

player of the time would have received quite this level of support from the Union. They were helped in their cause, of course, by the overwhelming backing for their actions by the majority of the public and press for whom he was undeniably the "Prince of Three-Quarters".

Looking back over his 60 years as a critic, in 1948, Townsend Collins ("Dromio") was still of the opinion that, "when every deduction is made, Arthur Gould stands alone." The wheel, however, keeps turning. In his last three internationals, Arthur was partnered by the superlative Gwyn Nicholls, the player whom the Welsh public would soon anoint their new "Prince of Centres".

But as rugby's first superstar, Arthur Gould remains unquestionably pre-eminent in the long history of the game.

Appendix

Gould Brothers' International Matches & Scoring Record

Robert Gould (P11 W2 D2 L7) Captain *1

Date	Opponent	Location	Result	Score	Other Gould
28.01.1882	Ireland	Dublin	**Won**	2 goals 2 tries to nil	
16.12.1882	England	Swansea	**Lost**	2 goals 4 tries to nil	
08.01.1883	Scotland	Edinburgh	**Lost**	3 goals to 1 goal	
05.01.1884	England	Leeds	**Lost**	1 goal 2 tries to 1 goal	
12.01.1884	Scotland	Newport	**Lost**	I dropped goal 1 try to nil	
12.04.1884	Ireland	Cardiff	**Won**	1 dropped goal 2 tries to nil	
03.01.1885	England	Swansea	**Lost**	1 goal 4 tries to 1 goal 1 try	A J Gould
10.01.1885	Scotland	Glasgow	**Drawn**	No score	A J Gould
02.01.1886	England	Blackheath	**Lost**	1 goal 2 tries to 1 goal	A J Gould
08.01.1887	England	Llanelli	**Drawn**	No score	A J Gould
26.02.1887	Scotland*	Edinburgh	**Lost**	4 goals 8 tries to nil	A J Gould

George Herbert Gould (P3 W2 D0 L1) Captain * 0

Date	Opponent	Location	Result	Score	Other Gould
05.03.1892	Ireland	Dublin	**Lost**	9-0	A J Gould
04.02.1893	Scotland	Edinburgh	**Won**	9-0	A J Gould
11.03.1893	Ireland	Llanelli	**Won**	2-0	A J Gould

Arthur Gould (P27 W10 D3 L14) Captain * 18

Date	Opponent	Location	Result	Score	Other Gould
03.01.1885	England	Swansea	**Lost**	1 goal 4 tries to 1 goal 1 try	R Gould
10.01.1885	Scotland	Glasgow	**Drawn**	No score	R Gould
02.01.1886	England	Blackheath	**Lost**	1 goal 2 tries to 1 goal	R Gould
09.01.1886	Scotland	Cardiff	**Lost**	2 goals 1 try to nil	
08.01.1887	England	Llanelli	**Drawn**	No score	R Gould
26.02.1887	Scotland	Edinburgh	**Lost**	4 goals 8 tries to nil	R Gould
12.03.1887	Ireland	Birkenhead	**Won**	1 dropped goal 1 try to 3 tries	
04.02.1888	Scotland	Newport	**Won**	1 try to nil	
02.03.1889	Ireland *	Swansea	**Lost**	2 tries to nil	
01.02.1890	Scotland	Cardiff	**Lost**	5-1	
15.02.1890	England*	Dewsbury	**Won**	1-0	
01.03.1890	Ireland*	Dublin	**Drawn**	3-3	
02.01.1892	England*	Blackheath	**Lost**	17-0	
06.02.1892	Scotland*	Swansea	**Lost**	7-2	
05.03.1892	Ireland*	Dublin	**Lost**	9-0	G H Gould
07.01.1893	England*	Cardiff	**Won**	12-11	
04.02.1893	Scotland*	Edinburgh	**Won**	9-0	G H Gould
11.03.1893	Ireland*	Llanelli	**Won**	2-0	G H Gould
06.01.1894	England*	Birkenhead	**Lost**	24-3	
03.02.1894	Scotland*	Newport	**Won**	7-0	
05.01.1895	England*	Swansea	**Lost**	14-6	
26.01.1895	Scotland*	Edinburgh	**Lost**	5-4	
16.03.1895	Ireland*	Cardiff	**Won**	5-3	
04.01.1896	England*	Blackheath	**Lost**	25-0	
25.01.1896	Scotland*	Cardiff	**Won**	6-0	
14.03.1896	Ireland*	Dublin	**Lost**	8-4	
09.01.1897	England*	Newport	**Won**	11-0	

Gould Brothers' International Scoring Record	Tries	Conversions	Drop Goals
Arthur Gould	4	1	2
George Herbert Gould	2	/	/
Robert Gould	/	/	/

Bibliography

(a) Books

Billot, John; *History of Welsh International Rugby* (Cardiff, 1999 edition).

Collins, Tony; *The Oval World: A Global History of Rugby* (London, 2015).

Collins, W J Townsend, (ed.); *Newport Athletic Club: The Record of Half a Century 1875-1925* (Newport, 1925).

Collins, W J Townsend; *Rugby Recollections* (Newport, 1948).

Davies, D E; *Cardiff Rugby Club: History and Statistics, 1876-1975: "The Greatest"* (Cardiff, 1975).

Davis, Jack; *One Hundred Years of Newport Rugby 1875-1975* (Risca, 1975).

Ereaut, E J; *Richmond Football Club: From 1861 to 1925* (London, 1925).

Evans, Howard; *Welsh International Matches 1881-2000* (Edinburgh, 1999).

Godwin, Terry; *The Complete Who's Who of International Rugby* (Poole, 1987).

Griffiths, John; *The Phoenix Book of International Rugby Records* (London, 1987).

Jones, Peter; *Newport Rugby Greats* (Stroud, 2016).

Lemon, Eric; *Wales Rugby Records to March 2022* (Sydney, Australia 2022).

Lewis, Steve; *Images of Sport: Newport Rugby Football Club 1874-1950* (Stroud, 1999).

Lewis, Steve; *The Priceless Gift* (Edinburgh, 2005).

Marshall, Rev. F (ed.); *Football: The Rugby Union Game* (London, 1894 edition.).

Parry-Jones, David; *Prince Gwyn: Gwyn Nicholls and the First Golden Era of Welsh Rugby* (Bridgend, 1999).

Pierce, Duncan, Jenkins, John M and Auty, Timothy; *Who's Who of Welsh International Rugby Players* (Bath, 2018).

Prescott, Gwyn; *This Rugby Spellbound People: the Birth of Rugby in Cardiff and Wales* (Cardiff, 2015).

Richards, Alun; *A Touch of Glory: 100 Years of Welsh Rugby* (London, 1980).

Roderick, Alan; *Newport Rugby Greats* (Newport, 1995).

Ryan, Greg; *Forerunners of the All Blacks: The 1888-89 New Zealand Native Football Team in Britain, Australia and New Zealand* (Canterbury, New Zealand, 1994).

Smith, David and Williams, Gareth; *Fields of Praise: The Official History of the Welsh Rugby Union 1881-1981* (Cardiff, 1980).

Thomas, Wayne, *A Century of Welsh Rugby Players*, (Birmingham, 1979).

Tyson, Dick, *London's Oldest Rugby Clubs* (London, 2008).

Van Esbeck, Edmund, *Irish Rugby 1874-1999: A History* (Dublin, 1999).

(b) Newspapers

Aberystwyth Observer
Athletic News
Belfast Newsletter
Bristol Magpie
Cambrian, The
Cardiff Times
Chums
Daily Mail
Daily News
Daily Telegraph
Dublin Evening Herald
Dublin Evening Telegraph
Edinburgh Evening News
Evening Express
Football Sun
Freeman's Journal
Glamorgan Times
Gloucester Citizen
Gloucestershire Echo
Graphic, The
Hull Daily Mail
Hull News
Illustrated London News
Illustrated Sporting and Dramatic News
Irish Times
Leeds Mercury
Liverpool Mercury
London Morning Leader
London Star

Manchester Guardian
Monmouthshire Merlin
Newcastle Chronicle
News of the World
Pall Mall Gazette
Pastime – The Football Journal
Pearson's Weekly
Penarth Chronicle
Referee, The
Scottish Athletic Journal
Scottish Referee
South Wales Argus
South Wales Daily News
South Wales Daily Post
South Wales Echo
Sporting Chronicle
Sporting Life
Sporting Sketches
Sportsman, The
Star of Gwent
Tenby Observer
Weekly Mail
Welsh Athlete, The
Western Daily Press
Western Mail
Western Morning News
York Herald
Yorkshire Evening Post
Yorkshire Post

(c) Minute Books

International Board Minutes
RFU Minutes
WFU (WRU) Minutes

(d) Miscellaneous Sources

Arthur Gould Scrapbook
Census Returns
Newport Street Directories
Newport RFC: www.blackandambers.co.uk

Index

S

Salisbury RFC 40

Salford RFC 93-4, 128, 130, 141

Samuel, David 84, 111

Scottish Athletic Journal 38

Scottish Referee, The 77, 152

Scottish Rugby Union (SFU) 135, 155, 175-6

Seddon, Robert 53

Sheffield Park (East Sussex) 69

Shepherd, William "Bill" 99-100

Simpson, H J 29, 155

Skipper Gould 149, 159, 163

Smith, James Aikman 175-6

Somerset RFU 62, 74

South Wales XV 15, 22-3, 35, 41, 50

South Wales Argus viii, 9, 49, 105, 127, 131, 149, 154, 157, 166, 188

South Wales Cricket Club 6, 14

South Wales Challenge Cup 7, 10-1, 14-5, 18-9, 25, 31, 49

South Wales Daily News viii, 25, 29, 31, 34-5, 41-2, 61, 65, 77, 85-7, 89, 144, 153-5, 188

South Wales Echo 36, 41, 64, 66, 87, 143, 145, 159, 181

South Wales Football Union 11

South Wales Press 157

Sporting Chronicle 103, 105

Sporting Life 43-4, 68, 71, 92, 119, 137, 148, 152, 157, 167, 193-4

Sporting Sketches 214

Sportsman, The 97, 105, 120, 150, 157, 161

St. Helen's Ground (Swansea) 18, 21, 26, 36, 73, 90-1, 133, 137, 163, 180

Stadden, William "Buller" 30-1, 41-2, 46, 57-8, 64-6, 75, 77-80

Star of Gwent 19, 51, 75, 82, 86-7, 163

Stephens, J R ("Old Stager") vii, 34, 37-9, 42-3, 45, 47-8, 52-4, 56, 63-4, 73, 76, 83, 89, 91, 98-100, 102-3, 108-9, 112, 115, 120, 124, 126-7, 130, 135-7, 139, 143-4, 147-9, 151-2, 154, 156, 158, 160, 162, 162, 174-5, 178, 183, 188, 192, 204

Stoddart, Andrew 42

Stoddart, Wilfred 175

Stradey Park (Llanelli) 52, 54, 84, 111-2, 129, 158

Stroud RFC 123

Stuart, Angus 46

Surrey County RFU 74, 98

Swansea RFC 7, 11, 23, 25-7, 30, 41, 48-9, 51, 53-5, 57, 68, 72-3, 75-7, 84, 86-8, 90, 111, 115, 125-7, 130-1, 137, 143, 159, 163, 169, 181, 193, 196

Sweet-Escott, Ralph 138

Swinton RFC 88, 163

T

Taylor, Charles "Charlie" 27-9, 37-8, 40-2, 44-6, 50, 52, 54-5, 57

Taylor, Ernest 175

Tenby Observer 157

Thomas, C J "Charlie" 75, 77-8, 81, 84, 87, 94, 129, 133

Thomas, George 58, 72, 84, 94, 133

Thomas, W Llewelyn 87, 121, 133, 135, 138-40

Thomas, Willie H 46, 53, 78

"Thornbury" (Clytha Park, Newport) xii, xvi, 157, 181-4, 195, 208, 212

Transvaal 168, 211

Tredegar Hall (Newport) 158

Tredegar, Lord 95

Tredegar RFC 198

Treharne, Edward 16

ST DAVID'S PRESS

Also by Gwyn Prescott

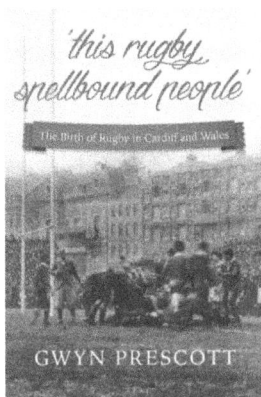

'this rugby spellbound people'
The Birth of Rugby in Cardiff and Wales

"...scrupulously researched [and] well written...Gwyn Prescott has given [rugby in Wales] a history to be proud of." **Huw Richards, scrum.com**

"Prescott paints a meticulous picture of Welsh rugby's growth in Victorian Britain" **Rugby World**

"...a fascinating piece of research and a major contribution to the history of rugby." **Tony Collins**

The Birth of Rugby in Cardiff and Wales is the essential guide to the importance of rugby in Cardiff and to the significance of Cardiff to the development of Welsh rugby in the 19th century.

978-1-902719-43-6   304pp   £16.99   PB

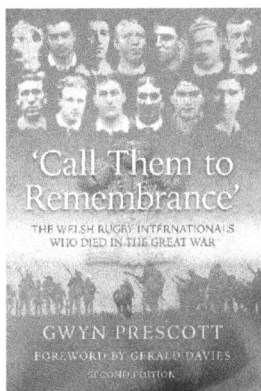

'Call Them to Remembrance'
The Welsh Rugby Internationals
Who Died in the Great War
(Second Edition)

'These pages contain an unexplored and untold tale which, from the deepest anguish of the suffering born of their unquestioning bravery, pierces the heart...This book is [an] acknowledgment of the sacrifice made by 13 Welshmen...Theirs was a sacrifice which needs to be told...Gwyn Prescott, with meticulous and sympathetic attention to detail, tells the story. This narrative is an essential record'.

Gerald Davies, from the Foreword

It is estimated that the First World War claimed the lives of 40,000 Welshmen, all of them heroes whose sacrifice is acknowledged by a grateful nation. 'Call Them to Remembrance', which includes over 120 illustrations and maps, tells the stories of 13 fallen heroes who shared the common bond of having worn the famous red jersey of the Welsh international rugby team.

978-1-902719-82-5   180pp   £19.99   PB
978-1-902719-90-0   180pp   £19.99   eBook

St David's Press

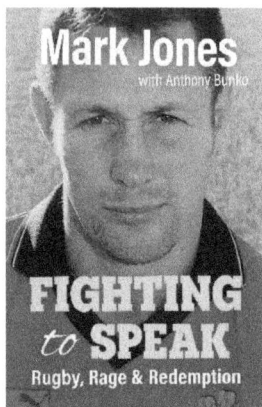

Fighting to Speak
Rugby, Rage and Redemption

Shortlisted for The Sunday Times Rugby Book of the Year (2023)

'I have nothing but the highest respect for Mark. His stammer did not make life easy for him and challenged his mental health, but his immense strength of character saw him beat his demons and win his battles.' **Jim Mills**

A talented and ferocious player, and one of the acknowledged 'bad-boys' of rugby, Mark Jones' on-field brutality was a direct consequence of the off-field torment he suffered with a debilitating stammer. *Fighting to Speak* reveals the journey of a miner's son with a stutter who succeeded to play rugby at the highest level and defeat his demons.

978-1-904609-018	250pp	£13.99	PB
978-1-904609-025	250pp	£9.99	eBook

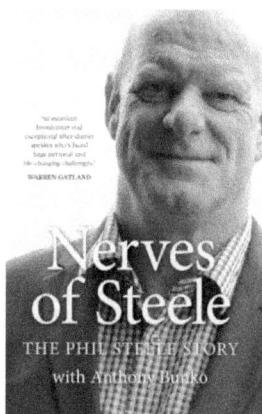

Nerves of Steele
The Phil Steele Story

'I've been lucky enough to get to know Phil during my time as Wales coach. He is an excellent broadcaster who genuinely wants Wales and Welsh players to excel and I respect his friendly and personal approach. I also admire the fact that he has been able to do this while facing personal and life changing challenges.' **Warren Gatland**

Known to thousands of rugby fans as a knowledgeable, passionate and witty broadcaster, and as an entertaining and popular after-dinner speaker, Phil Steele's confident demeanour and humorous disposition mask a life-long battle against depression and anxiety heightened by heartbreak and tragedy in his personal life.

978-1-902719-50-4	208pp	£13.99	PB
978-1-902719-53-5	208pp	£9.99	eBook

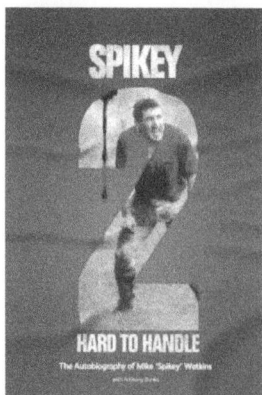

Spikey: 2 Hard to Handle
The Autobiography of Mike 'Spikey' Watkins

'One of the most inspirational leaders that Welsh rugby has ever produced' **Mike Ruddock**

'No one trained harder, no one played harder...heart of a lion' **Terry Holmes**

One of the most colourful and controversial characters in Welsh rugby history, Mike 'Spikey' Watkins remains the only player since 1882 to captain Wales on his debut, and win.

978-1-902719-40-5	251pp	£18.99	PB

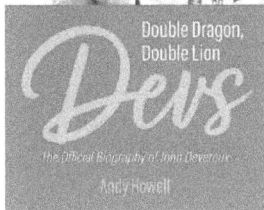

Devs
Double Dragon, Double Lion
The Official Biography of John Devereux

'a guy you wanted alongside you in the trenches, a hard man who wouldn't take a backward step and who you knew you could rely on.' **Jonathan Davies**

'John was up there with Billy Boston, who was the best player I've seen' **Dougie Laughton**

Capped for Wales as a 19-year-old student, John Devereux starred at the inaugural Rugby World Cup in 1987 and for the British & Irish Lions in 1989 before a big money offer lured him to rugby league with Widnes. A dual-code international - scoring six tries in eight games for Great Britain, and three tries in 12 games for Wales RL, Devs was also the last Wales union international to appear in a RL World Cup final when he lined up for Great Britain against Australia at Wembley in 1993.

Held in the highest regard by former teammates and opponents alike, John Devereux is revered by followers of rugby league and rugby union and, in his official biography, Devs, tells the fascinating story of his life in rugby.

978-1-904609-05-6	224pp	£13.99	PB
978-1-904609-06-3	224pp	£9.99	eBook

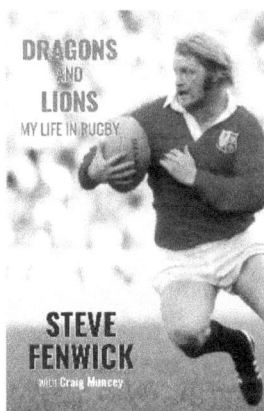

Dragons and Lions
My Life in Rugby

'A player I would go to war with.' **JPR Williams**

'One of the outstanding centres of the 1970s.' **Willie John McBride**

An icon of Welsh rugby and one of the stars of the great Wales team of the 1970s, Steve Fenwick won four Triple Crowns, two Grand Slams, played in all four Tests of the 1977 Lions tour to New Zealand, and won two Welsh Cups with Bridgend RFC.

Witty and engaging with a very dry sense of humour, in *Dragons and Lions*, his long-awaited autobiography, Steve Fenwick tells the story of the schoolboy from Nantgarw who became one of the most celebrated players in world rugby.

978-1-902719-856	200pp	£13.99	PB
978-1-902719-917	200pp	£9.99	eBook

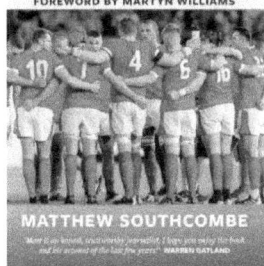

No Regrets
Welsh Rugby's Plan to Conquer the World

'Matt is an honest, trustworthy journalist. I hope you enjoy the book and his account of the last few years!' **Warren Gatland**

'Having followed Wales' every move over recent years, few journalists are better-placed to chronicle the team's journey over that period of time than Matt.' **Martyn Williams**

In *No Regrets - Welsh Rugby's Plan to Conquer the World*, acclaimed *Western Mail* rugby correspondent Matthew Southcombe reveals how the masterplan led to the 2017 tour success in Argentina, a clean sweep in the 2018 autumn internationals and, in 2019, a Six Nations Grand Slam, a record 14-game unbeaten run and a World Rugby #1 ranking. Hopes were high, amongst the squad and the nation, as the team headed to Japan with a genuine expectation winning the tournament.

978-1-902719-81-8	176pp	£13.99	PB

St David's Press

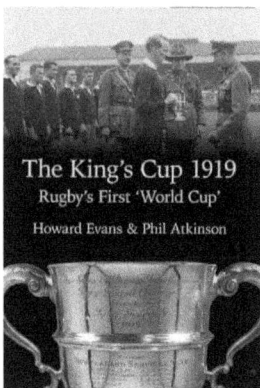

The King's Cup 1919
Rugby's First World Cup

'An intriguing retelling of a significant but largely forgotten chapter of rugby union history, superbly illustrated.'
Huw Richards

After the Armistice in November 1918 – with the forces of the world's rugby-playing nations and many of their stars still stationed in Britain – and with the public desperate to see competitive rugby played again, an inter-military tournament was organised. *The King's Cup 1919* is the first book to tell the full story of rugby's first 'World Cup' and is essential reading for all rugby enthusiasts and military historians.

978-1-902719-44-3   192pp   £14.99   PB

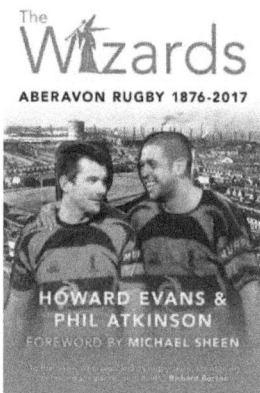

The Wizards
Aberavon Rugby 1876-2017

'I would rather have played rugby for Wales than Hamlet at the Old Vic. To that town, Aberavon and its rugby team, I pledge my continuing allegiance, until death.'
Richard Burton

One of the traditional powerhouses of Welsh first class rugby, Aberavon RFC has a long, proud and illustrious history, with 50 of its players being capped for Wales, the club winning many league titles and domestic cups, and - with Neath RFC - facing the might of South Africa, Australia and New Zealand. Aberavon RFC is a great rugby club and this is its story.

978-1-902719-66-5   256pp   £19.99   PB

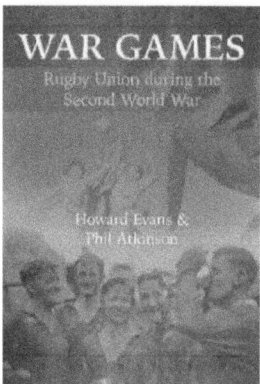

War Games
Rugby Union during the Second World War

Dedicated to 'all those in rugby who did - and who didn't - make it through those troubled times', *War Games* is a comprehensive and highly illustrated commemoration, packed with stories and statistics that for the first time chronicles the history of rugby - the men and the matches, from 'scratch' to international - during the Second World War. Essential and entertaining reading for followers of rugby and military historians alike, respected rugby authors Howard Evans and Phil Atkinson tell the tale - meticulously and with great affection for the game they love - of those men who played for fun but who, on too many occasions, lost more than a rugby game.

978-1-902719-67-2   302pp   £25.00   PB

St David's Press

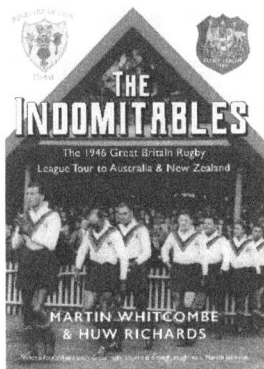

The Indomitables
Rugby League's Greatest Tour
The 1946 'Great Britain' Tour to Australia & New Zealand

'What a tour! What a story! Great rugby players and tough, tough men.'
Martin Johnson

'If you want to know why I and so many other league players wanted, more than anything, to be selected for an Ashes tour - then read this book. It's a sensational story of the greatest team that created the tradition we were all so proud to be part of.'
Andy Gregory

The 1946 Indomitables won the three Test series in Australia with two victories and a draw - an unbeaten record that has never been repeated - and remain Britain's most successful rugby league tourists. Lavishly illustrated with over 300 photographs, *The Indomitables* is the most comprehensive and authoritative account of the 1946 tour that made sporting legends of the 15 Englishmen and 11 Welshmen (including the captain, Gus Risman) who created sporting history and won the respect of the Australian nation.

These were *The Indomitables* – and this is their sensational story.

978-1-902719-702	500pp	£28.00	PB
978-1-902719-924	500pp	£25.00	eBook

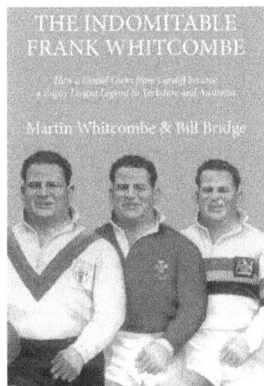

The Indomitable Frank Whitcombe
How a Genial Giant from Cardiff became a Rugby League Legend in Yorkshire and Australia

'Frank Whitcombe was a rugby league cult hero in the days before there were cult heroes. An eighteen-stone battle tank of a prop forward, he graduated from Welsh rugby union to become a pillar of the great Bradford pack of the 1940s. In the process, he became the first forward to win the Lance Todd Trophy, a member of the 1946 'Indomitable' Lions touring team to Australasia and had even driven the team bus to Wembley when Bradford won the 1947 Challenge Cup Final. This book is his story - it is essential reading for anyone interested in the history of rugby and the amazing men who made the game.' **Prof. Tony Collins**

'Frank Whitcombe became a Welsh international and a Great Britain tourist. He is widely regarded as an all-time great of rugby league.' **Fran Cotton**

978-1-902719-47-4	256pp	£19.99	PB
978-1-902719-59-7	256pp	£9.99	eBook

White Gold
Swansea RFC 1872-1887

'an incredible insight into the formation of Swansea RFC: its characters, games played and the evolution of the 'Swansea Style'.'
David Richards, Swansea, Wales and British & Irish Lions

Lavishly illustrated with many previously unpublished photographs, *White Gold* has been meticulously researched by club historian David Dow and is the most comprehensive study of the early days of rugby in Swansea ever published.

978-1-904609-07-0	580pp	£75	PB
978-1-904609-08-7	580pp	£38	PB
978-1-904609-09-4	580pp	£25	eBook

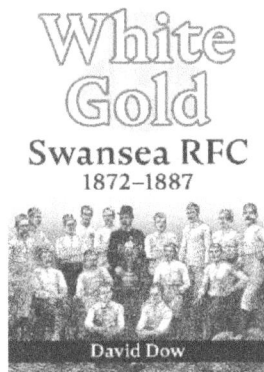

.

9 781904 609124